S0-BRN-735

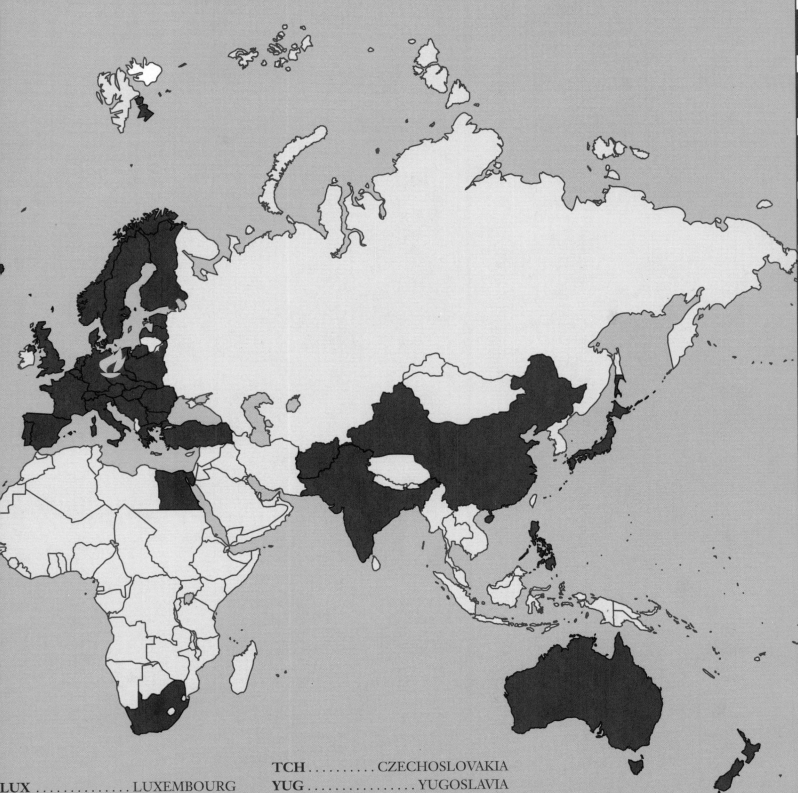

THE OLYMPIC CENTURY
THE OFFICIAL 1ST CENTURY HISTORY OF THE MODERN OLYMPIC MOVEMENT

VOLUME 11

THE
XI, XII, & XIII OLYMPIADS

BERLIN 1936
ST. MORITZ 1948

BY

GEORGE CONSTABLE

WORLD SPORT RESEARCH & PUBLICATIONS INC.

LOS ANGELES

1996 © United States Olympic Committee

Published by:
World Sport Research & Publications Inc.
1424 North Highland Avenue
Los Angeles, California 90028
(213) 461-2900

1st Century Project
The 1st Century Project is an undertaking by World
Sport Research & Publications Inc. to commemorate the
100-year history of the Modern Olympic Movement.
Charles Gary Allison, Chairman

Publishers: C. Jay Halzle, Robert G. Rossi,
James A. Williamson

Senior Consultant: Dr. Dietrich Quanz (Germany)
Special Consultants: Walter Borgers (Germany), Ian
Buchanan (United Kingdom), Dr. Karl Lennartz
(Germany), Wolf Lyberg (Sweden), Dr. Norbert Müller
(Germany), Dr. Nicholas Yalouris (Greece)

Editor: Laura Foreman
Executive Editor: Christian Kinney
Editorial Board: George Constable, George G. Daniels,
Ellen Galford, Ellen Phillips, Carl A. Posey

Art Director: Christopher M. Register
Production Manager: Nicholas Pitt
Picture Editor: Debra Lemonds Hannah
Designers: Kimberley Davison, Diane Farenick
Staff Researchers: Mark Brewin (Canada), Diana
Fakiola (Greece), Brad Haynes (Australia), Alexandra
Hesse (Germany), Pauline Ploquin (France)
Copy Editor: Anthony K. Pordes
Proofing Editor: Harry Endrulat
Indexer and Stat Database Manager: Melinda Tate
Fact Verification: Carl and Liselott Diem Archives of the
German Sport University at Cologne, Germany
Statisticians: Bill Mallon, Walter Teutenberg
Memorabilia Consultants: Manfred Bergman, James D.
Greensfelder, John P. Kelly, Ingrid O'Neil
Staff Photographer: Theresa Halzle
Office Manager: Christopher Jason Waters
Office Staff: Chris C. Conlee, Brian M. Heath,
Edward J. Messler, Elsa Ramirez, Brian Rand

International Contributors: Jean Durry (France),
Dr. Antonio Lombardo (Italy), Dr. John A. MacAloon
(U.S.A.), Dr. Jujiro Narita (Japan), Dr. Roland Renson
(Belgium), Dr. James Walston (Ombudsman)

International Research and Assistance: John S. Baick
(New York), Matthieu Brocart (Paris), Alexander
Fakiolas (Athens), Bob Miyakawa (Tokyo), Rona Lester
(London), Dominic LoTempio (Columbia), George
Kostas Mazareas (Boston), Georgia McDonald
(Colorado Springs), Wendy Nolan (Princeton), Alexander
Ratner (Moscow), Jon Simon (Washington D.C.), Frank
Strasser (Cologne), Valéry Turco (Lausanne), Laura
Walden (Rome), Jorge Zocchi (Mexico City)

Map Compilation: Mapping Specialists Inc., Madison,
Wisconsin
Map Artwork: Dave Hader, Studio Conceptions,
Toronto
Film Production: Global Film Services, Toronto
Marketing Consultant: Robert George

Customer Service: 1-800-451-8030

Bookstore and Library Distribution:
Firefly Books Ltd.
3680 Victoria Park Avenue
Willowdale, ON M2H 3K1
(416) 499-8412

U.S. Offices
230 Fifth Avenue, #1607
New York, NY 10001

Printed and bound in the United States by R. R.
Donnelly Co.

ISBN 1-888383-00-3 (25-volume series)
ISBN 1-888383-11-9 (Volume 11)

Library of Congress Cataloging-in-Publication Data

Constable, George.
    The XI, XII & XIII olympiads : Berlin 1936, St. Moritz 1948 / by
George Constable.
        p.   cm. -- (The Olympic century ; v. 11)
    "1st Century Project"--T.p. verso.
    Includes bibliographical references (p. 171 - 172) and index.
    ISBN 1-888383-11-9 (alk. paper)
    1. Olympic Games (11th : 1936 : Berlin, Germany) 2. Winter
Olympic Games (5th : 1948 : Saint Moritz, Switzerland) I. 1st
Century Project. II. Title. III. Series.
GV722 1936.C65 1996
796.48--dc20   96-10657
                                                                                CIP

CONTENTS

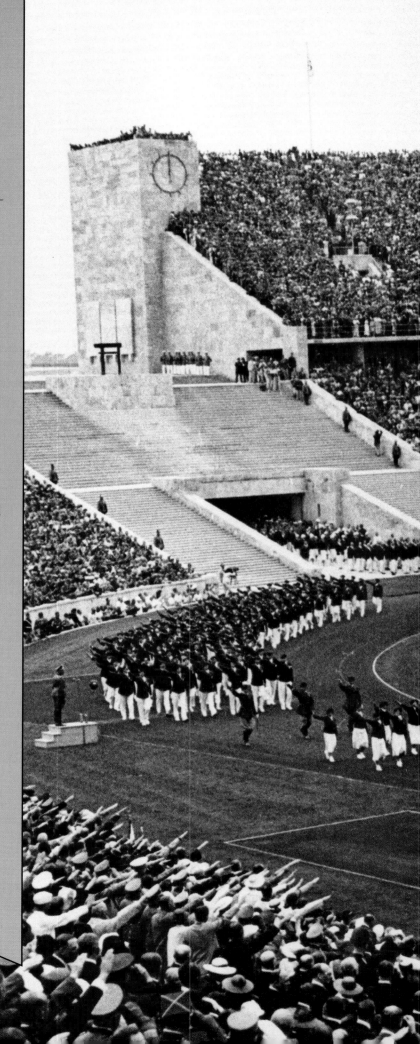

CITYWIDE CELEBRATION

Nazi authorities enthusiastically backing the Berlin Games wanted all Berlin, not just the 110,000 people at the Olympic stadium, to feel part of the Games' opening ceremony festivities. So, for August 1, planners developed an all-day celebration that lasted well into the night.

The morning phase showcased German youngsters. Children from every Berlin school district gathered on playing fields to run races, perform gymnastics, and play soccer and tennis matches. The climax was a massive demonstration at the Lustgarten that included a rally of Hitler Youth, with speeches by Propaganda Minister Joseph Goebbels and other prominent Nazi officials.

The opening ceremony itself began at 3 p.m. in the Olympic stadium. There were 50 delegations in the Parade of Nations. The French team won approval with its straight-armed salute *(right)* to Adolf Hitler as it passed his seat in the reviewing stand. The crowd went wild, inferring a Nazi greeting, but French officials quickly claimed a misunderstanding: Their athletes had given an Olympic salute, not a fascist one. (In fact, some historians suggest that the Nazis adapted their infamous *Sieg Heil* gesture from the Olympic salute, first used at Stockholm 1912.) After the remaining teams settled onto the infield and Theodor Lewald, organizing committee president, greeted the crowd, Hitler declared the Games open. A German wrestler, Rudolph Ismayr, took the athlete's oath.

The long-running gala picked up again at 9 p.m. when spectators returned to the Olympic stadium to watch the Festival Play. A precursor to pageants that would mark later opening ceremonies, the play featured student groups performing musical numbers and yet another series of athletic demonstrations—all to glorify the youth of Germany. The day's events served their purpose: Berliners returned home charged with enthusiasm for the upcoming Games.

FLAME OF PEACE, FLAME OF WAR

June, as always, brought a sensuous softness to Berlin in the summer of 1936, and July was gentler still. People strolled in the sun, gossiped outside the shops, picnicked in parks. But for all the quiet pleasures of the season, there was something unsettling in the air that summer, a sense of vast forces gathering. Far from Germany, armies were on the move: Japan had wrested Manchuria from China and was eyeing additional territory; Italy's fascist dictator, Benito Mussolini, had just seized Ethiopia. Close to home, Greece and Austria were roiled by political storms. And in Germany itself, a dark dreamer ruled. Chancellor Adolf Hitler and his minions in the National Socialist Party believed that history was turning and that they were the pivot. Their country had suffered a bitter defeat in the First World War, then lapsed into debility and drift. Now, said the Nazi leaders, the years of weakness were over. A new Germany had arisen, and the international community would have to acknowledge its greatness.

A significant step in that direction was about to happen. On August 1 the Games of the XI modern Olympiad would open in Berlin. More than 150,000 foreign visitors were expected, along with about 700 foreign journalists, and Hitler was determined that they be dazzled by the Third Reich, as he called his dominion.

Creating impressions of grandeur and potency was one of Hitler's foremost talents, and he didn't hesitate to spend freely in the cause. Even before the Games got under way, the bill for hosting the Olympics approached an unprecedented $30 million. The finest sports arenas in Olympic history were built for the occasion. Transportation systems were upgraded, thoroughfares were widened, and communications facilities improved. Berlin was brought to a high polish by cleaning crews and set aflutter with the new national flag bearing the Nazi swastika. The Games would launch with lavish and spectacular ceremonies, including a multinational pageant beginning at the very

The Olympic flame reaches Berlin's Lustgarten, August 1, 1936

A sketch from Carl Diem's diary explains the origin of the torch relay. While studying a book on antique monuments, Diem saw an illustration of winged runners adorning the entrance to the Academy in Athens. They were lighting torches at the altar of Eros, god of love. Later research led Diem to a passage in the *Auctor ad Herrenium,* an anonymous treatise written in 80 BC, describing a torch run.

font of Olympism, in the hills of the Peloponnesus in Greece.

That particular ceremony was conceived by Carl Diem, the man with the primary responsibility for organizing the Berlin Games. Diem, general secretary of the Berlin Olympic Organizing Committee, was a respected member of international sport circles—and a man with an acute sense of drama. His rite would draw its power from fire, an element woven deep into the ancient tapestries of both Greek and Teutonic myth. The sacred flame would ignite from the focused rays of the sun in the ruins of ancient Olympia, then be borne to Berlin by a relay of runners—conveyed from torch to torch along a route extending almost 2,000 miles across Europe. By this transfer of fire from the oldest Olympic site to the newest, the past would touch the present. A spirit would move across the ages.

The logistics were prodigiously complicated. On its way to Berlin, the flame would travel through seven nations: Greece, Bulgaria, Yugoslavia, Hungary, Austria, Czechoslovakia, and finally Germany itself. The national Olympic committees in the seven countries were charged with recruiting local runners, but Diem kept close control of all the preparations, shaping his mobile fire festival with Germanic precision. He decided that each torchbearer would run exactly one kilometer, and by means of a careful survey carried out in 1935, he determined that a total of 3,075 runners would be needed. In a directive he wrote, "The symbolic act of handing on the fire is planned by us as follows: We will give to all participating countries the number of torches they require, together with reserves. Every runner will be provided with a torch, and a second will remain at the hand-over point as a standby." Diem reckoned that, allowing for mountains and other barriers, runners should make an average time of five minutes per kilometer. "The whole project will be spoiled," he cautioned, "if the fire arrives too late."

The relay would require 11 days, with the flame reaching the Berlin stadium at exactly 5:20 on the afternoon of August 1. Taking no chances on tardiness, Diem built reserve time into the schedule—two-hour periods when the

flame would rest in a bowl on an altar in towns along the way. During these respites local officials could give speeches, and the populace might sing, dance, or hold parades in tribute to the Olympic spirit.

The torches themselves were, of course, a critical ingredient. Scholarly research indicated that the ancient Greeks had used wax or bundles of slow-burning stalks for conveying a flame in religious ceremonies, but Diem wanted something better—a failure-proof torch that would burn for about 10 minutes (to allow a margin for safety in each projected five-minute run) and couldn't be quenched by rain or wind. German scientists and engineers came through handsomely, designing an apparatus that had an incendiary device at the tip for quick ignition and burned magnesium as its principal fuel. The torch could even be dropped without going out: It was equipped with special wicks that would automatically shift the fire to backup fuel if the flaming magnesium fell off. Handles of chromed steel were supplied by Krupp, the German steelmaker. The entire torch, eminently photogenic, weighed 1 1/2 pounds and was just over 2 feet long.

On the morning of July 20, the glorious scheme was set in motion amid the tumbled stones of Olympia. As journalists from several nations looked on, a "high priestess" attended by 13 Greek girls in classical costume held a wand above a sun-focusing mirror supplied by the Zeiss company, Germany's famed optical firm. The wand burst into flame and was carried to an altar. After a few words from a Greek official, a German delegate declaimed: "O fire, lit in an ancient and sacred place, begin your race, and bring greetings to the youth of all the world, gathered together in my country. Bring greetings also to my Führer and to the whole of the German people." A Greek youth, clad only in briefs, then touched the tip of the first torch to the flame on the altar, turned, and began to run.

During the days that followed, the torchbearers

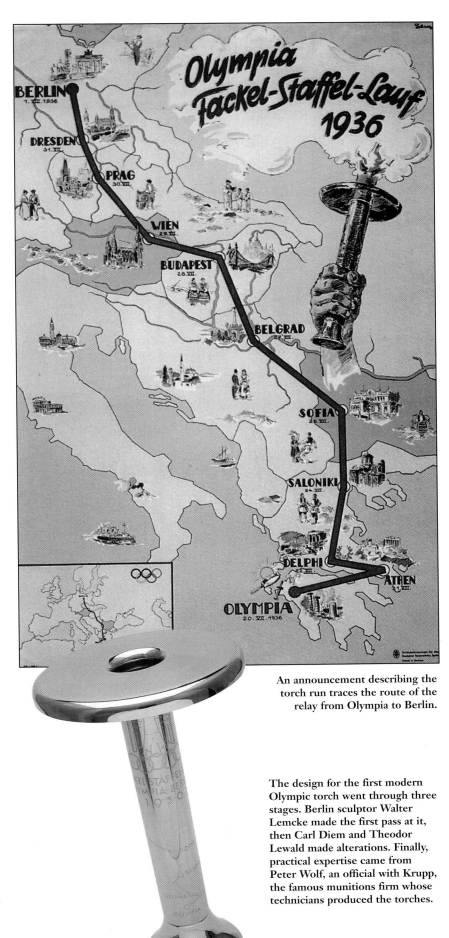

An announcement describing the torch run traces the route of the relay from Olympia to Berlin.

The design for the first modern Olympic torch went through three stages. Berlin sculptor Walter Lemcke made the first pass at it, then Carl Diem and Theodor Lewald made alterations. Finally, practical expertise came from Peter Wolf, an official with Krupp, the famous munitions firm whose technicians produced the torches.

A circle of Greek girls clad as ancient priestesses surrounds the Zeiss sun mirror during the 1936 torch-lighting ceremony at Olympia. The torch was ignited on July 20, 1936, 12 days before the start of the Games.

ran along a route connecting the capitals of all the participating nations. The runners sped over hills, through mountains, along the seacoast, across plains, and—for a stretch of 571 kilometers—beside the railway tracks of the Orient Express. A German radio team in a van accompanied the flame and reported on its progress to audiences back home. A second van carried a team of filmmakers led by brilliant young director Leni Riefenstahl, whose film *Olympia* would become the classic of Olympic documentaries. (Close by but unremarked was another vehicle. It carried Diem's insurance policy—a backup flame that had been lit in Olympia and could be put into service if, by some unimaginable mischance, the primary flame went out.)

Everywhere along the way, the drama of the relay stirred the people who watched. In Athens, much of the citizenry turned out to see the king of Greece pay honor to the flame. At several towns in Yugoslavia, officials were so long-winded

in reception ceremonies that the relay fell behind schedule; the torchbearers had to make up the lost time by riding on the running boards of cars for a while. In Yugoslavia, young men and old ran alongside the flame, sharing its mystical passage. In Hungary, Gypsies urged the sacred fire along with songs, and one of their chiefs in Budapest performed a special rite as further homage. In Austria, the president of the national Olympic committee clothed his stout figure in a baggy track suit, inserted himself in the human chain, and ran the first Austrian kilometer. The flame's arrival in Vienna brought huge crowds into the streets—and, to the discomfort of Olympic officials, also inspired an antigovernment demonstration by the city's many Nazi sympathizers. When the flame crossed the border into Czechoslovakia, 50,000 people witnessed the moment. In Germany, the roads were lined with celebrants along the entire route.

As the flame approached Berlin, some 30,000

A Greek in traditional peasant costume carries the torch in an early stage of the relay. Runners bore the flame for all but 25 kilometers of its route. For that stretch, all in Yugoslavia, it was carried by car to make up for lost time at earlier ceremonies.

young men and women gathered in the Lustgarten, a large square, to hail the Olympic flame with a special youth festival. This event had been organized by Joseph Goebbels, the head of Germany's propaganda ministry and one of Hitler's closest advisers. Gifted at his trade, the diminutive Goebbels addressed the crowd, finishing his speech with a theatrical gesture—a kind of summoning—and shouting: "Holy flame, burn, burn, and never go out!" Just then a roar began at the far margins of the crowd and rolled inward toward the center. Punctual to the minute, the sacred fire had reached the Lustgarten. Thousands of arms shot up in the Nazi salute.

The flame rested on an altar in the Lustgarten until late afternoon, then resumed its journey toward the Olympic stadium. The runners followed the city's main thoroughfare, broadened and given the name Via Triumphalis for the Games. The last runner of all was an embodiment of the Germanic ideal. Dressed in white, he was tall, slender, and flaxen-haired, a vision of athleticism and chiseled virility. He did not run alone: A V-shaped formation of seven runners accompanied him, providing a kind of living frame for his Nordic splendor.

At the stadium, celebrations had been going on for more than an hour. Hitler arrived at 4 p.m.; he

Adolf Hitler, flanked by Theodor Lewald *(right)* and Henri de Baillet-Latour, receives a bouquet of flowers from Carl Diem's daughter, Gudrun, as the Führer enters the Olympic stadium before the opening ceremony. Lewald and Baillet-Latour wear ceremonial Olympic chains commissioned by Berlin organizers as keepsakes for IOC members.

was wearing the brown uniform of a storm trooper and looked small and drab, but the stadium shook with exultant roars. A collective sigh followed as Carl Diem's five-year-old daughter approached the Führer, curtsied, and presented him with a bouquet of flowers. Finally, the opening ceremonies began in earnest. A march by Wagner was played. The teams tramped past the reviewing stand and assembled in the center of the stadium. Loudspeakers then delivered a recorded message from the founder of the modern Olympic movement, Baron Pierre de Coubertin, now 73

years old and unable to attend. "The important thing at the Olympic Games," said Coubertin, "is not to win, but to take part, just as the most important thing in life is not to conquer, but to struggle well."

After a speech from an Olympic official, Hitler stepped to a microphone and spoke the words everyone was waiting for: "I declare as open the Games in Berlin, to celebrate the XI Olympiad of the modern era." Distant artillery boomed a 21-gun salute. Flags of the attending nations fluttered around the stadium's rim. Thousands of pigeons,

each trailing a colored ribbon representing a particular country, soared aloft. In front of a chorus of 3,000 white-clad singers, world-famous German composer Richard Strauss conducted a hymn he had written specially for this day.

As the last notes died away, the final torchbearer appeared at the eastern gate of the stadium. He was alone now and, blondly radiant, looked like a messenger from the gods. The crowd grew hushed, rapt. The torchbearer, seemingly struck by some divine wonderment of his own, paused to contemplate the 100,000 gathered mortals. Then he proceeded to the cinder track and, with his torch held high, ran around the oval to a set of stairs leading upward to a stone dais where a huge brazier rested atop a tripod. Supremely graceful, he climbed the stairway, approached the brazier, rose on his toes, and touched his torch to the fire bowl. A great flame bloomed, rippling in the breeze. It was done: The light of Olympia resided in Berlin.

But in that moment—and indeed in the whole enthralling spectacle of the torch relay—lurked the makings of a dreadful irony. Nothing could have been further from Adolf Hitler's heart than Baron de Coubertin's sentiment that "the most important thing in life is not to conquer, but to struggle well." Conquest was elixir to the Führer. Every one of the seven countries crossed by the peaceful Olympic flame would soon experience, by his will, a wholly different kind of conflagration: In 1938 Austria would be hauled into the Third Reich by political intimidation; in 1938 and 1939 a supine international community would allow Hitler to seize parts of Czechoslovakia; in 1939 Hungary would begin allying itself with the Third Reich, only to eventually become a battleground between German and Soviet forces; in 1941 German troops would pour into the Balkans, taking up strategic positions in a compliant Bulgaria, then smashing into Yugoslavia and Greece. And by the end of 1945, much of Germany itself would lie in ruins, a

shattered testament to a dictator's rapacity.

Coercion and conquest along the route of the Olympic flame were, of course, only a fraction of the horrors unleashed by Hitler. War would engulf much of the world and, in one way or another, claim perhaps 50 million lives. The Olympic movement itself would come near destruction, with the cancellation of four Games, two summer and two winter. Not until the winter of 1948 would athletes of the world gather again—in a Europe that was a moonscape of wreckage.

Middle-distance runner Fritz Schilgen turns to acknowledge the crowd after igniting the flame in the Olympic brazier. The honor of being the final torchbearer fell to the graceful Schilgen because officials thought he ran with a perfect gait.

It was all done in the name of destiny.

According to Nazi ideology, Germans were "Aryans," a race superior to all others—to Jews, Slavs, Gypsies, people of color, and various other strains that made up the National Socialists' eccentric categorization of humankind. From Nazi racial theories was derived an overarching imperative: Lesser human breeds must be subjugated or eliminated, and a racially purified Germany must take whatever land it needed to support its growing population. These actions had a cultural corollary, according to Hitler. As Germany dealt with inferior races and territorial needs, German culture would conquer, too. It would be universally recognized as the crowning glory of world civilization.

The Olympic Games were a small but cherished feature of this vision of destiny. Germans had long been fascinated with ancient Greece and had played the leading role in the archeological excavations of Olympia during the previous century. In their twisted way, the Nazi leaders shared the general interest in the classical world. Pondering the racial aspects of the matter, they concluded that the ancient Greeks had been Aryans themselves, with blue eyes and fair hair. Unfortunately, intermarriage with lesser races had rendered their descendants swarthy and had diminished their cultural vigor. When that happened, said Hitler, the torch of history was passed; Germans, the purest of Aryans, had served as "culture-bearers" for the world ever since classical times. It was only proper, therefore, that the Olympics were now being held in Berlin. Indeed, the Führer would later tell a subordinate that, once the international order had been rearranged in accordance with his political and racial theories, the Olympics would be staged in the Third Reich "for all time to come."

On the eve of Berlin 1936, the implications of nazism were poorly understood by most foreign observers, but some sensed grave danger and said so. Many of the journalists who came to Berlin were troubled by the adulation Hitler inspired, the way crowds saluted him ecstatically and shouted "Sieg Heil!" Noting the pro-Nazi demonstration that occurred when the flame passed through Vienna, the *New York Times* editorialized: "The Olympic torch is more like a firebrand than a symbol of the welding flame of international sport. It is only a flare illuminating dark shapes and bewildering prospects." To some commentators, the Olympic Games had taken on an ominous political meaning. In this Nazi fastness, with all the world looking on, Hitler's claims of Aryan superiority would be put to a crucial test.

A central figure in the 1936 Olympics—whether as a test of Nazi ideology or simply as a test of athletic ability—was an African-American named Jesse Owens. He had only a sketchy notion of Hitler's claims, but he knew plenty about racism.

Owens was born in 1913 in the cotton country of north-central Alabama, the son of an impoverished sharecropper and the grandson of slaves. In America's Deep South, strict segregation of blacks from whites was either law or sacred custom in every aspect of life—in education, in sports, in where a person could sit in a movie theater or on a bus, in where one could work or eat a meal or get a drink of water or even go to the bathroom. Most white southerners in those days—and indeed, many white Americans—were no less convinced than Adolf Hitler of the superiority of their own race, the inferiority of others. In later life, Jesse Owens would remember his father telling him, "It don't do a colored man no good to get himself too high because it's a helluva drop back to the bottom."

Jesse was the youngest of 10 children and rather sickly in his early years, but he grew into a sturdy, handsome boy, brimming with optimism. He may have inherited his sunny temperament from his mother. In the early 1920s, at her urging, the

family moved to Cleveland, a city that had been known for its antislavery sentiments before the Civil War and had long been favored by Alabama blacks seeking a better life.

As it happened, Jesse and Cleveland were already linked: The boy had been christened James Cleveland Owens. That changed after the move north. When he enrolled in elementary school, a teacher asked him his name. He responded, "J. C. Owens, ma'am." Not understanding his Southern drawl, she recorded it as "Jesse." The name stuck.

In junior high school, Jesse's natural athleticism caught the eye of a physical education teacher, Charles Riley, who began giving the boy special training in track. Soon the two of them grew close: Riley drew Jesse into his own family and

became a sort of surrogate father—a relationship that would endure for many years. Riley was also an excellent coach, and in this case he had a pupil with astonishing physical gifts, among them an effortless running style. Another top American sprinter would later say that Jesse Owens "was the smoothest runner I have ever seen and the most physically coordinated. When he ran, it was like water flowing downhill." Jesse could also jump: In 1928, still only in his mid-teens, he soared 22 feet 11 3/4 inches (7 meters) in the long jump and 6 feet (1.83 meters) in the high jump. In June 1933—grown into a smoothly muscled young man standing 5 feet 10 inches tall and weighing 165 pounds—he won the long jump at the National Interscholastic championship meet in Chicago with a leap of 24 feet 9 5/8 inches

Berlin's Königstrasse is decked out in an incongruous mix of Olympic and Nazi regalia. At the time of the Games, the swastika had yet to become universally synonymous with evil.

Representing Ohio State, Jesse Owens sprints to the 220-yard dash title during the 1935 Big Ten championships at Ann Arbor, Michigan, the highlight of his breakthrough year on the U.S. track circuit. His exploits at Ann Arbor would make him an eagerly anticipated attraction at the Berlin Games.

(7.56 meters), then set two high-school world records, running the 220-yard dash in 20.7 seconds and the 100-yard dash in 9.4 seconds. The city of Cleveland gave him a victory parade when he returned home.

That same year, Owens entered Ohio State University. His early schooling had been haphazard, and he found reading and writing difficult, but he was willing to work hard and managed to stay afloat in his classes. In sports he was in a class by himself. During his freshman and sophomore years he went from victory to victory in local track meets. The high point—dizzyingly high—was the Big Ten championship meet in Ann Arbor, Michigan, on May 25, 1935.

Owens almost didn't take part that day. His back, wrenched during some horseplay, was

hurting him badly. Rubdowns and the warm weather helped, however, and after his first sprint he could run without pain. Perhaps in part because of the injury, his concentration was flawless and his timing perfect. In the long jump he soared 26 feet 8 1/4 inches (8.13 meters), a world record. In the 220-yard low hurdles—usually his weakest event—he flashed across the finish line in 22.6 seconds, another world record. In the 220-yard straight-course dash his time was 20.3 seconds, breaking a world record that had stood since 1924. And in the 100-yard dash he finished in an official time of 9.4 seconds, tying the world record. All three timers of that race actually clocked him at closer to 9.3 seconds, but the rules called for the time to be rounded to the higher tenth of a second. By any measure,

though, what he had accomplished was phenomenal—the greatest single day in track history, in the judgment of many experts.

Yet he didn't always win. Later that year, in a number of meets and in various events, Owens was repeatedly beaten by two other black athletes: Ralph Metcalfe of Marquette University, an Olympic silver medalist in 1932; and Temple University's Eulace Peacock, whose hard-driving style contrasted with Owens' fluidity. At the time, Jesse was troubled in his personal life. Few people knew that he was the father of a three-year-old girl by his high-school sweetheart. When a newspaper learned that the pair had never wed, he hastened to the altar, but the marriage was strained and would remain so. Still, he regained his old form by the following spring, and he

looked forward to the Olympics. Metcalfe would be another member of the U.S. team. Peacock, sadly, had been undone by injuries.

The Germans were familiar with Jesse Owens. His track heroics had been extensively described by the local press, but neither he nor his coach knew what sort of reception to expect in Berlin. They prepared for the worst. As Owens approached the Olympic stadium on the first day of competition, his coach said, "Don't let anything you hear from the stands upset you. Ignore the insults and you'll be all right."

Ready for whatever slurs came his way, Owens probably was not at all prepared for what he actually heard when he walked into the stadium—an enormous, deafening ovation. And every time he appeared thereafter, chants of "Yes-sa Ovens! Yes-sa Ovens!" would begin among the German spectators—their best effort at pronouncing his name. Whenever he stepped to the starting line, all eyes focused on him.

He would step to a starting line many times. On that first day's schedule were preliminary heats of the 100-meter dash, one of the glamour events of track; the Olympic winner was traditionally dubbed "the world's fastest man." Germany had an outstanding sprinter, Erich Borchmeyer, a great favorite with the crowd, but Owens' toughest competition was likely to come from his own teammate, Ralph Metcalfe.

During the course of the morning there were 12 preliminary heats, with 63 competitors. Owens had to wait almost three hours, until just before noon, before his heat—the last—was run. The waiting didn't bother him at all. He finished yards ahead of the other runners, clocking 10.3 seconds, equal to the world record. In the next elimination round, at 3 p.m., he appeared to overturn the world mark when he darted down the course in 10.2 seconds, but because of a following wind the time was discounted as a record.

The semifinals and finals in the 100-meter dash took place the next day—Monday, August 3.

THE GAMES AT A GLANCE

	August 1	August 2	August 3	August 4	August 5	August 6	August 7	August 8	August 9	August 10	August 11	August 12	August 13	August 14	August 15	August 16
OPENING CEREMONY	■															
ATHLETICS (TRACK & FIELD)		■	■	■	■	■	■	■	■							
BASKETBALL							■	■	■	■	■	■	■	■		
BOXING										■	■	■	■	■	■	
CANOEING							■	■								
CYCLING						■	■	■		■						
DIVING										■	■	■	■	■		
EQUESTRIAN SPORTS												■	■	■	■	■
FENCING	■		■	■	■	■	■	■	■	■	■	■	■			
FIELD HOCKEY							■	■	■	■	■	■	■	■	■	
FOOTBALL (SOCCER)			■	■	■	■	■			■		■			■	
GYMNASTICS											■	■	■			
MODERN PENTATHLON		■	■	■	■											
POLO			■	■	■	■	■									
ROWING											■	■	■	■		
SHOOTING						■	■									
SWIMMING										■	■	■	■	■	■	■
TEAM HANDBALL							■	■	■		■		■	■		
WATER POLO										■	■	■	■	■	■	
WEIGHT LIFTING		■	■		■											
WRESTLING		■	■	■			■	■	■							
YACHTING				■	■	■	■	■	■	■						
CLOSING CEREMONY																■
DEMONSTRATION SPORTS																
BASEBALL												■				
CHINESE BOXING						■					■					
CYCLING							■	■	■							
GLIDER PLANES				■												
GYMNASTICS (SPECIAL DISCIPLINES)		■	■		■	■	■	■								

Conditions didn't favor outstanding times. The weather was cool and cloudy, and a shower passed over the city around midday. When the semifinals were run a little later, Owens was slower than usual, although he won easily. About 2 p.m. rain fell again. The track was not only wet, but it had also been badly churned up in places by distance runners.

The six 100-meter finalists included three from the U.S. team: Owens, Ralph Metcalfe, and Frank Wykoff. Germany's Borchmeyer had also made it to the finals, along with Lennart Strandberg of Sweden and Martinus Osendarp of the Netherlands. Carefully, each of them dug small "toe holes" in the cinders with trowels provided for that purpose; starting blocks weren't yet available for sprinters.

The starter, Franz Miller, had already earned the runners' appreciation for his perfect steadiness as, at two-second intervals, he called out the start sequence and fired his pistol. Now he signaled the climactic moment. As Owens would later recall: "The starter stepped back about ten paces and he hollered in a loud German voice, 'Aufdieplatz,' and when he hollered, 'Aufdieplatz,' every man went to his mark. And when the starter suddenly said in a soft voice, 'Fertig,' every man came to set position. Every muscle in his body was strained. The gun went off."

Owens was not always good in his starts, but

now his mind was finely focused. At the sound of the gun he surged away from the line. Most of the others also got a smooth start, but Metcalfe stumbled slightly as he came out of his crouch. After the first 10 meters or so, Owens reached full stride and, showing the fluency that other runners marveled at, began to pull away. Metcalfe still seemed to have a chance, and at the three-quarters mark he put on a burst of speed, making up ground on the leader. But it was too late. Amid a storm of noise, Owens crossed the line a yard ahead of Metcalfe. Clocked at 10.3 seconds, Owens had once again tied the world record, despite a sodden track. Osendarp of the Netherlands was third. Borchmeyer finished fifth behind Wykoff.

That victory would become part of the Owens legend—a one-man show of Olympic greatness never to be forgotten. But more than one legend was born that day. An ugly tale related to the victory would soon find its way into print and live on for decades: It was said that Hitler went out of his way to snub Owens; having made a great show of extending his personal congratulations to white victors, the Führer supposedly refused to shake the hand of this black man.   •

In fact, the snub never occurred, at least not in the way the story was told. The tale arose out of Hitler's behavior on the first day of competition—a banner day for the Germans. In past Olympics, no German man had ever won a gold medal in track and field, but on that Sunday, Hans Woellke took first place in the shot put, and another German won the bronze. A proud Hitler summoned both of them to his box in the stadium and pumped their hands vigorously. A little later he accorded similar honors to three Finns when they finished first, second, and third in the 10,000-meter run, and he also congratulated two German women, Tilly Fleischer and Luise Krüger, for finishing one-two in the javelin throw before his arrival. One other final, in the high jump, remained on the day's schedule, but with darkness descending and rain threatening, Hitler left the stadium before the winner was determined. The president of the International Olympic Committee, Count Henri de Baillet-Latour of Belgium, perceived his departure as a slight. The next day Baillet-Latour sent an emissary to the Führer. Hitler was told that he must congratulate either all the winners or none. The

Demonstrating his unique straight-backed running style, Jesse Owens leads the competition by a yard at the finish of the 100-meter dash. His time of 10.3 seconds would remain the Olympic standard until Rome 1960.

directive had to be obeyed, since Hitler was not an Olympic official but only a guest of honor. Thus beginning that Monday and continuing throughout the Games, he treated all winners alike: He shook none of their hands. The alternative of congratulating blacks or Jews or other such subhumans was presumably unthinkable.

Hate was Adolf Hitler's stock-in-trade. He had been fomenting it and spewing it and exploring its outer reaches ever since Germany lost the First World War. Some of his hate was directed at the victors and the harsh peace terms of the Treaty of Versailles—a settlement calling for crippling reparations payments stretching far into the future, and also designed to block any revival of German

military power. Some hate was directed at supposed internal enemies who, in various ways, conspired to weaken or rule his adopted country (he was Austrian by birth). Foremost among the internal enemies were Jews, but Communists, Roman Catholics, Freemasons, and many other foes were on the list.

During the 1920s, Hitler's hatemongering went unheeded by most Germans; the National Socialist Party remained small, although violent, intimidating its opponents with a force of brown-shirted street brawlers called storm troopers. But after the Wall Street crash of 1929 sent economic shock waves across the world and pitched German society into further disarray, the Nazis flourished. In elections held in 1930, when unemployment stood at four million, Nazis won

Germans on the winners' podium, along with attendants that include Theodor Lewald *(front, right)*, give a Nazi salute during the medal ceremony for the women's javelin medalists. IOC president Baillet-Latour *(front, left)* keeps hold of his hat. Tilly Fleischer *(top step)* was the first of 33 German gold medalists at Berlin.

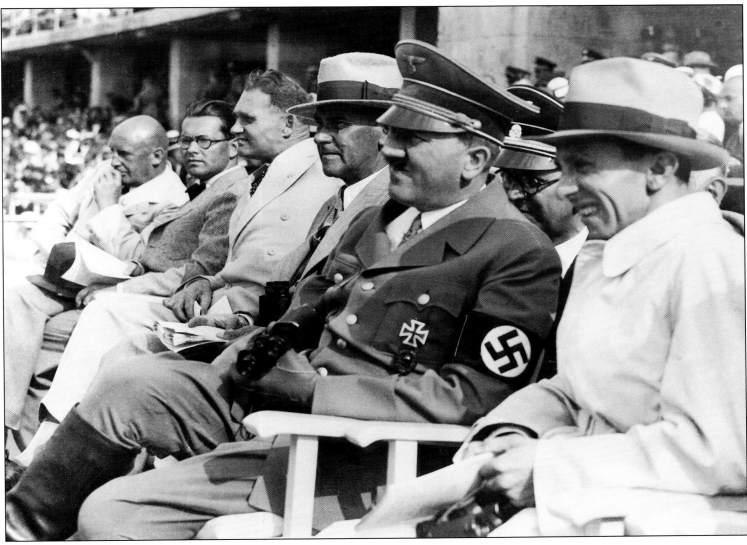

the second-highest total of seats in the Reichstag, the national parliament. Two years later unemployment reached six million, and Hitler closed in on total power.

A spellbinding orator, the Führer convincingly promised to restore the economy and expunge the disgrace of the Treaty of Versailles, meanwhile ridding the Fatherland of all the elements that undermined Aryan greatness. Germany would rise again, its internal fissures healed, its international dignity restored.

Despite Hitler's rhetorical talents, the Nazis lost ground in the elections of November 1932. Still, they were powerful enough to be desirable political allies, and in 1933 Germany's aging and ineffectual president, former field marshal Paul von Hindenburg, named Hitler chancellor, his second in command of the government. Later that year, after fears of social unrest coalesced

around a fire in the Reichstag building, Hitler persuaded the legislature to let him rule by decree. He promptly outlawed all political parties but his own and set up the first concentration camps, where enemies of the state could be detained indefinitely. In 1934 Hindenburg died. Hitler took his place and named himself "Führer" (leader) of the German people. He outlawed strikes and took control of all governmental institutions, all police forces, all newspapers.

However extreme his measures, Hitler's popularity soared—and not just among the malcontents first attracted to nazism. Now many professionals were caught up in the Führer's fire, among them teachers and university professors. Students were fascinated by him. Children joined youth organizations and learned Nazi social views. And, by and large, both the Catholic and Protestant churches cooperated with his regime.

Hitler was an avid spectator at the Berlin Games, taking in as many events as his schedule would allow. The sports fans watching with him—*(from left)* Julius Streicher, Philipp Bouhler, Rudolf Hess, Wilhelm Frick, and Joseph Goebbels—were already becoming notorious as leaders of the Nazi regime.

OLYMPIC BUST, SOCIALIST BOON

One athlete at Berlin became a minor legend even though he didn't win any medals. Germany's Werner Seelenbinder was a national champion Greco-Roman wrestler in the light heavyweight class. He was also an outspoken socialist and anti-Nazi.

Born in 1904 to a working-class family in Stettin, now a part of Poland, Seelenbinder developed both his muscles and his politics while hauling produce for his father's grocery business: He was attracted by workers' groups, and wrestling coaches were attracted by his strength. Seelenbinder became a well-known figure in socialist sporting circles during the 1920s, and he joined the Communist Party in 1928. When the Communist-hating Nazis came to power in 1933, the popular wrestler came under close government scrutiny. When he failed to give a fascist salute after winning a national tournament, Seelenbinder landed in jail. Released, he was nevertheless a marked man. His eligibility for matches was often contested, yet he was still wrestling in 1935 when the Germans held their Olympic trials. Seelenbinder was by then 31—seemingly over the hill—but he surprised everyone by winning the light heavyweight division.

Socialist companions, confident he would win at Berlin, urged Seelenbinder to make an antifascist gesture on the medals stand. He agreed, but first he had to get there. He didn't. Pinned in his first match, he fell from medal contention. The moment was lost.

On February 4, 1942, Nazi authorities arrested Seelenbinder and charged him with treason. He spent the next three years in prison camps until his execution by guillotine in 1945. After the war, leaders in East Germany turned the unlucky Seelenbinder into a Communist martyr. Schoolchildren learned about his life, stadiums were named after him, and annual competitions were held in his honor. His ideals rather than medals made him a symbol of East German sport.

Meanwhile, Jews were systemically persecuted. Hitler loathed them. In *Mein Kampf* (My Struggle), a manifesto composed in 1923 during a stay in prison for revolutionary activities, he had written that it was the goal of Jews "to bolshevise Germany—i.e., to rot away German national intelligence, and so crush the forces of German labor under the yoke of Jewish world finances, as a preliminary to extending far and wide the Jewish plan of conquering the world."

As soon as he won power in 1933, he acted on these views. Jews were barred from public office or work in the civil service; they were banned from the stock exchanges, journalism, filmmaking, teaching, and farming. But that was just the beginning. Under the so-called Nuremberg Laws, proclaimed by Hitler at a party rally in 1935, Jews were deprived of their citizenship and forbidden to marry German "nationals."

If his vicious, police-state governance appalled some Germans, even they had to admit that Hitler was delivering on his promise to revive the nation. He had only a minimal understanding of economics, but he nevertheless managed to bring prosperity to Germany through vast public-works projects and a massive rearmament

program: By 1935 unemployment was down to 1.7 million (although about half of the country's Jews were now pauperized). He also made good on his vow to throw off the yoke of the Versailles treaty. On March 7, 1936—five months before the opening of the Olympic Games in Berlin—he sent troops into the Rhineland, a 30-mile-wide zone of German territory that had been designated by the treaty as a permanently demilitarized buffer zone between Germany and France. The French government briefly thought about going to war to drive the Germans out, then thought better of it. After the French backed down, Hitler pushed his rearmament program even harder.

But because he needed time to get ready for any bolder move, he disguised himself as a man of peace. In marching into the Rhineland, he said, he merely wanted to correct an old injustice; the Rhineland was German, after all. Other nations should not take alarm at his rapid rebuilding of German military strength. On the contrary, the world could count on Germany remaining a constructive member of the international community; a strong, prosperous Germany would contribute to international stability.

The world listened and did nothing.

In a modest way, sport had figured in Hitler's vision of a resurgent Germany from the very start of his political maneuverings. For the Führer, athletics held more complex meanings than who won or lost in competitions. The point, he said in *Mein Kampf*, was to strengthen the young Aryan: "Through his bodily power and agility he must fortify his faith in the invincibility of his whole race and nation."

As time went on, other Nazis fleshed out this idea. A year before the Berlin Games, the government issued a handbook aimed at teaching athletes proper political attitudes. "National Socialism cannot permit even a single phase of life to remain outside the general organization of the nation," it stated. "Every athlete and sportsman in the Third Reich must serve the State." Having made that clear, the handbook turned to the subject of race, focusing on Jews, as usual. "Among the inferior races, the Jews have done nothing in the athletic sphere. They are surpassed even by the lowest of the Negro tribes."

Before the National Socialists came to power, most party leaders viewed the Olympics with contempt—"an infamous festival dominated by Jews," wrote one. It never occurred to the Nazis that they would one day find themselves hosting the Games. Nor did it occur to members of the International Olympic Committee when they awarded the 1936 Games to Germany. That step was taken in mid-1931, two years before Nazi ascendancy. At the time, a centrist coalition ruled the Reich. But even without Nazi extremism to give it pause, the IOC hesitated in its decision, conscious of past troubles with Germany.

The difficulties had begun with an Olympic misfire long ago. Before the outbreak of World War I, Berlin had been tapped to host the 1916 Games. As the time approached, it seemed possible that the fighting would end soon enough to allow the event to go forward. But the war went on, and the Games were never held.

The Germans expected to attend the next Olympic gathering, Antwerp 1920, but the Belgians, who had suffered horribly during the war, had other ideas. Caught in the middle, the IOC decreed that the host city could determine who was invited, and Antwerp left Germany off the list, along with Austria, Hungary, Turkey, and Bulgaria. Paris followed suit by excluding Germany from the 1924 Olympics. Not until 1928 and the winter festival at St. Moritz did German athletes rejoin the Games.

The return greatly pleased two men who had been closely involved with the ill-fated 1916 Games: Theodor Lewald and Carl Diem. Both men had glittering credentials in the sports world. From 1913 onward, Diem, who began his career

Carl Diem *(far left)* and **Theodor Lewald** *(seated across the table from him)* convene a meeting during the early planning stages of the Berlin Games. Neither man had connections to the Nazi party, and both had Jewish associations—facts that threatened their positions as leaders of the Berlin organizing committee. The IOC forced Hitler to keep them on.

as a sports journalist, had been a leading figure in German sports unions and federations. He was also the motive force in founding the German College for Physical Education, an institution for the scientific study of sport and the training of physical education teachers. Because sport was his profession, Diem could not be a member of the IOC. Nevertheless, he was highly influential in the international Olympic movement and a close friend of IOC leaders. After World War II he would go on to become the world's leading authority on sports history and theory. Lewald, the very model of a Prussian public servant, had been since 1919 the leader of Germany's most important sports union. He became an IOC member in 1924 and was also the president of the German National Olympic Committee.

Both Diem and Lewald had worked hard for the Olympic reinstatement in 1928, but they weren't satisfied merely to be back in the movement. They had been bitterly disappointed by the loss of the 1916 Games and were determined to win Germany another chance to be host. Their persuasion was largely responsible for the IOC's 1931 decision to launch the XI Olympiad in Berlin. Best of all from their point of view, Lewald and Diem would once again be heading

up Germany's effort to produce the Games. Lewald would be chairman and Diem general secretary of the Berlin Olympic Organizing Committee—or so they thought.

When the IOC voted in 1931 to have Berlin host the 1936 Games, Hitler was still short of the absolute power he craved. At that time his attitude toward a cosmopolitan athletic festival on the sacred soil of the Reich was scornful. The Olympics, he said, were "an invention of Jews and Freemasons." If the National Socialists were in charge, he declared, the Games would not be held in Germany. But by the time Nazi rule became a reality the following year, he was already changing his mind. Given his genius for image making, he could hardly fail to grasp the Games' potential as an international showcase for the new Germany. What better way to display to the world the fruits of Nazi policies—a strong, prosperous, disciplined nation? Sedentary and uninterested in sports himself, Hitler nevertheless recognized the mass appeal of the Olympics, not to mention their potential for spectacle in the service of politics.

The roles of Lewald and Diem were another matter, however. From the Nazi point of view, the two men were fatally flawed: Diem's wife was

one-quarter Jewish, and Lewald was himself half Jewish. Some party leaders urged that these racially dubious personages be severed from the Olympic effort. Others urged caution, since Nazi anti-Semitism was notorious abroad and had already prompted talk of relocating the 1936 Games. The deciding factor in this argument was the International Olympic Committee itself: IOC president Baillet-Latour wrote Hitler that if Lewald and Diem were removed from their posts on the Olympic organizing committee, the 1936 Games would not be held in Berlin. So Lewald and Diem stayed on. However, their Jewish connections couldn't be overlooked. To make the necessary point, the Nazis saw to it that Diem and Lewald were stripped of their positions with German sports organizations, and Diem lost his post as vice-rector of the college he had helped to found. Lewald was forced to give up the presidency of the German Olympic Committee, ceding the job to a man named Hans von Tschammer und Osten, a party hack who got the title of Reichssportführer (leader of German sport).

The IOC was dismayed at the treatment of Lewald and Diem, two distinguished men regarded outside Germany as invaluable members of the international Olympic family. IOC members were also alarmed by reports of Nazi discrimination against Jewish athletes. In April 1933, a top player on the German Davis Cup tennis team was dropped because he was Jewish. In May, Jews were excluded from Germany's

Cabaret-style shows in the Hindenburg House at the Olympic Village drew large audiences during the Games. Even nonathletes such as Village commandant Werner von und zu Gilsa *(left)*, a high-ranking Wehrmacht officer, and Reichssportführer Hans von Tschammer und Osten *(second from left)* spent an evening watching a performance. The Wehrmacht had oversight responsibility for the Village during the Games.

13,000 gymnastic associations, a fixture in the nation's sports. In June, the Reich's minister of education announced that Jews could no longer belong to youth and welfare organizations or use any of their facilities. That summer, many cities began excluding Jews from public swimming pools. In the autumn, Jewish athletes were informed that they could compete only against other Jews, and they would not be allowed to travel abroad for matches. As the Nazi newspaper editor Julius Streicher put it, "We need waste no words here, Jews are Jews and there is no place for them in German sports."

In the face of all this, the IOC, meeting in Vienna in 1933, demanded assurances that German Jews would be allowed to try out for the 1936 Games. The Nazis, now eager to hold on to the Games, authorized Lewald to provide a written guarantee. Its language was careful and legalistic: "As a principle, German Jews shall not be excluded from German Teams at the Games of the XI Olympiad." But the principle wasn't worth much, since German tryouts for the Olympics would be open only to athletes belonging to sporting clubs—clubs that now excluded Jews—and the few all-Jewish sports clubs in Germany were already being harassed by the police. Still, some Nazis were embarrassed at making any concession at all. When Reichssportführer Tschammer und Osten addressed a gathering of sports officials in Germany, he was defensive: "You are probably astonished by the decision in Vienna," he noted, "but we had to consider the foreign situation."

The foreign situation involved more than just the feelings of IOC members. Athletic organizations in a number of countries—among them Sweden, Switzerland, Holland, and Czechoslovakia—had begun discussing the possibility of boycotting the Games, thus wrecking Germany's hour of Olympic glory and rejecting all that the Nazis stood for. In those countries the protest movements were never more than embryonic.

Nor did would-be boycotters make much headway in Britain, where sporting officialdom was largely made up of conservative aristocrats, many of whom sympathized with the Nazi cause. "There are a lot of well-meaning busybodies who are trying to mix sport with politics," fumed one. "All I have to say to them is, 'Hands off sport, politicians.'" Elsewhere, however, the boycott threat was very real. The Republican government of Spain firmly blocked Olympic preparations and eventually approved the staging of rival games—the so-called Peoples' Olympiad, scheduled to be held in Barcelona in July of 1936. Even more worrisome to the Germans was the possibility that the United States, a nation that had always gleamed bright in the Olympic firmament, might refuse to send its athletes to the Third Reich.

The U.S. boycott movement had support at the highest levels of the amateur-sports establishment. In November of 1933 the Amateur Athletic Union (AAU)—national governing body for track and field—voted to decline Germany's invitation to the Olympics unless German Jews were allowed to train and compete. This resolution had teeth: IOC regulations required that the AAU sign off on the eligibility of would-be Olympians. Eligibility also had to be approved by the American Olympic Committee (AOC), which was headed by a man who backed the AAU resolution, Avery Brundage. A former Olympic athlete and now a successful Chicago businessman, Brundage was destined to play a key role in this debate—and he would continue to figure pivotally in Olympic affairs for years to come.

In mid-1934 the German government made a conciliatory move: Reichssportführer Tschammer und Osten announced that 21 Jewish athletes had been nominated for Olympic training. This peace offering was greeted with suspicion in the United States. In hopes of settling the matter once and for all, the AOC decided to send Brundage to Germany for a firsthand look.

THE PEOPLES' OLYMPICS

Antifascists of all stripes were opposed to holding the Olympic Games in Nazi Germany. Several of these opponents, whose boycott efforts fell short, started movements to hold competing games. Exiled German artist Max Ernst put together an art competition and show in Amsterdam billed as The Olympics without a Dictator. In Prague, workers' groups held a track and field exhibition with athletes from Sweden, the United States, France, and German émigrés. But the contest that drew the greatest attention was the Olimpiada Popular, or Peoples' Olympiad, scheduled for Barcelona from July 22 to 26, 1936.

Often misconstrued as a workers' event, the Peoples' Olympiad was created by socialist-friendly Catalonian sports groups as a response to fascist oppression. It was billed as the only festival that would reaffirm the Olympic spirit of brotherhood and fair play. Organizers expected as many as 6,000 athletes from 23 national groups to take part in a program as large as that of the Olympics, and competitors and journalists from around the world converged on Barcelona in late July. The last practice for the opening ceremony took place on July 18, and all seemed ready for the celebration. But the next day, Communist forces attacked the government and started the Spanish Civil War. The goodwill that the event promised was the first casualty. The Peoples' Olympiad never took place.

A poster promotes the Olimpiada Popular, a sport festival designed to protest the Berlin Games.

Brundage's inspection tour turned out to be a cursory and well-filtered glance. He spoke no German and had to use interpreters at all times. In his few brief meetings with representatives of Jewish sports clubs, Nazi officials were always on hand. He talked with Tschammer und Osten, liked him, and took away written assurances that Jewish athletes were getting fair treatment. Brundage, who had been intimately involved with amateur sports in America ever since competing in the Stockholm 1912 pentathlon and decathlon, badly wanted the boycott movement to fizzle. So he saw in Germany what he wanted to see, ignored any inward doubts, and hurried home with a favorable report to the AOC. The group accepted his assessment and voted for participation.

The following year, the senior U.S. member of the IOC, General Charles Sherrill, made his own tour of Germany. Like Brundage, Sherrill concluded that the Germans were proceeding in good faith. But he went further, commenting that Nazi handling of Jewish athletes was nobody else's business. "As for obstacles placed in the way of Jewish athletes or any others in trying to reach Olympic ability," he told a reporter, "I would have no more business discussing that in Germany than if the Germans attempted to discuss the Negro situation in the American South or the treatment of the Japanese in California." Anyway, the issue was moot, in the view of Sherrill, who admired Hitler. "There was never a prominent Jewish athlete in history," he opined.

But in America the boycott movement still gathered strength. Many American Catholics favored it, viewing the Nazis as weird neopagans. Many labor unions supported it, seeing Hitler as hostile to the workingman. And American Jews found the prospect of U.S. involvement utterly

abhorrent after finding their German coreligionists stripped of citizenship and redefined as "subjects" by the Nuremberg Laws. The depth and breadth of the movement was stunning to the likes of Brundage and Sherrill: A poll revealed that 43 percent of all Americans favored staying away from Berlin. Most significant of all, the AAU still withheld its approval.

Brundage, domineering by nature, began to question the motives of anyone who disagreed with him. At one point he suggested that his critics were hapless tools of "Jewish propaganda." On another occasion he wrote: "Many of the individuals and organizations active in the present campaign to boycott the Olympics have Communistic antecedents. Radicals and Communists must keep their hands off American sport." Strong views and strong language were customary with him, and now he showed little restraint.

A critical moment arrived in December 1935, when the executive committee of the AAU convened in New York for a final vote on the question of Olympic participation. The president of the organization, Jeremiah Mahoney, argued strenuously for a boycott, but Brundage—Mahoney's predecessor as AAU president—had been working hard behind the scenes. By a narrow margin, the committee voted to send American athletes to Berlin. Shortly afterward, Mahoney resigned and Brundage took his place. Now that Avery Brundage was in charge of both the AAU and the AOC, the danger of the United States' spoiling Germany's party was past.

As it turned out, there would be absentees from the party, for a variety of reasons. The USSR, at odds with most of the international community, had never approved of the Olympic movement and had been holding rival games called "Red Sport International" since 1921. Brazil, riven by factional politics, sent two teams to Berlin, but Olympic officials couldn't decide which squad was eligible, and both left. In Spain, plans for the Peoples' Olympiad went forward; these alternative games were heavily backed by the international labor movement and billed as a "final gesture of protest against the Hitler Nazi Games in Berlin," but they were undone at the last minute by the outbreak of the Spanish Civil War.

While the boycott movement waxed and waned during the three years prior to Berlin 1936, the German government kept its eye on the main goal—making the Games display the dynamism of the Third Reich. "Preparations," said Hitler, "must be complete and magnificent." The indefatigable Carl Diem carried most of the organizational load, but even the Führer was happy to help—as, for example, after his briefing on plans for the Olympic stadium in the autumn of 1933. A stadium already existed; it had been built for the aborted 1916 Games on the grounds of the Grünewald racecourse eight miles west of the center of Berlin, but its seating capacity was insufficient for the present purposes. A well-known architect named Werner March, whose father had designed the original, was enlisted to enlarge it. The commission proved uncomfortable. When Hitler examined March's model and visited the site, he railed against what he saw as architectural timidity. (The Führer had aspired to be an architect in his youth, and he deemed himself an expert in the field.) The old stadium was to be razed and a new, bigger one erected, he decreed. Moreover, the racecourse must be relocated and room made for an assembly area where grand ceremonies could be staged.

The resulting stadium, lavishly faced in stone and fitted in steel, was the largest ever built, able to hold 100,000 spectators. It had a 400-meter red-cinder track, and the track and its infield were set 45 feet below ground level, giving the 71 tiers of seats an unusually low profile. They rose a mere 54 feet above the ground. The adjacent assembly space, the Mayfield, could hold a quarter of a million people. At one edge of the

WHERE THE GAMES WERE PLAYED

Olympic Swim Stadium

Olympic Stadium

Dietrich Eckart Open-Air Theater

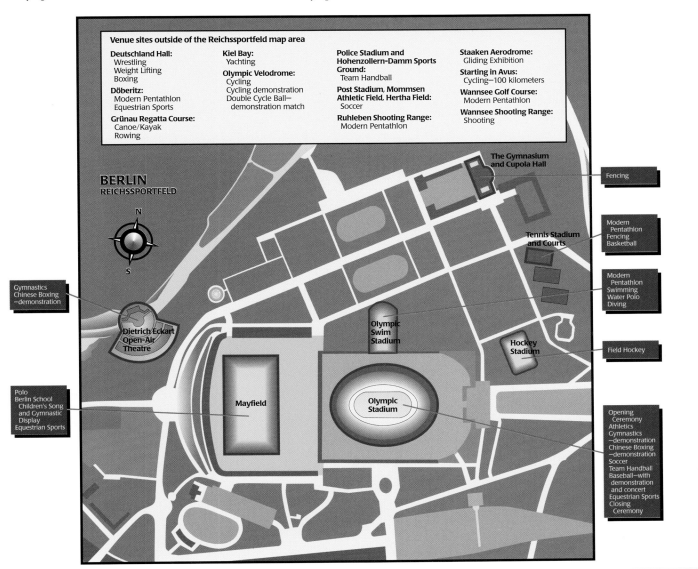

Venue sites outside of the Reichssportfeld map area

Deutschland Hall:
Wrestling
Weight Lifting
Boxing
Döberitz:
Modern Pentathlon
Equestrian Sports
Grünau Regatta Course:
Canoe/Kayak
Rowing

Kiel Bay:
Yachting
Olympic Velodrome:
Cycling
Cycling demonstration
Double Cycle Ball—
demonstration match

Police Stadium and Hohenzollern-Damm Sports Ground:
Team Handball
Post Stadium, Mommsen Athletic Field, Hertha Field:
Soccer
Ruhleben Shooting Range:
Modern Pentathlon

Staaken Aerodrome:
Gliding Exhibition
Starting in Avus:
Cycling—100 kilometers
Wannsee Golf Course:
Modern Pentathlon
Wannsee Shooting Range:
Shooting

BERLIN REICHSSPORTFELD

A primitive TV camera with a telephoto lens follows Olympic action for the first time. The TV coverage was a free service commissioned by the organizing committee. Today, revenues from worldwide rights to televise the Games have surpassed one billion dollars.

field was a 243-foot tower, and at its top hung a nine-and-a-half-ton bell inscribed "Berlin 1936" and bearing the legend *Ich rufe die Jugend der Welt*—"I summon the youth of the world." The Olympic bell was Theodor Lewald's idea.

Vast as they were, the main stadium and the Mayfield represented just a small fraction of the Olympic complex. Immediately adjacent to the stadium was the impressive swimming and diving venue, where, from a pair of opposing grandstands, 16,000 people would have a superb view of the water sports. Close by were soccer fields, polo fields, and a constellation of additional arenas. At an open-air amphitheater, Grecian in style, 25,000 people could sit on stone tiers and watch gymnastic competitions. A small stadium to the northeast was dedicated to field hockey. On the south side was a riding ring with a paddock and stables. The entire complex covered almost 350 acres.

Elsewhere in and around Berlin were additional Olympic venues, created in the same expansive spirit. A few miles away from the main complex stood the Deutschland Hall, where 20,000 spectators would view weight lifting, boxing, wrestling, and a number of other sports. At Grünau in the east of the city, a 2,000-meter rowing course, broad enough to accommodate six boats abreast, was laid out on a lake, and stands for 20,000 spectators were constructed along the shore. Only one sport would take place at any appreciable distance from Berlin: The nearest suitable yachting venue was at Kiel, a great naval base and longtime yachting center 300 miles to the north, on the Baltic Sea.

Along with superior facilities, the Germans aimed to impress visitors with superior technology. For track events they devised a photoelectric timing mechanism that would be activated by the starter's pistol; the pistol would also trigger the

world's largest stopwatch, a behemoth 11 feet in diameter, mounted in the stadium to give the spectators instant results. For viewing at a distance, the planners arranged to transmit closed-circuit television images to theaters and halls throughout Berlin. Novel as it was, the nascent medium proved to be a disappointment: The television cameras were huge and produced miserable results. During the Games one reporter would complain, "All that you can see are some men dressed like athletes but only faintly distinguishable, like human beings floating in a milk bath."

Carl Diem had visited Los Angeles for the 1932 Games and had been most impressed by that city's creation of an Olympic Village. Thus he and other planners prepared carefully for the housing of the athletes—though with mixed results. The principal women's facility was a spartan dormitory located in the main complex and guarded by a high fence. Its supervisor was a Prussian noblewoman who turned out to be a stern disciplinarian with scant interest in her charges' physical comfort.

By contrast, the quarters for the men were practically paradisiacal. Diem decided that male athletes would be housed in a community built from scratch about nine miles west of the stadium in a sylvan landscape of oak, birch, and pine trees; gleaming lakes; and gentle hills. This Olympic Village boasted houses made of brick and stone, roofed with red tiles, each having 10 or 12 double bedrooms. (The Los Angeles dwellings that had inspired Diem in the first place were hovels by comparison.) The Village also included several large buildings for meals and meetings, training facilities, an infirmary, and a Finnish-style sauna beside a lake. To attract birds, rabbits, and other wildlife, feeders were dotted about the grounds. Not all wildlife was welcome, however: Mosquitoes were eradicated everywhere within flying distance.

In devising this Village, the planners' concerns for the comfort of the residents reached down to the tiniest details. It was stipulated that each house would have two stewards speaking the language of the athletes living there. Bedding was chosen with national preferences in mind: The Americans would get mattresses, sheets, and blankets; the Japanese would have mats, the Europeans their goose-down comforters. Food, too, would be attuned to national palates, with the Czechs getting pork fat in their meat dishes, the British given grilled meat and plainly cooked vegetables, and

Post-office buildings such as this one were converted into closed-circuit TV houses for spectators who couldn't buy tickets to Olympic events. The television coverage was a technological miracle of its time, even if the fuzzy pictures it provided were less than satisfying.

American athletes strolling ahead of uniformed Germans enjoy the serene grounds of the Olympic Village. Ironically, World War II would turn the site into a training camp for bomber pilots.

the French able to order steak Châteaubriand, along with suitable wines.

The government looked to the well-being not only of the athletes, but of more ordinary visitors. Berliners were told to try to please all their guests, giving seats to women in buses or trains "even if the woman looks like a Jewess." To make sure that foreigners could find their way around the city without trouble, the organizers arranged to have interpreters, identified by

badges, at key locations. As opening day approached, known pickpockets and other troublemakers were rounded up. Vendors were warned against price gouging, and the currency exchange rate offered near-windfall benefits to tourists. Special police detachments were assigned to keep an eye on boardinghouses and hotels of shady repute. And in both Berlin and the surrounding countryside, people were ordered to clean up rubbish, paint their houses, plant flowers, and fly the national flag.

On the eve of the great sport festival, Propaganda Minister Joseph Goebbels told an assemblage of foreign journalists that in Berlin they would find plentiful evidence that the German people were thriving under the Nazis. The resurgence of his nation was authentic, he said. In truth, some of the arrangements were decidedly artificial. Farm laborers were told to stay out of sight during work breaks because visitors might think they were malingering. People condemned to forced labor had to be altogether invisible; a directive to the appropriate authorities stated: "Political prisoners and inmates of concentration camps are in no circumstances to work on the land from 1 July to 1 September." In accordance with Hitler's wishes, Goebbels

Located in the western suburbs of Berlin 10 miles from the Reichssportfeld, the Olympic Village, still under construction in this April 1936 photograph, became an idyllic setting for the male athletes.

also tried to mute the virulent anti-Semitism that the Nazis had encouraged for years. Realizing how visitors might react to the sight of a sign that said "Jews are not wanted here" or a scrawled anti-Semitic slogan on a wall, the propaganda minister ordered wholesale erasure—until the foreigners left, anyway. He also saw to it that the most venomous of Nazi newspapers, *Der Stürmer*, was removed from display during the weeks leading up to the Games.

Deceptive or otherwise, the preparations for the Olympics had the desired effect. Virtually all of the 150,000 foreigners who arrived in Berlin for the Games were mightily impressed by what they saw. Even before they began, these Olympics had established new standards—in the scale and design of the sport facilities, the accommodations for the athletes, the beauty of the torch relay, and the pomp of the opening ceremonies. In terms of participation, too, the Berlin Games overshadowed any previous Olympics. Fifty nations were represented, the most ever. The teams were far bigger than ever before, comprising 3,738 men and 328 women. By almost any measure, the scene was spectacularly

set. Now would come the essence of the great sporting spectacle, two weeks of competition that would show athletes performing on the highest plane of physical possibility. And in that regard, too, these would prove to be the greatest Games since the start of the modern Olympics.

As in previous Games, track and field competitions made up the most popular portion of the Olympic agenda. They were scheduled to take place in the first week, and they proved a rich feast indeed.

It was a mostly male show: The track and field program included only six events for women. In these contests, the host nation did extremely well. The very first gold medal of the Games, awarded on Sunday, August 2, went to German javelin thrower Tilly Fleischer, a great local favorite. Hers was a dramatic come-from-behind victory. In an early round, Fleischer was very nervous and her throw was woefully short. But she did better on her next try, and in the last round, as the largely German crowd urged her on with a chant of "Til-ly! Til-ly!" she made the greatest throw of her life, heaving the javelin 148 feet 3 inches

Germany's Tilly Fleischer takes the final step of her run-up for the javelin throw. When she launched her spear 148 feet 3 inches (45.18 meters), she became the first German woman ever to win an Olympic gold medal in a field event.

The *Olympia Zeitung*, or Olympic Newspaper, a daily created to report on the Games, headlines the discus victory of Germany's Gisela Mauermayer. Published in German, English, and French, the paper was printed from July 21 through August 19, 1936. It profiled athletes, promoted tourist attractions in and around Berlin, and gave a wrap-up of each day's results.

Offizielles Organ der XI. Olympischen Spiele 1936 in Berlin

5. AUGUST 1936
NUMMER 16
Preis 20 Pfennig

OLYMPIA ZEITUNG

Nun auch Gisela Mauermayer
Paula Mollenhauer Dritte beim Diskuswerfen

Am Dienstag für Deutschland:

1 Goldene
1 Silberne
2 Bronzene

Die deutsche Meisterin bei ihrem siegbringenden Wurf am Dienstag Nachmittag

The German Woman Champion's winning throw on Tuesday afternoon

La championne allemande réalisant son jet victorieux, mardi après-midi

(45.18 meters). Another German woman, Luise Krüger, won the silver. Poland's Maria Kwasniewska was third.

In the discus throw, Germany's Gisela Mauermayer—a superb athlete and also a famed beauty—won easily, as was expected of the holder of the world record; she pleased the crowd with an Olympic record of 156 feet 3 inches (47.63 meters). But German women also had some disappointments. In the 4 x 100-meter relay their anchor runner dropped the baton, allowing the Americans to gain the gold. In the high jump, Dora Ratjen of Germany was the favorite, but Ibolya Csák of Hungary won with a leap of 5 feet 3 inches (1.6 meters). (Among Nazi spectators, the disappointment over Ratjen's poor showing was probably all the more bitter because Csák, the winner, was a Jew.) Ratjen could do no better than fourth—somewhat surprising in light of a later revelation: It turned out that "Dora" was not a woman, but a sexually ambiguous person with certain characteristics of both genders. (Years later, Ratjen would have surgery to resolve the question in favor of maleness and would adopt the first name Heinrich.)

The premier women's track and field event was

Hungary's Ibolya Csák stretches over the bar during the high jump competition. Csák, along with two other athletes, reached 5 feet 3 inches (1.60 meters) to tie for first. Improving by half an inch during the jump-off, Csák claimed the gold medal.

The field lurches two yards behind America's Helen Stephens as she wins the 100-meter dash. Stephens dominated the sprints and could have been equally potent in the shot put, another of her specialties, had it been on the women's program. Instead, she entered the discus. She finished 10th.

the 100-meter dash, and here the Americans were heavily favored. On their team was Helen Stephens, a lanky 18-year-old Missouri farm girl whose precocious accomplishments rivaled those of Jesse Owens. As a child, Stephens loved to run and routinely beat the boys in races home after school. She grew to a height of 6 feet, well-knit and strong, good at every sport she tried. When she was 15 and a high-school freshman, she amazed a coach by running the 50-yard dash in 5.8 seconds, the world record at the time; she also tied the world record for the standing broad jump during a practice session in gym class. Two

years later, the coach entered this wonder-girl in four events in the AAU championships in St. Louis. As he expected, no one could touch her. She won the shot put, tied the world record in the 50-yard dash, and set a world mark in the 200 meters and in the standing broad jump. A rival surfaced on that occasion, a veteran competitor named Stella Walsh, born Stanislawa Walasiewicz in Poland. Although she had grown up in America, Walsh had represented Poland at Los Angeles 1932, winning a gold medal. At the AAU championships she had finished second in the 50-yard dash. Once more running for

Poland, Walsh would have a rematch with Stephens in Berlin.

Unfortunately for Walsh, Stephens was even more awesome as an Olympian. In an early heat of the 100-meter dash, the Missouri prodigy finished 10 yards ahead of everyone else; her time, 11.4 seconds, was a half-second faster than the Olympic record (held by Walsh), but officials said it was wind-aided. No matter: In the finals, Stephens clocked 11.5 seconds—a world record. Stella Walsh finished second, about two yards back. Little did anyone know it, but in St. Louis and Berlin, Helen Stephens had reenacted her

childhood victories over the opposite sex. Forty-four years later, Stella Walsh—then 69—was shot to death, the victim of a robbery attempt. The subsequent autopsy revealed that she, like Dora Ratjen, was more man than woman.

In contrast to the women's scanty schedule, the track and field program for men was crammed with action. The rapid succession of preliminary rounds and finals—often with several events going at once—kept the spectators enthralled during the first week of the Games.

The Germans fared especially well in events requiring strength. Hans Woellke's victory in

The sidearm position of the
javelin shows Gerhard
Stöck compensating for
windy stadium conditions.
A strategic low-trajectory
throw gave him the gold.

The German men continued their surprising showing in the field events when Karl Hein posted a personal best 185-foot-4-inch hammer throw to win that event. Countryman Erwin Blask also established a personal record to finish second.

the shot put on the opening day was an upset; American Jack Torrance held the world record and was expected to win, but he had come to Berlin overweight and out of shape, and his best throw in the finals was far short of Woellke's toss of 53 feet 1 3/4 inches (16.2 meters). In the hammer throw, Germany's Karl Hein took the gold with a heave of 185 feet 4 inches (56.49 meters)—a stupendous effort, breaking the Olympic record by almost two meters.

The Germans didn't expect to win the javelin throw. That event had been dominated by Finland and Sweden in previous Games, and a similar outcome seemed likely after four preliminary rounds in Berlin: Germany's Gerhard Stöck was in fifth place, behind three Finns and a Swede. Then Stöck changed strategy. Noting that a capricious wind in the stadium was affecting the airborne javelins, he went for a lower trajectory—and hurled the spear 235 feet 8 inches (71.84 meters) to edge out his rivals.

In the discus throw the Germans discovered that upsets could go the other way. On their team was the man who held the world record, Willy Schröder. He wasn't big, but his high-speed spins more than compensated for his lack of size—when they didn't go out of control. In Berlin technique failed him. Schröder's best throw was more than 5 meters short of his world mark, nowhere near good enough to win a medal. The winner was an American, Kenneth Carpenter, who threw the discus 165 feet 7 inches (50.48 meters).

Finland's hour came, as expected, in the distance races. Finnish teams had always excelled in the middle- and long-distance Olympic runs, and the 1936 team seemed bent on upholding the tradition. The first of these events was the 10,000 meters. For most of the race a Japanese runner led, setting a pace so punishing that all but four other runners—three Finns and an Englishman—were out of contention before the halfway point. At 6 kilometers the Finns attacked, taking the lead. The Japanese runner held on and managed to reach the front again. But on the last lap the Finns, demonstrating the pacing and teamwork that Paavo Nurmi had raised to an art in earlier Games, sprinted past the leader and came home one-two-three: Ilmari Salminen first, in a time of 30:15.4, followed by Arvo Askola and Volmari Iso-Hollo.

Four days later, Iso-Hollo handily won the 3,000-meter steeplechase, with compatriot Kaarlo

Finnish teamwork holds off the challenge of Japan's Kohei Murakoso *(running fourth)* in the 10,000-meter run. Two decades of Finnish domination in distance events culminated with a sweep in the 10,000.

Tuominen right behind him. That same day, Finland's Gunnar Hoeckert took the gold in the 5,000-meter race, and teammate Lauri Lehtinen won the silver; 10,000-meter winner Ilmari Salminen was in position to gain another medal in this event, but a traffic jam formed on the last lap. As the runners jostled one another, Salminen tripped and went down, recovering to finish a disheartening sixth.

Britain, too, reaped a satisfying share of medals. The outstanding British squad for the 4 x 400-meter relay was expected to bring home the gold. It did, but only after its second runner, Godfrey Rampling, overcame an eight-meter deficit on his leg and pounded past the American front-runner; the next two Britons widened the margin to finish in 3:09, just off the Olympic record and two seconds better than the American team.

Britain also had high hopes for the 50-kilometer walk, vesting them in Harold Whitlock, a 32-year-old automobile mechanic from London. Whitlock was the quintessential amateur: He had no coach, trained alone, and had taken a holiday leave without pay to come to Berlin. His style was to stay behind the leader for most of the distance, "eager in the chase and voracious

for a kill," as he put it. But the contest proved a little more complicated than he had anticipated.

Like the other competitors, Whitlock expected to restore his energies with drinks of a glucose mixture at prearranged stations along the way. The first such station was at the 20-kilometer mark; to Whitlock's dismay, no British attendant was there. He pressed on and found the man at the 25-kilometer mark, but the attendant had no glucose refreshment; all he could offer was tea, mixed with condensed milk and revoltingly sweet. Whitlock drank a bit and picked up his pace, taking the lead after 31 kilometers. Then he began to feel awful, his mouth dry, his stomach knotted. Relief came only when he threw up all the tea. With that, he quickened his pace again, lengthened it near the stadium, and entered the arena amid thunderous cheers. The reason was soon apparent. He crossed the line in a time of 4:30:09.2, beating the Olympic record by an astonishing 20 minutes.

The British had come to Berlin expecting to do well in the 1,500-meter run. In the field was an outstanding New Zealander, a slim 27-year-old former Rhodes scholar named Jack Lovelock; but the best of the British entrants, Sydney

Wooderson, had beaten Lovelock four times in five races the previous autumn and spring. Unfortunately, Wooderson injured his ankle; he competed but failed to survive the preliminary heats. In the finals Lovelock faced two other strong runners, Olympic record holder Luigi Beccali of Italy and top American miler Glenn Cunningham. Through the first three laps Lovelock bided his time, staying close to the leaders. Usually he saved his strength for a sprint in the last 60 yards or so, but with about 300 yards to go he suddenly exploded past the front runners. Taken by surprise, Cunningham and Beccali desperately tried to stay with him. But Lovelock was in the best condition of his life and seemed to float along. He surrendered no ground and even allowed himself a gratifying look back over his shoulder as he neared the finish. His winning time was 3:47.8, a full second below the world record.

The United States had always been a track and

A drink of oversweetened tea goes to Great Britain's Harold Whitlock near the halfway point of the 50,000-meter walk—and it would create problems for him later in the race. Whitlock's strategy was to let others set the pace, then attack from behind. His tactics proved faultless at Berlin, as he beat his closest competitor by nearly two minutes.

field powerhouse, and in spite of a few disappointments the American team would also excel at the Berlin Games. Even so, some U.S. victories had aspects of an ordeal. In the pole vault, for example, competition got under way about 10:30 on the morning of August 5 and was still going on under floodlights and a cold drizzle 12 hours later. By then it had come down to a battle between two Americans, Earle Meadows and Bill Sefton, and two Japanese, Shuhei Nishida and Suoe Oe. Watched by a small, chilled audience, all four weary vaulters managed to clear 13 feet 10 inches (4.25 meters); then all missed their first try at 14 feet 4 inches (4.35 meters). Meadows made it over the bar on his second try, setting a new Olympic mark. The others each got two more attempts, failed both, and began a jump-off to determine the order of finish behind the

victor. When Sefton was eliminated, Nishida and Oe declined to break their tie. Their team leader did it for them, judging that Nishida should be awarded the silver, Oe the bronze. Later, back in Tokyo, the two had a jeweler divide and rejoin the medals so that each had half silver, half bronze.

Another harrowing contest was the decathlon, not only because of its fiercely demanding nature—two days of throwing events, jumps, races, and the pole vault—but also because of a misunderstanding at the very end. From the outset the 10-part competition was dominated by three Americans: Robert Clark, Glenn Morris, and Jack Parker. That spring, Morris, a 24-year-old car salesman from Colorado, had set a world record with 7,880 points during the Olympic trials back home. (The total was particularly impressive, since he was a novice in the sport; the Olympic event in Berlin would be only his third decathlon.) Despite his immense natural talent, however, Morris found himself trailing Clark after the first day of the event in Berlin—though by only 2 points.

The second day played to Morris's strengths as a runner and hurdler, and by finishing first in the sixth contest, the 110-meter hurdles, he gained the overall lead. He was still leading going into the final event, the 1,500-meter run, and he seemed sure to win the gold medal. The big question remaining was whether he would win with a world-record point tally. Before the start of the race, an announcer informed the stadium that for Morris to set the record he would need a time of 4:32. That was faster than he had ever run in his life. He gave it his all, battling into the lead on the second lap and holding on by sheer will. "His features were strained and drawn," one reporter later wrote. "Every step was painful, but still he came on, running only with his heart. His feet were leaden." After crossing the line he collapsed, fearing that his effort had not been good enough.

Morris's winning time was announced as

4:33.3—a personal best, but more than a second short of what the announcer had said was required for the decathlon record. Then the announcer spoke again. He had made a terrible mistake, he told the crowd; the computations had been faulty. The American had indeed won, with a world-record total of 7,900 points.

A triumph by an American like Glenn Morris was palatable to the Nazis in the audience. After all, the new decathlon champion was tall, handsome, and white, someone they could admire. But Hitler and other Nazi officials felt otherwise

about most of the Americans who took medals in track and field.

Ten of the 66 men on the U.S. track and field team were black; their haul of medals—eight gold, three silver, and two bronze—would exceed the track and field total of any other nation (and all of their 56 teammates). From the outset, Hitler was privately contemptuous: One underling later recalled that after Jesse Owens took the gold in the 100-meter dash, the Führer said, "The Americans should be ashamed of themselves, letting Negroes win their medals for

New Zealand's Jack Lovelock *(black uniform)* **waits in the middle of the pack in the 1,500-meter run. America's Glenn Cunningham** *(No. 746)* **took the lead with 400 meters to go. Lovelock passed him 100 meters later and sprinted all the way to the finish.**

Frozen in concentration, America's Glenn Morris stands ready with his vaulting pole. The pole vault was one of his worst events in the decathlon, but he was so strong in the other nine specialties that the only concern was whether he would set a world record. The decathlon victory at Berlin earned Morris the 1936 Sullivan Award, given to the best amateur athlete in the United States. Among those he beat for the honor was Jesse Owens.

them." As the victories accumulated, some Nazis openly vented their frustration. Midway through the competitions the official party newspaper, *Der Angriff* (The Attack), described the medal winners as America's "black auxiliaries" and said (with some truth) that the U.S. would have fared badly without them. Wincing at this propaganda blunder, Goebbels publicly rebuked the newspaper, signaling that Nazi racism should, for the time being, run submerged.

In a number of events the African-Americans made their exploits look easy. On the first day, for example, Cornelius Johnson—a California college student who was favored in the high jump—hardly seemed to pay attention during the preliminary rounds and didn't even bother to take off his sweat suit until the final jumps. Johnson

was tall and fast and had tremendous spring in his legs, and he cleared every intermediate height without effort. In the finals, having at last deigned to remove his warmup clothes, he catapulted over a bar set at 6 feet 8 inches. Two of his American teammates, David Albritton—also black—and Delos Thurber, cleared 2 meters to take the silver and bronze respectively. All three broke the Olympic record. Albritton had done it with an ankle injury.

Another amazing display occurred in the finals of the 800-meter race. In the qualifying rounds the fastest time had been posted by African-American John Woodruff, a freshman at the University of Pittsburgh. Woodruff was a newcomer to track with an awkward, erratic running style and minimal skill at pacing. Before the finals his coach told

A group of African-American athletes and their friends pose outside the Olympic stadium in Berlin. Rare on U.S. Olympic teams before the 1930s, black athletes made up almost one-sixth of the U.S. track and field team at Berlin. David Albritton *(second on left)* was a silver medalist. Cornelius Johnson *(third from right)* and Archie Williams *(second from right)* won golds.

The giant strides of America's John Woodruff *(left)* power him toward the front of an 800-meter heat. Woodruff, a relative newcomer to track, didn't bother to try conserving energy during races. He willingly took to outside lanes to avoid traffic.

him to avoid trouble by going out front early and staying there. But Woodruff failed to take this advice, and he soon found himself in a bad position, trapped in a pocket near the back of the field after 300 meters. His solution was highly original: He slowed his pace to little more than a fast walk, letting all the other runners go past. The track ahead was now clear, but he was far behind. Moving to

an outside lane, he sprinted, eating up the lost ground in 10-foot strides and grabbing the lead with a lap to go. Then he relaxed again; another runner reclaimed the lead, and a third boxed Woodruff in on the outside. But nothing could contain this novice. At the end of the last turn he reached a clear lane with a great, outward leap. By now he was exhausted, yet he somehow hung on

to win by 2 meters in a time of 1:52.9—not outstanding, but altogether remarkable considering his unorthodox detours and pacing.

The spectators might marvel at a Woodruff, but for sheer track and field genius, no one came close to Jesse Owens. His smooth and compact stride was beautiful to see. He delighted the public with his manner off the track as well as on it: He was cheerful, gregarious, obliging to photographers and autograph hunters—a thoroughly likable, low-key individual who, despite Nazi racism, quickly became the darling of both the media and the crowd. His blazing times in the 100-meter dash whetted the audience's appetite for the 200-meter event, next on his crammed schedule. Obligingly, Owens in the first qualifying heat set an Olympic mark of 21.1 seconds—a world record for running the distance around a turn. He clocked the same time in the next run, then won his semifinal at a slightly slower pace. In the finals he had some tough competition from Mack Robinson, another black American. Robinson (the older brother of Jackie Robinson, who would be America's first black major-league baseball player) equaled Owens' new Olympic mark in his semifinal.

The finals were run at 6 o'clock on a cold, damp evening. At the gun Owens and Robinson were both fast off the line, matched by the top Dutch sprinter, Martinus Osendarp. Then Owens began building an edge. As the runners came out of the turn and entered the straightaway, he was two yards ahead, and he continued to widen his lead as the battle for second place raged behind him. Flying along, he finished a stunning four yards in front, establishing a world record of 20.7 seconds. Robinson took second, and Osendarp finished third, just as he had in the 100-meter dash.

For many spectators, Jesse Owens' greatest moment came in the long jump. He had set the world record with a leap of 26 feet 8 1/4 inches (8.13 meters) the previous year (a record that would hold for more than 25 years), and he expected to have no trouble qualifying; he would be allowed three tries to jump a little more than 23 feet. His strongest rival figured to be a German named Lutz Long—tall, blue-eyed, blond, and hugely popular in his homeland. Long qualified easily. Owens, on the other hand, soon found himself in danger of elimination. As was customary in American meets, he made a practice jump, only

Jesse Owens' performance in the 200-meter dash was even more impressive than in the 100. He won the longer sprint by four yards. A German official described his style in winning as "playful superiority."

During a break in competition, Germany's Lutz Long talks strategy with Jesse Owens. Long held the long-jump lead until Owens regained the top spot on his penultimate jump. It was the only time Owens was challenged during the Games.

to learn that, under the international rules here, it counted as one of his three attempts. He then tried in earnest, but he fouled by stepping over the takeoff mark.

What happened next is wrapped in myth. As Owens later told the story, Lutz Long approached and introduced himself in English, a language he spoke quite well.

"Glad to meet you," Owens said. "How are you?"

"I'm fine," Long supposedly replied. "The question is: How are you?"

""What do you mean?"

"Something must be eating you," said Long. "You should be able to qualify with your eyes closed." As Owens remembered it, the two of them then talked, with Long saying that he didn't believe in the Nazi ideas of Aryan superiority. Long then suggested that Owens, on his last qualifying attempt, take off from a point several inches behind the mark, just to be safe.

"The truth of what he said hit me," Owens would relate later. "I drew a line a full foot in back of the board and proceeded to jump from there. I qualified with almost a foot to spare."

Jesse Owens was a great storyteller, and embellishment seems very likely in this case, since reporters didn't notice the American hero talking with Long. It's indisputable that the two men formed a close bond during the Games, but their friendship probably bloomed sometime after the long jump.

Lutz Long proved a tremendous competitor. In the next-to-last round he jumped 25 feet 8 2/3 inches (7.84 meters), a European record; Owens congratulated him—then jumped 25 feet 9 1/2 inches (7.87 meters), more than an inch farther. Now came the finals, with each man getting three attempts. Long was short on his first try. Owens was nowhere at all: He aborted his first attempt. Then, as the crowd grew eerily silent, Long gathered all his energy, sprinted, launched himself into the air, and landed 25 feet 9 1/2 inches away in the pit. Now he was tied with Owens. The applause was deafening. When the stadium quieted again, Owens crouched, flashed down the line, leaped out in his distinctive low-trajectory style, and broke the tie with a mark just over 26 feet. Long had one more chance, but in his determination to make the most of it, he overran the takeoff, eliciting a groan from the audience. Owens had won, but he jumped again, now competing only against himself. He soared 26 feet 5 1/2 inches—8.06 meters—providing

Owens steadies himself in midair as he soars over the long-jump pit. His winning jump of 26 feet 5 1/2 inches (8.06 meters) would have qualified him for the final round of every Olympic long jump ever held.

onlookers with the sort of thrill that they had come to expect from him. The first person to offer congratulations was Lutz Long. Wrote Owens later, "You can melt down all the medals and cups I have, and they would be a plating on the 24-carat friendship I felt for Lutz Long at that moment."

If the long jump showed friendship transcending the murkier currents of Nazi Germany, the 4 x 100-meter relay—the last event for Jesse Owens—left an opposite impression, a sense that the Nazi infection might have spread into American ranks. Owens hadn't expected to run the relay. According to some accounts, it had been decided prior to the Games that the U.S. foursome for the event would consist of Foy Draper, Marty Glickman, Sam Stoller, and Mack Robinson. After Robinson qualified for the 200-meter dash, his place was taken by Frank Wykoff, who had run relays in two previous Olympics (earning a gold medal both times). To determine the running order, a time trial was held on a practice

POLITICS AND PATRONAGE

The Olympic Art Competition at Berlin suffered from the poor reputation the Nazis already had with the art world: Outside Germany, overblown Nazi taste was deemed so bad that many talented artists declined to enter. Protesting politically as well as aesthetically, artists from three nations—France, Spain, and Estonia—boycotted altogether. Nevertheless, there were entries from 22 countries. The usual media were contested: architecture, painting, sculpture, literature, and music, with subdivisions for more specific disciplines. The jury was hardest on the entries in the four painting divisions, awarding only one first prize, and that for an advertisement. Architectural offerings won more respect, with Werner March taking a gold medal for his design of the Reichssportfeld.

However tepid the field, one of its sculptors gained an important fan. Germany's Arno Breker won a silver medal with his *Decathlon Athlete*, a neoclassical piece that caught the eye of Adolf Hitler. Breker was not a fascist of any sort; indeed, he spoke out against the Nazi purges of so-called degenerate art. But Germany was in the midst of a classical revival, with its focus on the ideal human form, and Breker caught the wave. The government commissioned several of his works for municipal projects

Germany's Arno Breker, sculpture silver medalist at Berlin 1936, works on a project in his Jäckelsbruch studio in 1942.

after the Games, allowing him to comfortably ride out the war creating reliefs of majestic Aryan-inspired figures. In spite of his dubious patronage, Breker maintained friendships with artists throughout Europe and never lost their respect. Even so, much of his work was destroyed at the end of the war. He remained popular, however, and continued to produce well-received works into the 1980s. He died in 1991.

field at the Olympic Village: Stoller won, Glickman was second, and Draper finished third. It never occurred to Stoller or Glickman that their places in the relay might not be secure.

What allegedly happened next is generally connected to two facts that have nothing to do with sprint times. Fact one: Foy Draper, like Frank Wykoff, was a product of the University of Southern California, where he had been coached by Dean Cromwell, who now happened to be a coach of the Olympic team. Fact two: Sam Stoller and Marty Glickman were Jews—the only Jewish members of the U.S. track and field squad.

As Glickman later remembered the key moment: "The morning of the day we were supposed to run, we were called into a meeting by Lawson Robertson, the head track coach, and Dean Cromwell, the assistant head, and we were told that because of a rumor that the Germans had been hiding their best sprinters and saving them to upset the American team in the relay, that Sam and I would be replaced by Jesse and Ralph Metcalfe. I said we'll win by 15 yards no matter who runs, but they said, 'You'll do as you're told and that's the way the team's going to be.'"

Others had somewhat different recollections: that the changes happened in two stages, with Glickman first being removed for Owens, then Stoller for Metcalfe. In any case, the reasons for the shifts—if indeed there were shifts—were never satisfactorily explained, especially the inclusion of Draper even though he had run slower than both Stoller and Glickman in the practice session. The coaches said he had "more experience." Glickman, lastingly embittered, later insisted that the switch was jointly engineered by Cromwell and Avery Brundage "to save Hitler and his entourage the embarrassment of having Jews on the winning podium."

According to Glickman, Owens protested the decision when it was announced, saying, "Coach, let Marty and Sam run. I've had enough. I've

won three gold medals. Let them run, they deserve it. They ought to run." To this—recalled Glickman—one of the coaches replied, "You'll do as you're told."

Owens himself would privately dispute Glickman's version, saying that all the sprinters had been told back at the Olympic trials in New York City that the fastest four of their number would be on the relay team. Similarly, Brundage would avow that the relay team members were picked well before the Games and that the lineup never changed.

In any case, the outcome of the race itself brought no surprises. Owens, the lead runner for the American foursome, was five yards ahead when he passed the baton. Metcalfe then widened the gap to seven yards. Draper built the lead to 10 yards, and Wykoff, the anchor runner, crossed the line about 12 yards in front. The winning time was 39.8 seconds, a world record.

Jesse Owens had now won four gold medals, and done it in a way that left reporters groping for suitable superlatives. In inclement conditions he had tied the Olympic record in the 100-meter dash, set new Olympic marks in the 200-meter dash and the long jump, and shared in the setting of a world record in the 4 x 100-meter relay. He was, all agreed, a hero beyond compare. Owens, in turn, was deeply gratified by the response to his performances and by his overall treatment in Berlin. "The German people," he would later say, "were tremendous."

The last event of the track and field program was the marathon, an occasion for memorable performances ever since a Greek peasant, Spiridon Louis, thrilled his countrymen with an upset win in the first modern Games in Athens in 1896. Afterward, Louis returned to the obscurity of his village. Now, four decades later, the organizers of the Berlin Games had tracked him down and brought him to Germany to present Hitler with a laurel wreath from Olympia as part of the opening ceremonies. He was in the stands on August 9, 1936, watching and remembering.

The Berlin 1936 competitor's badge (left) was worn by athletes. The Honorary Olympic Service Medal, Second Class (center), was awarded to the Germans and foreigners who helped with the daily organization of the Games. A visitor's pin (right), available to the public as a souvenir, used a depiction of the Brandenburg Gate with the Olympic rings.

The marathon was the supreme test of endurance—a run of 26 miles 385 yards (42,195 meters). To see the start and finish, a capacity crowd was in the Olympic stadium. Outside, a million more people lined the course. The cold, wet weather was gone; the sky was clear. At 3 p.m. 56 runners assembled for the start.

A man favored by many for the gold was a little Argentine, Juan Carlos Zabala; he had won the marathon in Los Angeles four years earlier, setting an Olympic record, and had been training in Berlin for months. Zabala could expect a battle from three Finnish entrants, tall men skilled in the Nurmi-taught art of working together to wear down the opposition. Britain had a likely contender—Ernest Harper, a tall and fastidiously groomed coal miner from Sheffield. Two runners representing Japan, Kitei Son and Shoryu Nan, were also reputed to be strong, clocking times in Asia that Europeans had yet to reach. Of the two, Kitei Son was considered the more formidable, although it was difficult to see why: He was bow-legged, weighed only about 120 pounds, and wore an expression of absolute impassivity. Arguably, his blank face concealed his shame and loathing at running for a nation he hated: Kitei Son's real name was Sohn Kee Chung, and he, like Shoryu Nan, was Korean. Japan had conquered Korea in 1910, and the two Koreans were forced to run under the flag of the aggressor country.

Zabala, smiling cheerily and plainly feeling at ease, jumped out to an early lead. After 4 kilometers he was 30 seconds ahead, and by 15 kilometers his edge had widened to 1 minute 40 seconds. At the halfway point, where the runners turned back toward the stadium, his lead dropped to 50 seconds, but he built it up again.

Kitei Son was running alongside Ernest Harper, who urged him not to worry, even though the Argentine was a speck in the distance. Son nodded, showing no emotion. Running well behind them, the three Finns seemed unperturbed; they cruised along, chatting and presumably plotting their fabled tactics. At the 25-kilometer mark, Zabala was 90 seconds ahead, but he was also weakening. The gap began to narrow as Son and Harper kept up their pace. At 28 kilometers—to Zabala's shock—they both passed him. The Argentine tried to stay with them, but his fast opening pace had exhausted him. He fell, picked himself up, struggled on, and finally dropped out of the race 4 kilometers later.

By then the Finns knew they were in trouble; they had waited too long to make their move. Their best hope was that one of them would finish third, but Japan's other runner, Shoryu Nan, fought them fiercely. Meanwhile, Son pulled away from Harper, who had developed a blister and was running with one shoe filled with blood.

In the stadium, loudspeakers reported on the runners' progress. Son approached, pounding through a tunnel beneath the stands, then emerging into the light. Two hundred meters later he crossed the line, still running strong, although his face was now tight with pain. Cheering hammered the air: The tiny Korean had set

an Olympic record for the marathon: 2:29:19.2. Spectators were still applauding when Harper finished more than two minutes later, followed by Shoryu Nan.

Afterward, when the Japanese flag was raised and the Japanese anthem played during the medal ceremony, Son and Nan bowed their heads. Son would later explain to reporters that the bowed heads were meant to express not reverence, but shame and outrage at Japan's forcible annexation of their country. The reporters showed little interest; they wanted to know about the race. Son obliged them with a statement that might have spoken for many others who had given their best during the first week of the Games. "The human body can do so much," he said. "Then the heart and spirit must take over." Perhaps he wasn't speaking only of sports.

OLYMPIA

Berlin 1936 spawned a cinematic classic: Leni Riefenstahl's *Olympia*. Riefenstahl's dramatic camera angles, her use of light and shadow, her rendering of perfect bodies in motion, captured the beauty of the athlete as no filmmaker had ever done before and that few have matched since.

Riefenstahl began in films as the beautiful heroine of a series of Alpine adventure stories. She became one of Germany's biggest stars, but her ambitions went beyond acting. In 1933 she produced, directed, and starred in *The Blue Light*, a fantasy film that caught the attention of Adolf Hitler. He and the young director became friends, and he urged her to create a documentary based on an upcoming Nazi party rally at Nuremberg. The result was *Triumph of the Will*, an award-winning work—and a potent propaganda tool for the Nazis. Given her political connections and her undeniable talent, Riefenstahl was an obvious choice for Olympic organizer Carl Diem when he sought a director to film the Berlin Games.

Germany's propaganda ministry backed the project, giving Riefenstahl unlimited resources. Engineers developed new camera equipment and film stock, and an 80-person crew shot virtually every moment of all 136 Olympic events, producing 250 miles of film. Some of the action was recreated after the events and later spliced into the live coverage for heightened drama.

Riefenstahl spent 10 weeks working 10-hour days just to view all the footage, followed by two years of painstaking editing to finish her masterpiece.

Olympia premiered in the summer of 1938 as a two-part epic, each segment almost three hours long. The film was acclaimed in Europe, but the American movie industry, sensitive to reports of Nazi horrors being perpetrated in Germany, ignored it.

Throughout her long life (she would be pursuing a new passion, underwater photography, into her nineties), Riefenstahl would remain an object of both scorn and veneration. Condemnation of her collaboration with some of history's greatest villains would follow her forever. But *Olympia* would endure as a testament to her genius.

Early in *Olympia*, the camera focuses on Myron's *Discobolus*. Then the ancient discus thrower dissolves into a living athlete *(right)* about to hurl the disk. The motif of joining the ancient and modern Games persists in the film with Riefenstahl's rendering of the torch run, beginning at Olympia, Greece, and proceeding to Berlin. With typical poetic license and scant regard for reality, the director idealized the relay, using handsome runners and scenic settings that were not, in fact, part of the official Olympic event.

Leni Riefenstahl herself is the willowy nude who heralds the beginning of part one of *Olympia*: "Festival of Nations." Track and field events make up the bulk of the three-hour segment, with Jesse Owens and Glenn Morris prominently featured. Riefenstahl's use of nude and partially nude figures along with images of athletes in action emphasizes the beauty of the human body at its physical peak.

The diving sequence in *Olympia* has earned Riefenstahl her highest praise. She inserted moments of reverse motion into the action above the water and expertly edited it to make it indistinguishable from forward movement. The technique served to extend the time the divers arced through the air and thus accentuated the graceful motion.

Scudding clouds give an ethereal feel to a gymnast working a routine on the pommeled horse. Disciplines apart from the track and field program, like gymnastics, were the subjects for part two of *Olympia:* "Festival of Beauty." The shot of this gymnast shows how Riefenstahl's camera angles swerved to make the athlete look bigger, more heroic, while backgrounds and lighting were used to maximize musculature. The clouds are a Riefenstahl trademark.

Shadow, like clouds, are ubiquitous in *Olympia*. These, cast by runners, make up part of Riefenstahl's marathon montage. Rather than merely record the race, the director focused on the faces and limbs of the athletes to create a visual metaphor of the marathon as a struggle of will. The shadows, with their own relentless pace, lend a mythic quality to the struggle.

DEUTSCHLAND ÜBER ALLES

On the printed program for equestrian events at the 1936 Games, the name of Lieutenant Konrad Freiherr von Wangenheim did not exactly leap from the page. Wangenheim was one of nine members of the German team—a fine rider, no doubt, but a newcomer to Olympic competition, with no particular reputation in his sport. Still, the name was distinctive in some ways. "Freiherr" meant that he was a baron—the scion, in his case, of an ancient, distinguished family in the Prussian state of Coburg-Gotha. That such a man should choose a military career was not unusual: Well-born Prussians had long formed the backbone of the German military establishment. In this role, they had forged a stern warrior's ethic, an amalgam of discipline, courage, and self-mastery. Among the leaders and street soldiers of the Nazi regime, such values were reduced to hollow parody, but in men like the little-known Lieutenant von Wangenheim, the ethic was strong. In Berlin that summer, it was his destiny to show the watching world an older, finer Germany.

Wangenheim was 26, a tall, slender young man with cosmopolitan interests and easy manners. Like his forebears stretching back to the days of knights, he had spent much of his life on horseback. When he joined the Wehrmacht, his riding skills earned him a place in the cavalry school in Hanover, the training ground for the national equestrian team. (At the Olympic level in those days, virtually all equestrians were cavalrymen; only two civilians competed at Berlin.)

In 1932, the Great Depression had kept Germany's equestrians out of the Games at Los Angeles; transporting horses across an ocean and a continent had simply been too expensive. With problems of money and geography now removed, the German riders were determined to make a strong showing. It wouldn't be easy. A record 17 nations had sent teams to Berlin, a number that reflected the militarism of the era. To prepare for the challenge, the

Lieutenant Konrad von Wangenheim and Kurfürst, Olympic gold medalists, 1936

An equestrian official's badge from Berlin 1936

Germans began full-time training a year and a half before the Games. They left nothing to chance, practicing on a cross-country course that was a precise replica of the Olympic layout—a ploy that greatly displeased their competitors when it became known. Still, there was no doubt that the German riders were good, and so were their horses. Wangenheim's mount was a powerful stallion of English lineage named Kurfürst.

The Olympic equestrian program began with team and individual competitions in dressage—the stately display of riders guiding their mounts through an almost balletic series of maneuvers—and in jumping. Then came the climax of the competition: three events, staged sequentially during the last three days of the Games. The first contest was dressage; the second a grueling, dangerous steeplechase; the third a jumping event in the Olympic stadium. Wangenheim was one of a trio of German horsemen competing both individually and as a team in the three-day marathon. To earn a team medal, all would have to finish each phase of the competition.

The young lieutenant got off to an erratic start. In dressage, he and Kurfürst were somehow out of tune and made a number of mistakes. But, knowing the strength of his horse, Wangenheim expected a different result in the endurance trial the next day. In the steeplechase, power and stamina would be more important than grace and subtlety: During the 36-kilometer (22.4-mile) course over difficult terrain, horses and riders would run a gauntlet of 35 obstacles. The most formidable of these was the fourth in the sequence. Challenging both nerve and balance, it required the horse to clear a fence and land in a small pond whose uneven depth invited falls.

That jump took a terrible toll. Of the 46 horses that attempted it, 18 fell in the water and 10 unseated their riders. Kurfürst was one of them.

Wangenheim, who had been riding superbly up to that point, fell hard as the big stallion crumpled beneath him. The officer came out of the water staggering, his left shoulder ablaze with pain. Ignoring it, he managed to catch his horse and remount. At least the animal seemed unhurt. About 100 yards farther on, however, Wangenheim was almost flung from the saddle again as Kurfürst brushed a tree. He managed to stay upright, but his left arm now hung limp and useless. He rode on one-handed, clearing all the remaining obstacles without a mistake. But at the finish he was ashen. Doctors examined him and discovered that he had suffered severe bruising—and a broken collarbone.

The endurance course had been a disaster for many teams. Barely half the horses that began the race completed it, and several had to be destroyed. Since a team medal depended on all team members finishing the full three days of competition, the field had been drastically whittled down. The Germans were well ahead on points, but their chances for a team medal had apparently vanished: The doctors told Wangenheim that he was through; in his condition he couldn't possibly take part in the jumping competition the next day.

Wangenheim's response was terse, and his tone brooked no argument: He would ride. The doctors patched him up as best they could, immobilizing his left arm with splints up to the shoulder. The next day, before he mounted, the sling and splints were removed, and the arm, tightly bound, was concealed under the young officer's uniform jacket. Most spectators knew nothing of his ordeal; indeed, he gave no sign of it. He sat erect in the saddle, the very picture of a proud Prussian, and he rode impeccably. He and Kurfürst cleared one jump after another, a beautiful unity of man and mount.

By the time Wangenheim and his horse had completed half the course, the mostly German crowd was already beginning to celebrate, seeing a team victory as certain. The rejoicing stopped cold when, without warning, Kurfürst slipped while making a short, sharp turn at an obstacle. The horse slammed against the barrier, fell onto his side, and lay there dazed. Wangenheim, flung clear, also lay motionless. Grim silence settled on the stadium. Then, slowly, Wangenheim rose to his feet, his sharp, pale features clenched against the renewed agony snaking along his left side. He moved to Kurfürst. The horse kicked, tried to get up, then collapsed again—an ominous sign. But, no more than Wangenheim, Kurfürst would not stay down. The stallion renewed his struggle and somehow regained his footing. Wangenheim remounted, and the two set off again. Working as one, they sailed flawlessly over 12 more jumps amid a storm of applause.

That ovation was nothing, however, compared with the tumult that followed a revelation from the stadium loudspeakers. There was something the onlookers should know, the announcer said: Lieutenant Wangenheim had fractured his collarbone the previous day but had insisted on riding. There was no need to explain why—that he did it for his team, for his country, for the ancient notions of duty and honor that bound a Prussian officer. Many Germans in the stadium, caught up in Hitler's rabid nationalism, must have seen the hero of the moment as the perfect exponent of the master race. They applauded him as such. Other Germans, perhaps, knew better. They knew they had been watching the best and bravest of Germany—a Germany vanishing now, and yet on this day manifest in the person of young Lieutenant Konrad Freiherr von Wangenheim. These Germans cheered too. They cheered their hearts out.

Whatever their politics, Germans had rarely known such exultant Olympic moments. Historically, there had been little cause for them to regard the international sports festival with much affection. Some remembered the wartime canceling of the 1916 Games planned for Berlin. Fresher and more bitter were memories of the postwar ostracism of Germany from the Olympic fold. Nor did reinstatement

A bath was Konrad von Wangenheim's penalty for mishandling Kurfürst through a perilous water jump. The fall knocked him out of contention for an individual medal; nevertheless, he finished his ride to keep the Germans eligible for team honors.

Arm in a sling, Konrad von Wangenheim accepts congratulations from his teammates after Germany's equestrian victory.

bring much satisfaction. In the most recent Games, Los Angeles 1932, the Fatherland's entries were disappointing: Germans won just four gold medals. A weight lifter took one, a bantamweight wrestler another, a rowing crew a third. The fourth medal was earned in a cultural competition, a part of the Olympic menu that had never excited much interest.

But Berlin 1936 was a different story altogether. Looking back, the abiding image of those Games would be of Jesse Owens and the other talented black Americans who gave the lie to Hitler's lunatic fiction of Aryan supremacy. And rightly so. Nevertheless, memories muddied by the horrors wrought by Germany in World War II tend to overlook an ineradicable fact: As such things are reckoned, the Germans won the 1936 Games, and won them decisively. The host country amassed more medals—89—and more gold medals—33—than any other country. The exact German tally included 26 silver medals and 30 bronzes. The United States, with its excellent teams in track and in swimming and diving, finished in second place—respectably, but well off the pace: 24 golds, 20 silvers, 12 bronzes.

German victories may have been scarce in some of the glamour events—no master-race sweep in track, for instance—but in equestrian (all six golds to Wangenheim and his colleagues in that sport), in field competitions, in gymnastics, in field hockey, in rowing and canoeing, in boxing, in weight lifting, the Fatherland's medal count steadily mounted. German fans celebrated new heroes, champions from all strata of society, from the aristocratic Wangenheim to a baker from Nuremberg who distinguished himself in gymnastics, and a slaughterhouse worker from Wuppertal who was ferocious in the boxing ring. Without doubt, the Berlin Games were a triumph for Germany—not just politically, but athletically as well.

Perhaps anticipating the glory to come, Olympic enthusiasm in Germany was at a fever pitch even before the Games began. Advance ticket sales told the tale: Virtually all tickets for the 21 events scheduled for the Olympic stadium were sold before opening day, as were seats for the swimming contests. In fact, planners had every reason to expect that total sales would bring in the maximum possible audience, 4.5 million spectators. Fans who weren't lucky enough to attend the Games avidly followed their progress in the newspapers. The German press had devised a simple method to rank nations by

The Olympic stadium decorates the diploma given to medalists at Berlin 1936.

Berlin sculptor Otto Placek created the design for the commemorative medal. The front shows five athletes, one for each continent represented at the Games, pulling the rope of the Olympic bell. The bell, with its inscription summoning the world's young athletes, filled the back.

The Berlin winners' medals used a time-honored motif: the goddess Nike holding a laurel wreath. B. H. Mayer, a Pforzheim jewelry firm, produced 960 of the awards for competitors.

points, allocating three points for a gold medal, two for a silver, one for a bronze.

The public was immensely gratified when German athletes took a gold and a bronze in the shot put and both gold and silver in the women's javelin throw on the very first day, along with a bronze in weight lifting. Day 2 would bring a gold and a silver in the hammer throw and a silver in weight lifting, day 3 a silver and two bronzes in wrestling. And, for the host country, the best was yet to come. There would, for instance, be two double-digit days for the nation's medal counters: 10 medals, including four golds, on day 7, and, four days later, an amazing 12 medals, among them five golds.

Joy over Germany's athletic successes seemed to buoy Berliners to ever-greater heights of hospitality toward their foreign visitors. The darker truths of Nazism were largely invisible to the outsiders—

and most were disinclined to think about political issues anyway; they were having too good a time. Not only were the competitions beautifully staged and brilliantly contested, but the whole city seemed attuned to the comfort of its guests.

Among the Olympic visitors were many dignitaries and celebrities, and the government saw to it that, in their hours away from the Games, they were entertained on an epic scale, the better to persuade them that Germany under the Nazis was the very hub of civilization. Members of the International Olympic Committee, in particular, found themselves whirled along in a torrent of social events.

Afterward, the official IOC report detailed some of the highlights: "A new record was established in receptions and festivities, which followed one another without interruptions. Amongst the most prominent of these were the

The Pergamon Museum was the site of a lavish reception for Olympic dignitaries during the Games. The museum is notable for housing the restored altar of the Pergamon temple, a wonder of the Hellenic world. The altar was carried piece by piece from its original home in Asia Minor.

gala in the Pergamon Museum, the banquet given by His Excellency Dr. Lewald in the Berlin Palace, the luncheon given by the Mayor of the City of Berlin, the receptions by Prime Minister Göring and Dr. Goebbels, Minister of Propaganda, at the Zoo Reception Hall, the State Opera House and Potsdam, the festivities to which the Reich Sport Leader invited the officials as well as the athletes, the dinners given by Field-Marshal von Blomberg, Reich War Minister, and Herr von Ribbentrop, Ambassador at Large of the Reich, those held at the Union Club and Embassies of the various countries represented, not to speak of the charming luncheons given by Herr von Tschammer und Osten at his villa 'Ruperhorn', and the programme prepared by civil and naval authorities in Kiel on the occasion of the visit of the International Olympic Committee." This was merely a sampling of the social marathon.

Goebbels shone as a party giver. Witty, intelligent, and well educated (qualities in short supply among the Nazi leadership), he could charm the most sophisticated of the visitors. He was diminutive—hardly more than five feet tall—and he walked with a pronounced limp, the consequence of a bout with polio that had left one leg four inches shorter than the other. But he had rapidly climbed the Nazi ladder by virtue of his

talents as a writer and orator—and his appropriate set of loathings. In an address to the party faithful at a rally that year, for example, he had railed, "Bolshevism is a pathological and criminal madness clearly originating from Jewish sources and led by Jews with the object of annihilating European civilization." When he expressed such views, all of Germany paid heed: This little man held absolute control over the press, book publishing, radio, movies, and every other vehicle for shaping public opinion.

Goebbels' style in entertaining was sumptuous. The Potsdam bash mentioned in the IOC report was held on an island in the middle of the river Havel. Joined to the riverbanks for this occasion by a pontoon bridge, the island was a picturesque place, having once been a private preserve of Prussian kings. Goebbels added to its attractions by stringing the trees with myriad lights, some in the pattern of giant butterflies. As his 2,000 guests arrived, they passed before an honor guard composed of torch-holding female dancers dressed as Renaissance pages. Champagne flowed from fountains scattered around the island, and music burbled from several dance bands. Goebbels, dressed in a double-breasted white gabardine suit, moved easily among the crowd with his wife, Magda. They were an affectionate couple, though Magda was said to be

THE BOXER REBELLION

Many visitors to Olympic Berlin were in no way repelled by the Nazi presence. For instance, South Africa's Sidney Robey Leibrandt (*left*) found much to admire. Leibrandt was a policeman from Potchefstroom and a sturdy light heavyweight boxer. During the Games, he broke his hand in the quarterfinals but nevertheless won his bout—and the right to meet France's Roger Michelot in the semifinals. The one-handed aspirant was no match for Michelot, the eventual gold medalist. Still, Leibrandt's Olympic experience moved him to return to Berlin in 1938 to study physical education. He was so taken by the Nazi regime that when he found that his training qualified him to become an SS paratrooper, he signed on. When the Nazi leadership learned of his ties to South Africa, it entrusted him with a special mission: to mobilize the Afrikaners in his former homeland; to overthrow the pro-English government there; and to liberate Namibia, a border territory and former German colony. The act that would set everything in motion would be the assassination of J. C. Smuts, South Africa's prime minister.

Leibrandt landed on the coast of Namibia in April 1941. He made his way to Pretoria and contacted leaders of a militant Afrikaner group, but then his plans went wholly awry. The Afrikaners notified the police, who captured Leibrandt in an ambush. He was convicted of treason and condemned to be hanged—a sentence later commuted to life in prison. After a change in government in 1948, he would win his release. He died, largely forgotten, in 1966.

in love with Hitler, and Goebbels was a notorious philanderer.

Hitler gave a party, too—a banquet in the grotesquely ornate dining room of the Chancellery. (The Führer, never one for understatement, had functioned as the decorator.) White-stockinged footmen hovered about, and the guests were announced by a majordomo who wore a court sword and carried a cocked hat. Sadly, Hitler's social skills were far inferior to those of his propaganda minister. His conversation was generally a monologue, and he had a decidedly boorish way at the table, being a health nut. At this banquet he turned down all offerings and ordered spinach and a poached egg.

For sheer ostentation, the winner of the entertainment sweepstakes was Hermann Göring, air marshal, prime minister of Prussia, and second in power only to Hitler himself. Göring was a massive, gluttonous man with a taste for morphine, a love of rouge and fancy uniforms, an eclectic sex life, and a genius for spending money. During the Berlin Games he gave several parties, one of them on the grounds of the Air Ministry. To lend interest to that setting, he ordered the construction of an 18th-century village, complete with inns, artisans' shops, and a bakery. Lest his guests grow bored with the village, he threw in additional amusements. One was a deafening exhibition of stunt flying just overhead. A more sedate diversion was dancing by the ballet corps of the Berlin Opera. But the most piquant touch, all agreed, was the sudden unveiling after dinner of an entire fun fair, with merry-go-rounds, shooting galleries, and booths where lovely actresses in Tyrolean costume dispensed beer and wine. When a jaded socialite among the guests heard someone remark that there hadn't been a party like this since the days of Louis XIV, he shook his head and said, "Not since Nero."

Athletes were invited to a number of these galas. Some found the experience disconcerting. Missouri farm girl Helen Stephens, for example, could hardly believe the sybaritic tone of a garden party given by Goebbels at his country estate. For this bash, attended by the cream of Berlin society, the propaganda minister had laid on seven dance pavilions and an archipelago of

champagne bars. Göring was there, conducting a private party of his own, as Stephens discovered.

During the evening, the star sprinter later recalled, a messenger summoned her and fellow Missouri runner Harriet Bland into Göring's presence. "Now this party was later written up by the press as one of those orgies, and that's what it was," Stephens related. "We get inside the door and there's Göring sitting on a great big divan with a couple of gals sitting there in dubious attire. He had a table in front of him, and I knew things weren't according to Hoyle when one of those girls slithered up from under the table. Then I realized this black thing he had on was his kimono, and he was sitting there in his shorts." Stephens' alarm grew exponentially when Göring suggested that she and Bland make themselves comfortable in an adjacent room, where he would get to them in time.

The sprinters were spared this private audience by a German officer who, finding the proceedings distasteful himself, contrived to extricate the two Americans while Göring's attention was elsewhere. Looking back on the experience, Helen Stephens said, "I'll tell you one thing. Those Nazis were living high on the hog. They were excessive in everything—food, sex, every material thing."

But if Stephens was put off by all this excess, American swimmer Eleanor Holm reveled in it. Göring was a barrel of laughs, in her view, as was Goebbels, whom she specified erroneously as "the one with the club foot."

"I was asked to all the Nazis' big receptions and cocktail parties," Holm recalled later. "It was a fantastic Olympics, spectacular! I had such fun." But Eleanor Holm was a special case. By the time she reached Berlin, the whole world knew how much she loved to party, and the whole world knew that some of the consequences had not been fun at all. She had, in effect, fouled out of the Games.

Considering her tremendous talents as a swimmer, hers was a calamitous fall. In 1936 she was only 23 years old and had already swum in two

Olympics. As a 14-year-old high-school student in Brooklyn, she had tied for fifth place in the 100-meter backstroke at Amsterdam 1928. Four years later at Los Angeles, she won that event, setting a world record. By the time she was selected for the 1936 team, she had won 29 national championships in various events and owned six world records.

Holm had a pretty face and an even better figure, and she was ambitious. When Hollywood came calling after her Olympic victory at Los Angeles, she jumped at the chance for a future in film. Warner Brothers offered her $500 a week—a sizable sum at the time. The studio also

The grounds surrounding the famous Brandenburg Gate *(left)* swelled with tourists during the Games. Distinguished by its huge colonnade and topped by a statue of the goddess Nike, the Brandenburg Gate was designed by neoclassical architect Carl Gotthard Langhans in 1793 as a symbol of Prussian eminence. In 1961 it would be incorporated into the Berlin Wall, becoming a symbol of Berlin's postwar division.

supplied her with a drama coach, although the plan was to have her do more on-screen swimming than acting. Holm had other ideas. She deemed pool parts too confining—not to mention a threat to her amateur status: She wanted to keep on competing. In 1933, despite the offer of more money, she chucked Hollywood and married a nightclub band leader named Art Jarrett. Together they toured the country; Eleanor sang with her husband or other bands and swam during the day to stay in shape. "I train on champagne and cigarettes," she told reporters.

The life of a nightclub chanteuse was not as lucrative or glamorous as that of a Hollywood starlet, but Holm enjoyed the free-and-easy atmosphere, the lack of regimentation, the independence, the kind of people she met, the chance to indulge her passion for being outrageous. Unfortunately, this lifestyle's virtues were not those usually associated with Olympic competition. Thus when she boarded the SS *Manhattan* in New York on July 15 for the trip to Germany, she was dismayed and displeased at her accommodations.

Like the rest of the 350 athletes on board, Holm was assigned a third-class cabin, which she had to share with two other swimmers—dull little nobodies, in her worldly opinion. Everybody

Banished American swimmer Eleanor Holm collaborates on a story with Pierre Russ, chief of the International News Service's Berlin bureau. Holm was in Berlin to defend her backstroke title from Los Angeles 1932, but a fondness for partying got her ejected from the team, forcing her to report rather than swim.

important or interesting, including the press and America's Olympic officials, was in first class, and Eleanor Holm felt that she should be there too. She would be happy to pay the difference, she told the Olympic officials. Their leader, the redoubtable Avery Brundage, turned her down. Brundage was a moralizer who found it hard to comprehend how a nightclub singer could be an athlete. He had tried to remove her amateur status two years earlier, and he certainly was not going to indulge her now.

But the sassy Miss Holm was not to be denied. On the third night of the voyage, she—alone among the athletes—joined a party in the first-class lounge; an executive of the United States Lines, owners of the ship, had invited her. She stayed until 6 a.m., drinking with reporters and having a wonderful time. Of no concern to her whatever were the rules of behavior spelled out for the athletes before they set off for Germany: "It is understood of course," these instructions said, "that all members of the American Olympic Team refrain from smoking and the use of intoxicating drinks and other forms of dissipation

while in training." When Holm got a warning from Olympic officials the next day, she dismissed it and continued to merrily dissipate in first class. Her journalist friends suggested that she be careful—advice as useful as telling the wind not to blow.

On July 23 the SS *Manhattan* made a stop in Cherbourg, France. That afternoon and evening Holm partied nonstop, finally weaving back to her third-class cabin with the help of a male friend. Their progress was observed by the team chaperone, the formidable Ada Taylor Sackett. Sensing disapproval, Holm said nothing at first, but on reaching her cabin she opened the porthole and let forth an artful and varied stream of obscenities. Her roommates hauled her back in and steered her to her bunk. Too late. The shocked Mrs. Sackett invaded the cabin at midnight with the team doctor and the ship's doctor in tow. Holm, decisively passed out, could not be roused. In a subsequent report, one of the doctors said that she was in "a deep slumber which approached a state of coma." It was a clear case, he said, of acute alcoholism.

An emergency meeting of the American Olympic Committee was convened that very night. Brundage and the others listened gravely to the reports of roistering, the medical opinions, and some allegations that Holm had smoked and gambled as well. (She had in fact won heavily in a game of craps with her pals.) In the morning, Holm—awake at last—learned that the committee had removed her from the team. She hastened to Avery Brundage's stateroom in hopes of changing his mind; when he wouldn't answer her knock, she talked through the door. Brundage was immovable. Nor did he relent when the press spoke up for her. Nor did he budge when half of the athletes on board signed a petition requesting her reinstatement.

American papers made the most of the story, suggesting that Brundage was a heartless prude and running large and engaging pictures of Eleanor in a bathing suit. Even the *New York Times* sniffed in its fusty way that Holm "had the universal sympathy of the masculine element" on board, while "the Olympic arbiters who sentenced her had none. Theirs was a stern ruling."

A combination of sympathy and business sense prompted the International News Service to hire Holm to cover the Games as a reporter. She struggled with her feelings at first. Sitting in the Olympic stadium as the U.S. team marched in review on opening day, she wept. But she was also defiant, issuing a public challenge to whoever won the 100-meter backstroke; over the past seven years, she had never been defeated in that event. (She no longer had the world record, however; her best time, 1:16.3, had been recently topped by 17-year-old Ria Mastenbroek, a Dutch swimmer who had knocked half a second off the record.) Then Holm's anger seemed to ebb, and she refocused on having a good time. "I enjoyed the parties, the Heil Hitlers, the uniforms, the flags," she later said. "Göring was fun. He gave me a sterling silver swastika. I had a mold made of it and I put a diamond Star of David in the middle."

When the final of the 100-meter backstroke was held, Holm was in the stands, shouting encouragement to a former American teammate. The American had no chance against the likes of Ria Mastenbroek, but the stocky Dutch swimmer had problems of her own, losing precious seconds when she ran afoul of one of the ropes that marked her lane. Even if the rope hadn't thwarted her, Mastenbroek might still have lost to her own teammate, 16-year-old Nida Senff, who had produced the best times in the preliminaries. In this race Senff sped into the lead,

A happy Nida Senff of the Netherlands shares a laugh with her coach, Mrs. S. W. de Dood-Koenen. Dutch swimmers who didn't respond to the grueling practices of famed national coach Ma Braun came to de Dood-Koenen, who was known as a good handler of temperamental athletes.

The Netherlands' Ria Mastenbroek touches the wall first at the finish of the 100-meter freestyle. She would win three gold medals at these Games, which were dominated by Dutch women swimmers. Their success is attributed to an early acceptance of swimming as a women's sport in the Netherlands and a thriving women's swimming-club culture that began in 1917.

widened it, and looked like a sure winner. Then she missed touching the wall on the turn. She went back, dropping all the way to sixth place. Yet, to the crowd's amazement, she made up the ground, regained the lead with 20 yards to go, and finished in front. Despite doubling back at the turn, she had clocked a respectable 1:18.9—better than Eleanor Holm's gold-medal pace in Los Angeles four years before. Ria Mastenbroek, recovering from her encounter with the rope, finished second, bettering Holm's Los Angeles time as well.

Swimming and diving events had always been a big Olympic draw, and the organizers had prepared accordingly. Their enormous new natatorium stood right next door to the Olympic stadium, on the north side, and was connected to it with a broad stripe of paving—the better for alternating between venues, if one were so lucky as to have tickets to events in both. (Few were that fortunate; the government had to turn 100,000 would-be spectators away from the swimming competitions alone.) The arena's capacious grandstands faced each other across the pool deck, which had two pools, one for swimming and one for diving. The arrangement provided excellent viewing for spectators, but judges had a problem: In the swimming events they had to stand in a position that allowed them to sight along the finish line, and there simply wasn't enough room for clear viewing. The result was a series of placement disputes—thoroughly justified, since the judges' determinations did not always agree with photographs of the finish.

In the women's swimming events, however, one fact was beyond argument: Notwithstanding the results in the 100-meter backstroke, Ria Mastenbroek was the best all-around female swimmer in the world in the summer of 1936. In the 100-meter freestyle she was up against another outstanding Dutch swimmer, Willy den Ouden, who had set a world record of 1:04.6 six

months earlier. That record, as it happened, would last 20 years, but Mastenbroek, unintimidated, beat Ouden in every preliminary round. The final called for a remarkable come-from-behind effort. At the 50-meter turn, Mastenbroek was in fifth place and appeared to be out of it. Then, with only 10 meters to go, she put on a tremendous sprint and surged to victory in the time of 1:05.9, an Olympic record.

Mastenbroek needed a similar closing rush in the 400-meter freestyle. In that race she trailed a 15-year-old Danish swimmer, Ragnhild Hveger, for almost the entire distance, catching her at the very end and finishing 1 meter (a little over a yard) in front in the time of 5:26.4. (In later years, Hveger would be virtually unbeatable, setting or resetting 42 world records.) Mastenbroek had a somewhat easier experience in the 4 x 100-meter freestyle. Germany led that race until the halfway mark, when Willy den Ouden put the Dutch team in front by a narrow margin. Mastenbroek swam the final leg, merely maintaining the slender lead at first, then, with 20 meters to go, speeding far ahead. With that victory, her haul of medals reached three golds and one silver. At the Berlin Games only Jesse Owens would do better.

A noteworthy development in swimming in these Games was the appearance of the butterfly stroke. Years later, in 1952, it would receive Olympic recognition as a separate swimming style that warranted its own set of competitions, but at the time the butterfly was treated as a variant of the breaststroke—a loophole, in effect. In the breaststroke, swimmers had always pushed their hands forward together into the water from the breast, then pulled hands and arms backward, on or under the water. The butterfly was a radical departure: Hands and arms were arched forward above the water's surface, substantially saving energy and quickening the stroke speed.

Unfortunately for some of the innovators, the butterfly was hard to do. The only woman to try

Members of Japan's 4 x 200-meter relay team pose for a victory picture. Masanori Yusa (*left*) and Shigeo Arai (*right*) also won silver and bronze medals respectively in the 100-meter freestyle.

it in Berlin was a Brazilian, who finished a trial heat in the 200-meter breaststroke in such a state of exhaustion that she broke down and was pulled weeping from the pool. The final of the breaststroke suggested that—for the women, anyway—youthful vigor was a more effective weapon than stroke technique: Third place went to a 12-year-old Danish girl, Inge Sörensen, and second to 14-year-old Martha Geneger of Germany. Still, the seniors had the last word. The winner, with a time of 3:03.6, was Hideko Maehata of Japan. She was 22.

The butterfly variant was used with more success among the male swimmers. One of the

practitioners was a German, Erwin Sietas, whose efforts in the 200-meter breaststroke inspired near riots in the stands. He was not quite good enough, however, finishing second to Japan's Tetsuo Hamuro, whose winning time was 2:41.5, an Olympic record. Another Japanese swimmer took third.

The strong Japanese showing in the event was not a surprise. Japan's team had dominated the men's swimming events four years earlier at Los Angeles, and in Berlin only the United States had any hope of mounting a successful challenge. The two teams knew each other well. Prior to the Games, American and Japanese teams

had repeatedly traveled back and forth across the Pacific to compete—and also to see if the opposition had developed any valuable new techniques. The familiarity between the two teams produced one odd sartorial note in Berlin: The American swimmers appeared in tank suits adorned with the Rising Sun. It turned out that the suits had been acquired during a meet in Japan and were now serving Olympic duty because the U.S. team had lacked the funds to outfit itself afresh.

Even before the two teams went at each other in Berlin, American coach Robert Kiphuth spoke of his great respect for the abilities of the Japanese swimmers—a result, in his judgment, of "unique physical characteristics and hard work." Pressed to explain, he said that there were "two outstanding characteristics of Japanese swimming—a remarkably high stroke, by which I mean a considerable number of complete strokes per minute, and a remarkable ability to maintain this high stroke over a considerable distance." In addition, Kiphuth opined, "the Japanese boys aren't interested in girls. They regard their swimming as a matter of national honor, and they work like the devil."

Whether or not interest in girls was a factor, the Japanese men performed brilliantly in Berlin—as did the Americans. Event after event

proved to be a two-nation story. In the 400-meter freestyle, Jack Medica of Seattle came from behind to overtake Japan's Shumpei Uto on the last lap and win the gold in an Olympic record 4:44.5. Uto, only a tenth of a second back, won the silver, and his teammate Shozo Makino took the bronze. In the 1,500-meter freestyle, Medica took the silver, sandwiched between two Japanese. The gold medalist was Noboru Terada, with a time of 19:13.7. Uto took the bronze. In the 100-meter backstroke, Americans Adolf Kiefer and Albert Vandeweghe finished 1-2, followed by Japan's Masaji Kiyokawa. And so it went, with mostly tidbits left over for the teams of other countries.

In one race, however, the Japanese-American duopoly was dramatically broken. As their entrants battled it out in the 100-meter freestyle, an unheralded Hungarian swimmer named Ferenc Csik—a 22-year-old medical student—slipped past them in an outside lane and went on to victory. His winning time of 57.6 seconds was by far the fastest of his life.

When it came to diving, the American men had the edge. Their style had an elegance and theatricality missing in the Japanese, who tended to be rigid and intense. In springboard diving, performed from a board three meters above the water, the favorite was Marshall Wayne of Miami—tall, blond, big-shouldered, and narrow-waisted,

Japan's Noboru Terada makes a turn during the 1,500-meter freestyle. Lap counters tell him how many hundred meters he has finished. Today a whistle signals athletes when they have 100 meters to go.

Richard Degener of the United States arches into a dive during the springboard competition. Degener won 15 national titles between 1932 and 1936. American coaches consider him one of the greatest divers of all time.

with movie-star looks and a cool confidence to match. Unfortunately for Wayne's many fans, another American, Richard Degener of Detroit, capped a solid performance with an optional dive—a full twist with a one-and-a-half somersault—that earned 19.55 points, very close to perfection. Wayne couldn't match it and had to settle for the silver; another American took third. But redemption for Wayne came in the platform diving, done from a height of 10 meters: He finished well in front.

In women's diving, the Japanese women garnered no medals. A newspaper back home explained, with notable lack of chivalry, that "the Japanese girls quite obviously were at a disadvantage in that their legs are somewhat short and their bodies not as well proportioned nor symmetrical as their taller rivals." The American women were totally dominant, taking the first three places in the springboard event and the first two in the platform event. The springboard winner was a 13-year-old Californian named Marjorie Gestring, who carried a doll for good luck and stuck close to her mother. Her youthful innocence was obvious, even without the doll: During the boat trip to Europe, she asked the ship's doctor for some pills to combat seasickness. The doctor produced a pill, stirred it in a glass of water, and handed the glass to the girl, saying, "Drink this." She seemed somewhat taken aback but drank it.

"Now you'll be all right," said the doctor.

Marjorie Gestring blinked and said, "But I'm not seasick. It's for my mother."

The wildest event held in the swimming arena was water polo, played (usually with some

spillage of blood) with seven men on a side. Considering the violence of the sport—much of it underwater and thus impervious to close refereeing—it was perhaps fitting that the key match, between Hungary and Germany, took place in a violent rainstorm. A star on the Hungarian team was Oliver Halassy, who had won a silver medal at Amsterdam 1928 and a gold at Los Angeles 1932. He had only one leg; the other had been amputated after an accident when he was 11 years old. As the two teams battled in the driving rain, spectators were so enthralled that not a single person left the stands. The result was a 2-2 tie. In the end, Hungary was awarded the gold and Germany the silver because of their comparative performances in other matches.

Of the various aquatic sports on the Olympic program, the best for Germany turned out to be rowing, held on a 2,000-meter course at Grünau. In past Games, the strongest rowing nations had

The champions in the women's platform diving pose at poolside: Germany's Käthe Köhler (left) won the bronze and America's Velma Dunn (center) the silver. Dorothy Poynton Hill (right), the American gold medalist, was the defending Olympic champion at the young age of 21.

been the United States, Canada, and Great Britain (birthplace of the sport), but the German rowers now had an advantage: They had developed superior equipment—sculls and shells that were much lighter than those of their competitors, making possible ultraquick starts.

One event after another saw a German victory—the single sculls, the pair-oared shell without coxswain, the pair-oared shell with coxswain, the four-oared shell without coxswain, the four-oared shell with coxswain. In one day, Germany won more rowing events than it had in all its previous Olympic history: seven medals—five golds, a silver, and a bronze.

Just a few contests eluded the German grasp. In one of them, the eight-oared shell with coxswain, the American crew, from the University of Washington, nipped the Italians and Germans by the narrowest of margins. Describing this victory, the *New York Times* waxed positively Homeric: "Courage boiled high and gray, cold waters were churned into white-flecked foam by the fury of their efforts." And in the double sculls, a British twosome overtook the Germans after 1,800 meters and sprinted past to win by three boat lengths. One of the British rowers in that victory was Jack Beresford, 37 years old and competing in his fifth Games. In all those Olympic efforts, he had never failed to win a medal, usually gold. "He was very vicious in a

Hungarian water polo players swarm the Belgian goal en route to a 3-0 victory and a second consecutive Olympic title. Hungary brought two innovations to water polo in the 1930s: the center-forward position, which gave its teams an extra attacker on offense, and the passing game. These changes, coupled with the national enthusiasm for water polo, made Hungary such a power in the sport that between 1932 and 1964 it would win the Olympic water polo tournament five times.

A heat of the four-oared shell with coxswain hits full stroke at the rowing course at Grünau. To ensure that Grünau had the proper Olympic spirit, organizers created a secondary torch relay that carried the flame to the rowing stadium. A similar run took a torch to Kiel, a harbor city 215 miles north of Berlin, the venue for the yachting events.

boat," said an admiring teammate. "He never knew what it was to pack up. He never knew what it was to let a man pass him."

Grünau was also home to canoeing, which was making its first Olympic appearance as a medal event. Two types of craft raced: kayaks (propelled by a double-bladed paddle) and Canadian canoes (propelled with a single-bladed paddle). The Austrians did particularly well, picking up three gold medals. But Germany also fared nicely with two golds, three silvers, and a pair of bronzes.

Fortune smiled on the Germans again in the yachting events at Kiel, on the Baltic. This seaside town, flanked by white beaches and picturesque birchwoods, had been a favorite gathering place for European yachtsmen for decades, and it was also a great naval center. Before the regatta began, a note of military harmony was sounded when a British cruiser arrived, carrying

the bell of a German warship that had been captured in World War I and then scuttled. The return of the bell, said the British captain, was "a gesture of the friendship which exists between the navies of our two nations." When Hitler arrived on August 10, the British cruiser greeted him with a 21-gun salute. Such amity was conspicuously absent from the regatta, however. Vehement protests abounded, and the judges' attempts to sort out the competitors' claims met with general contempt.

The races were held in series of seven on two courses: Smaller boats stayed in the quiet confines of Kiel's harbor; bigger boats vied in the outer bay. The smallest class, the Finn, consisted of 12-foot dinghies, sailed single-handed; a Dutch sailor won, with a German second and a Briton third. Next up in size was the Star class. The Star, a swift and graceful sloop with a two-man crew, had been

developed in the United States, but the Americans did miserably. Germany won the gold medal by a wide margin.

In the outer bay, six- and eight-meter yachts battled messily. The six-meter races produced a virtual tie among Great Britain, Norway, and Switzerland. So unhappy were the combatants with the judges' various rulings that an appeal was made to a higher jury. That tribunal supported the judges in awarding the British first place and the Norwegians second, but the Swiss had to give way to the Swedes for the bronze because their helmsman was found to lack clear amateur status. The eight-meter races yielded even more wrangling. Italy ultimately received the gold on the basis of a movie taken from a balloon. However, this cinematic evidence failed to resolve quarreling over second and third place, and an extra race was arranged. As a result of the highly unorthodox overtime, Norway got the silver. Germany had to settle for the bronze—a severe disappointment, since the German boat had been leading until the last day.

The contention at Kiel paled beside some of the goings-on in soccer. Passion was no novelty in that sport, but for sheer unrestrained emotionality, the soccer games at Berlin 1936 were record breakers. In an early match between the

Germany's Ernst Krebs paddles his kayak to the 10,000-meter championship, an event that would be discontinued after Melbourne 1956. Germany, Austria, and Czechoslovakia dominated the nine inaugural kayak and canoe events of the Berlin Games, winning seven gold medals. Canada, birthplace of both specialties, fared poorly, winning only one event.

A yachting badge from Berlin 1936

Yachts of the Finn class compete at Kiel. The Finn class boats are the only ones in Olympic yachting that are sailed by one-person crews.

U.S. and Italy, for example, the Italians drew a number of admonitions from the referee for excessively rough play. One American was felled by a violent kick to the stomach, and another was deliberately shoved and tore the ligaments in his knee. In spite of these conspicuous infractions, the Italians were only able to score a single goal by halftime; the Americans were blanked.

As the bad behavior continued in the second half, the referee, a German, three times ordered one of the top Italian players to leave the game. The player refused, amid loud proclamations by his teammates that the referee was incompetent. Eventually the Italians felt that some physical expression of displeasure was needed. They gathered around the referee, pinned his arms to his side, and clapped hands over his mouth to indicate that they were fed up with his warnings. After a while the game resumed, and the Italians won 1-0, a score that was allowed to stand despite bitter American protests.

True mayhem erupted in the quarterfinal game between Austria and Peru. Most of the contest was fought fair and square. In the last 15 minutes Peru scored two goals to achieve a 2-2 tie. This necessitated a 15-minute overtime. Neither team was able to score during that period, and another overtime was ordered. By then the Peruvian fans had worked themselves into a frenzy, and when the second overtime failed to resolve the issue, they poured onto the field. The mob's exact intent was unclear, but the general aim seemed to be bringing

about the only acceptable outcome: victory for Peru. Allegedly, one of the Peruvian fans showed a revolver. If so, he didn't use it, but an Austrian player was attacked and bloodied. Amid the ruckus the game went on, with the Peruvian fans helping out their players. The mob-buttressed team scored two goals in quick succession.

The Austrians lodged an official protest, directed to a jury composed of members of FIFA, the international football federation. After deliberation the jury nullified the result and ordered the match replayed two days later. The arbiters further specified that no spectators would be allowed to watch the game. The Austrians showed up on schedule, guarded by a small army of Berlin policemen. However, the Peruvian team ignored the rematch: As far as the South Americans were concerned, they had already won. Austria was declared the victor.

At that point, the dispute spread into the political arena. Back in Lima, Peru's leader, General Oscar R. Benavides, summoned his nation's Olympic officials and instructed them to pull the entire Peruvian squad out of the Games. Meanwhile, thousands of demonstrators gathered to throw stones at the German consulate. Benavides fed their wrath with a denunciation of "the crafty Berlin decision," and he assured the mob that all Latin-American nations would follow Peru in withdrawing from further competition. But such solidarity was not to be. When the Peruvian athletes righteously boarded a train for Paris, having refused all diplomatic efforts at peacemaking, they were alone.

Speechifying continued in Lima for a while, but apologies sent from Berlin had a soothing effect: The German diplomats blamed everything on rigid international football officials who failed to comprehend Peruvian honor. Eventually, General Benavides decided that he had wrung sufficient political benefit from the situation, and he let it drop. His last word on the subject was to declare that the demonstrations

Leaping to get a head on the ball, an Austrian player forces the action during the soccer final against Italy. Disputes marred the early rounds of the tournament at Berlin, but the last match was a thriller. Italy took the gold medal with a 2-1 overtime victory.

in Lima had been stirred up by Communists.

In other team sports, tempers were generally held in check. Field hockey matches proved quite civilized, in part because they were often so one-sided that wrangling was pointless. India had by far the strongest team; the Indians had learned the game from British colonists and developed a style of ball control that amazed and dismayed their opponents. In Berlin they made 38 goals and allowed just one against them. The sole goal by the opposition came in the final and was scored by the German team. This tiny dent in their armor so miffed the Indians that they immediately

An Indian field hockey player slaps a shot past the German goalie in the tournament final. At Berlin 1936, India was in the midst of an undefeated field hockey streak that began at Amsterdam 1928 and would continue until Rome 1960. During that time, India would win 26 straight Olympic field hockey matches.

Dhyan Chand was the star of India's talent-rich field hockey team. He, along with teammate Richard Allen, played on three gold-medal Olympic field hockey squads.

went on a goal-scoring rampage, winning 8-1.

Although disappointed by the outcome, Germans in the crowd were pleased at having been able to watch one of the greatest field hockey players of all time, at the top of his game. He was Dhyan Chand, who, just short of his 31st birthday, was playing in his third Olympic Games. (His team had won gold in all three.)

As a child, Chand had cut branches off date palm trees to use as sticks for hockey practice. He was a legend in his own country, subtle on the field but a single-minded pragmatist: Once asked how his team intended to win, he replied, "We score goals." In Berlin he personally accounted for 11 of his team's 38 goals, including three in the final match against Germany.

After that game, Chand received a summons for a private audience with Hitler. The terrified Indian went sleepless the night before the meeting: He had heard that the Führer tended to shoot people he didn't like. Chand was relieved to find that Hitler was not, in fact, moved to homicide by the Indian victory over the Fatherland. He merely wanted to congratulate the star player.

Hitler also urged Chand to move to Germany and accept a high post in the Wehrmacht. So reported Chand's family, anyway. The story seems a little dubious, since the swarthy Chand could never have been mistaken for an "Aryan" in the Hitlerian mode. In any case, the story goes, Chand declined, and the Führer was understanding about the Indian's reluctance to leave home.

Just as India wholly dominated field hockey, Argentina ruled polo. The Argentines had left nothing to chance: Many months earlier, they had shipped 56 ponies to Berlin to become acclimated. Such foresight was hardly necessary. In a fair showing of their superiority, they blanked the British in the final, 11-0.

Basketball figured to be a similar story. It was, of course, an American game. Its basic rules had been codified back in 1891 by Dr. James Naismith, who organized games at a YMCA gymnasium in Springfield, Massachusetts, using peach baskets for hoops. The sport tore through the United States, but despite its popularity, it never gained a firm foothold in the Olympics until 1936. At Berlin, 22 national teams were entered, more than for any other team event. A proud Dr. Naismith traveled to Germany to witness the competition, only to discover to his chagrin that he was virtually unknown outside his own country. No reception was planned for him, and officials had not even bothered to supply him with tickets to the games. The American players came to the rescue, getting him tickets and honoring him with a small but enthusiastic parade.

These good-hearted American players had an unusual basketball background. Back home about half of them worked for Universal Studios in Hollywood. In a series of tournaments, Universal's company squad had fought its way to the top of

A British player leans into a shot against Argentina in the polo final—but to no avail. The British lost 11-0. Five countries entered teams in the tournament, the most ever for polo, but the chronically low number of entries caused the sport to be dropped from the Olympic program after Berlin.

the amateur ranks. Not only were the Hollywood hoopsters experienced and tournament-tough, they were also big, with an average height of 6 feet 6 1/2 inches. But when they arrived in Berlin, they saw that size and experience might not count for much. Somehow the Germans had fastened on the idea that basketball was an outdoor sport: All the games would be played on clay courts used for tennis. Moreover, the German balls were so light that a mere zephyr could throw a shot far off course, and so poorly balanced that any spin induced a wobble.

Adapting as best they could, the Americans reached the final without a loss. That last contest,

against Canada, proved a real challenge—because of nature, not the Canadians. The game took place in the rain, with spectators huddled under umbrellas and the players sloshing around the clay court. Dribbling on the marshy surface was out of the question, and passing and shooting became progressively harder because of yet another deficiency of the ball: It was made of untanned leather and, as U.S. team captain Francis Johnson remembered, "took up water like a sponge." Footwork, he added, deteriorated to mere floundering. "Being a clay court, when you went to stop, you couldn't; you'd just slip and slide along. Our uniforms got discolored pretty good from these slides through the mud." Another player said simply, "It was insane." The United States won by the spectacularly low score of 19-8.

Another American pastime that traveled to Berlin was baseball. It had been demonstrated in some earlier Games; on those occasions, however, the athletes weren't baseball players but members of the track and field team. In Berlin real baseball players would represent the game, and there was no doubt that the winners would be American: Only Americans, two teams' worth, would be playing. The Japanese had hinted at sending a team but never did.

German knowledge of baseball was minimal at best. One indicator of local ignorance appeared in a guidebook explaining Olympic sports. This guide noted that baseball would be especially festive because Americans liked to bring in marching bands to enliven the "interval." Apparently the idea of an interval was born when Germans observed a demonstration football game at Los Angeles 1932 and noted that bands marched at halftime. If American football had an interval, it surely stood to reason that baseball had one too.

A Berlin newspaper tried to enlighten the public in advance by running a week-long series about baseball's mysteries. Its title was "Baseball: Was es Das?" Merely finding German words to describe the sport was a major creative challenge.

An American player tries to block a Canadian shot in the finals of the basketball tournament. On an outdoor clay court turned to mud by rain, the Americans won 19-8, beginning an Olympic undefeated streak that would last until 1972.

Hungary's Imre Harangi lands a jab to José Padilla of the Philippines *(right)* during their lightweight bout. Doctors cautioned Harangi against boxing because his nose had been severely damaged in earlier fights. He ignored the advice, kept his nose out of harm's way, and won a gold medal.

As one of the American players, Herman Goldberg, later recalled, "Left field was translated as *linkausen*, meaning 'way out in the left side.' A pitcher was *der werfen* (the 'thrower-in'). Bases translated as 'points of refuge.'"

Incredibly, when the demonstration game was held in the stadium on the evening of August 12, it was a historic sellout: With the possible exception of the throngs at the 1959 World Series games at the Los Angeles Memorial Coliseum, the crowd of more than 100,000 in Berlin ranks as the largest to date ever to watch a baseball game.

What the spectators saw was not baseball at its finest. The game was played under lights—lights that were not designed to illuminate the trajectory of a high fly ball. "Any ball hit above 50 feet became invisible," right fielder Dick Hanna remembered. "One time I heard the crack of the bat and by the way the infield was looking, I knew the ball was heading in my direction, but it had disappeared in the dark. So I stood absolutely still, not knowing which way to go, and all of a sudden, the ball appeared out of the black. I moved my glove no more than an inch and the ball just plopped in. I was glad that was the only one that came my way."

As the game proceeded, it became obvious to the Americans that the German newspaper's instructional efforts had not done the job. "If anyone popped up to the infield and ran like crazy to get to first base, the crowd went mad," recalled player Bill Shaw. "Here's someone running down to first base and the crowds cheering—and it's a pop-up! But belt one out beyond second and go for extra bases and there's no reaction at all." A ground ball that rolled beneath a shortstop's glove elicited fits of laughter. Foul balls were wildly cheered.

Eventually, the spectators' struggle to comprehend the game exhausted them, and many drifted from the stadium. The final score: Americans 6, Americans 5.

Boxing was one sport in which expertise was broadly shared. Fully 31 countries sent boxing teams to Berlin. They competed in eight different weight divisions—191 boxers in all. The United States sent an eight-man team that fared poorly, winning only one medal, a bronze. Some American journalists attributed this to favoritism by the judges, most of whom came from central and eastern Europe—areas that, perhaps not coincidentally, supplied most of the winners. But the United States also

These four stamps are part of an eight-stamp issue created by the German government to help promote the Berlin Games.

may have been hurt by the loss of two boxers just before the competitions began. When reporters asked why the two had suddenly left, they were told that the athletes had become "homesick." Another explanation was widely rumored, however. It was said that they had been caught stealing from the lockers of other athletes in the Olympic Village and that American Olympic officials were given just two hours to get their thieving pugilists out of town.

Germany did better than any other country in the ring, winning two golds, a silver, and a bronze. The fine showing was no accident: In 1933 state-run boxing camps had begun training homegrown pugilists with regimens bordering on brutality. Among other rigors, some of the trainees had to endure long runs carrying 25 kilograms (about 55 pounds) in weights. Such workouts were so tiring that by nightfall the boxers could barely lift their legs. But by the time the Games arrived, German boxers were a tough and durable lot.

Particularly tough was heavyweight Herbert Runge, a slaughterhouse worker from the town of Wuppertal in the Rhineland. Runge was big—6 feet 3—and he was fast, with a lightning left hook. In his first Olympic bout he floored his Czech opponent 20 seconds into the first round. The next victory was a decision over an Englishman who had been favored to win it all. Runge got to sit out the third round of competition after a Hungarian fighter whom he had twice beaten in non-Olympic bouts had to drop

out with injuries. In the finals, on the night of August 15, the German won the gold with a jarring left in the second round to dispatch Argentina's Guillermo Lovell.

The crowd was ecstatic to have a German heavyweight champion—although it might have been a little less enthusiastic had it known of Runge's shaky standing with the Nazi regime. Whatever he owed to the state-run training camps, the big German had learned all he knew about boxing from a hometown trainer named Fred Buchanan. Buchanan was an American—a black American. The Nazis viewed this arrangement with considerable disdain. (At one point Runge would go all the way to Deputy Führer Rudolf Hess to petition against Buchanan's firing; he would win a temporary reprieve.)

For his part, Runge's feelings toward his country's New Order seemed tepid at best. His Olympic championship "fit Hitler and his guys' dreams," he would tell an interviewer years later, "even if I had black hair and wasn't really like the Germanic ideal." (After the Games, on the occasion of another victory in the ring, Runge was offered as a prize his choice between a leather bag and an autographed photograph of Hitler. He took the bag.)

The gymnastics competitions would see yet more German triumphs. Scoring in gymnastics was fearsomely complicated. Each team had eight members, and all of them competed in six events—free exercises, horizontal bars, parallel

bars, long horse vault, side horse, and rings, with both compulsory and optional exercises required within each event. The scores yielded three different sorts of results: individual class placement, individual all-around placement, and team placement. The magnificent German team would finish on top. One of its stars, Alfred Schwarzmann, was first in the long horse vault and finished high in three other events to rack up 113.1 points and win the individual all-around gold medal.

Schwarzmann, a baker from Nuremberg, had been nurtured in his sport by Germany's turnen movement. *Turnen* is the German word for gymnastics, albeit a brand of gymnastics bearing little resemblance to the modern sport. The turnen movement was as political as it was athletic, seeking to instill national pride and a sense of duty to the Fatherland. (The Turners, as followers of turnen were called, were among the earliest German organizations to support the Nazis.) Turnen's hallmark was a kind of mass calisthenics that stressed uniformity rather than individual excellence. Nevertheless, the discipline and agility that Schwarzmann derived from his turnen training stood him in good stead—at Berlin and later: Surviving wartime adventures as a paratrooper, he would return to Olympic gymnastic competition in 1952 at the Helsinki Games. There, at age 40, he would win a bronze medal.

Berlin 1936 saw the first women's gymnastics since Amsterdam 1928. The eight-woman teams competed in some of the same events as the men and also in several group drills with inflated balls and other hand-held devices. No individual

Floating to a perfect landing, Germany's Alfred Schwarzmann dismounts the long horse vault during the gymnastics competition. The Olympic gymnastics program had been in a state of flux since Athens 1896, but the men's competition at Berlin changed that: The six exercises featured for the first time in 1936 are still standard today.

ZEUS'S OAKS

Champions at Berlin found their hands full when they reached the top step of the winner's podium. In addition to the gold medal, the athletes were given an oak wreath and an oak seedling. In Greek myth, the oak is sacred to Zeus, king of the gods and the patron deity of the ancient Olympics. Charmed by the oak's classical associations, the Berlin organizers decided to give every 1936 champion a tree to take home as a living reminder of the Games. The saplings stood about 28 inches high and came in pots inscribed: "Grow to the honor of victory! Summon to further achievement!" Little was known about what became of the Berlin oaks until a 1994 survey published by James Constandt sought to uncover the mystery.

Most of the trees had vanished with time, but some had an interesting history. Several that were planted in Europe fell victim to World War II bombs. Others fell to the ax. At least two remain standing but neglected in city parks. A few, however, continue to hold places of honor. Students at Kyoto University can rest under the shade of triple-jump champion Naoto Tajima's oak. The Argentine polo team's tree thrives on the grounds of the Polo Association at Palermo, Argentina.

Particularly esteemed is the oak won by New Zealand's middle-distance runner Jack Lovelock. Planted in Timaru, New Zealand, on the grounds of the Timaru Boys High School, which Lovelock attended, it has flourished for more than 50 years, protected by law against any predation.

Egypt's Khadr Sayed El Touni holds a victor's oak seedling. The middleweight weight-lifting champion, El Touni had an impressive meet. He set three world records as he bested the gold medalist in the next highest weight class.

medals were awarded—only team honors. Again, the German team took the gold.

To the surprise of many observers, an American, Anthony Terlazzo, won a gold in weight lifting. In this sport—which, like boxing, was split into weight divisions—contestants were given three tries at three different lifts, the snatch, which involves bringing the bar from the floor to overhead in a single motion and holding it there; the clean and jerk, a two-part lift, with the bar first brought up to the shoulders and then lifted overhead with the aid of the legs; and the press, a similar two-part lift, but one that doesn't permit

the use of the legs. In his three best tries, Terlazzo, a featherweight, hoisted 687 1/2 pounds (312.5 kilograms), a world record. It was a remarkable feat in more ways than one. The United States hadn't even competed in the sport in most previous Games, and this was the first American weight-lifting gold medal ever—the first of a great many, as it turned out.

Other teams had a greater spread of talent, however. The Egyptian lifters produced the best overall performance, and the Germans were not far behind. Germany's Josef Manger won the most prestigious competition, the unlimited

weight division, lifting a world-record total of 904 pounds (410 kilograms).

More medals for the host nation came in cycling, although one victory, in the 1,000-meter sprint, was highly controversial. That particular event amounts to a tactical duel between two cyclists. For most of the distance they circle the track at a modest pace, trying to ride in a competitor's slipstream or gain some other positional advantage; then, with about 200 meters to go, they sprint furiously for the finish. The favorites

were Toni Merkens of Germany and Arie van Vliet of Holland. The finals consisted of two races between them. In the first race, van Vliet was on the verge of overtaking Merkens during the sprint when the German swerved to the right, either as a feint or as an intentional effort to block the challenger. The latter would have been an egregious foul, but the German judges didn't call it. After Merkens won the second race as well, the Dutch team lodged a protest. In an unprecedented decision, the judges declined to

The German team of Ernst Ihbe (*front*) and Carl Lorenz pedal toward a gold medal in the 2,000-meter tandem race. The Germans did well in cycling, but France's Robert Charpentier was the individual star of the Games. He collected gold medals for the individual road race, team time trial, and 4,000-meter team pursuit.

An electronic fencing piste connects Sweden's Hans Drakenberg *(No. 38)* and Belgium's Raymond Stasse during an épée duel. The German organizers introduced automated scoring to the Olympic fencing program.

disqualify Merkens but instead fined him 100 marks and let him keep his gold medal.

Trouble of a different sort occurred in the 100-kilometer road race. For the first time in Olympic history, all the cyclists—100 of them—started at the same time rather than adhering to the usual procedure of setting off at intervals to minimize the danger of collisions. For most of the race the dense traffic flowed well enough, but near the end, at a place where the road was perilously narrow, disaster struck. A Peruvian rider struggled with his three-speed gears (a recent innovation) and went down. His fall set off a chain reaction and took 20 other cyclists down as well, drastically thinning out the field and causing a number of injuries.

The finish was a wild sprint, won by Robert Charpentier of France; he beat a compatriot, Guy Lapebie, by the tiny margin of 0.2 of a second. But Lapebie was puzzled by his defeat. He was in front with 30 meters to go, then seemed to slow down inexplicably for a split second, allowing Charpentier to go past. A few months later he discovered the reason: A photograph of the finish showed Charpentier plucking his teammate's jersey from the back. That utterly unsportsmanlike tug, momentarily arresting Lapebie's charge to the finish, was the margin of victory.

Fencing was another mostly European show. The men fenced with three different swords: the foil, épée, and saber. For the épée bouts, in which the first touch is critical, the Germans had developed an electrical device that could measure a difference of just 0.25 of a second between two hits; in other contests, human judgment decided the outcome. Both individual and team medals were awarded. The Italian men reaped a golden harvest; behind them came the Hungarians, the French, and the Germans.

The women fenced only with foils—swords with flexible, rectangular blades—but their part of the program was, if anything, more dramatic than the male portion. All eyes were on Helene

Mayer, in part because of her enormous ability, and also because she was the only "non-Aryan" on the German squad in Berlin.

Born to a Christian mother and Jewish father, Helene Mayer had been raised in Offenbach, Germany, and grew up to be a tall, strong, athletically gifted girl with blond hair and green eyes. At 14 she won the German foil championship, and at 17 she took the gold medal in the foil at Amsterdam 1928. The following year she won the world championship, and she repeated as world champion in 1931. Mayer had a setback at the 1932 Olympics in Los Angeles, finishing in fifth place—but only because she was ill at the time. After that she decided to stay in California, where she studied international law and taught languages. Since she remained active in fencing, she expected to represent Germany at the Berlin Games, but she soon received a jolt, learning in late 1933 that she had been expelled from the Offenbach Fencing Club. Since only members of clubs could compete for the German team, Mayer was effectively barred from the Games. It made no difference that she was generally recognized as the greatest woman fencer on earth, or that she looked like the very archetype of Aryan womanhood.

The movement in America to boycott the Berlin Games altered the equation. In response to the threat of an American pullout, the German government promised that Jewish athletes would be allowed on the national team and that Helene Mayer would be among them. But when it came to making good on the promise, the Nazis stalled. Finally, in September 1935, General Charles Sherrill—one of three Americans on the IOC—demanded action. Sherrill wasn't particularly bothered by Nazi racism, but he was alarmed at the possibility that the boycott movement would succeed. In response to his appeal, Reichssportführer Tschammer und Osten invited two German Jewish athletes to return from abroad and join the national team. One was Helene Mayer; Tschammer und Osten saved face to some degree

The champion women's foil fencers were: Germany's Helene Mayer (*left*), Austria's Ellen Preis (*center*), and Hungary's Ilona Schacherer-Elek. All three women had impressive careers. Mayer competed at three Games, winning a gold medal and a silver. Preis took part in five Games, earning a gold and two bronzes. Schacherer-Elek would repeat as foil champion at London 1948 and win a silver at Helsinki 1952.

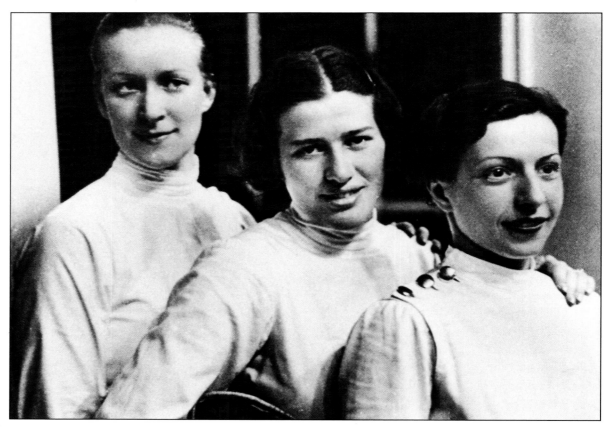

by noting that she had two Aryan grandparents. The other Jewish athlete was Gretl Bergmann, a world-class high jumper who had left her native Stuttgart to settle in England. Both accepted.

Having made the commitment, the Nazis did include Mayer. Bergmann was another story. On July 17, 1936, just two weeks before the start of the Games, the German Olympic Committee wrote her a letter saying that her performance was unsatisfactory and that she would have to step aside. In fact, the Nazis had rigged matters so that Bergmann never got a chance to compete in the qualifying trials, and they chose to ignore the German high-jump record that she had recently defended at a meet in Württemberg. She explained all this to the American consul general in Stuttgart, but nothing was done. Had she competed, she would very likely have won a gold medal: At Württemberg she had jumped 5 feet 4 inches (1.64 meters); the winning Olympic jump was 5 feet 3 inches (1.60 meters).

Helene Mayer said little about her decision to represent Germany in the Games. She knew that under the 1935 Nuremberg Laws she was no longer a German citizen: No one with Jewish blood could be allowed that honor, declared Hitler. But she had little interest in politics and resented efforts by American Jews to dissuade her from going to Berlin.

Ironically, Mayer's toughest competition would come from a Jew—Ilona Schacherer-Elek of Hungary, the European champion. In their two encounters during the finals, Schacherer-Elek bested Mayer both times. Mayer was able to score well against weaker opponents, and she defeated Austrian fencer Ellen Preis (the gold medalist at Los Angeles 1932) 5-4 in the final round. It wasn't enough. Schacherer-Elek's point total was higher, and Mayer finished in second place. When she mounted the dais during the victory ceremony in the Olympic stadium to accept her silver medal, she gave the crowd a fine, stiff-armed Heil Hitler salute. Then she went home to California. In the years ahead she would be the American champion many times, but she would never again compete internationally.

If fencing proved something of a disappointment for Germany, shooting made up for it: A German took first place in the firing of automatic pistols at moving targets 25 meters away, and another German was second; Germany also won a silver in target free-pistol shooting at 50 meters.

The show-stopper, however, was the performance by a Norwegian, Willy Rögeberg, in rifle shooting at 50 meters. His 30 shots produced the first perfect score ever seen in any competition anywhere.

One popular Olympic event, the modern pentathlon, was designed to test a broad spectrum of military skills. Its five phases were a kind of dramatization of a soldier delivering a message: He rides a horse five kilometers (about three miles) over an obstacle course, dismounts to fight with a sword, shoots his way out of a trap with a pistol, swims across a river, and completes his mission with a 4,000-meter run. (In reality, the five phases took place on different days.) One of the pentathletes in Berlin was the 1932 winner, Count Johan Oxenstierna of Sweden, a big, blond man who proudly noted to journalists that Swedes had taken both gold and silver medals in every Games except one since Stockholm 1912. (A Dane had managed to make off with a silver medal there.) "There is an enormous interest in the sport in Sweden," said the count. "The country is smaller and therefore everything is centralized. Most competitors are just a foot

Norway's Willy Rögeberg lines up a shot for the benefit of a photographer. In actual Olympic action at Berlin, Rögeberg won the small-bore rifle competition in flawless style, posting the first perfect round in the event's history. In the contest, marksmen have an hour and 45 minutes to fire 60 shots at targets 50 meters away.

away from the field, the woods, and usually the sporting complexes." Maybe, but it didn't help in 1936. Lieutenant Gotthardt Handrick, a German officer, trounced the opposition. Crowed a local newspaper, "Sweden was beaten; the blond Swede from Stockholm was crushed."

The pentathlon had come early in the Games, but it was part of a continuing trend: When all was said and done, Deutschland über Alles was indeed the story of the 1936 Olympics. According to the local press's method of scorekeeping, Germany's 89 total medals translated into 181 points. The United States had 124. Italy finished a distant third with 47. Mussolini berated the Italian athletes when they returned home.

It was inevitable, given the times, that the Nazis managed to co-opt these Olympic Games, to use them to showcase the Germany that Hitler wanted the world to see. Victories for German athletes meant glory for the Third Reich. A sparkling, bustling Berlin testified to a reinvigorated nation. Germany was, of course, tottering on the edge of an abyss as those Games drew to a close. But from such triumphant heights, only the most prescient could envision the catastrophic fall to come.

At the time, Berlin 1936 was generally considered a triumph for the entire world of sport. Almost everyone agreed that the Games had been the finest ever, with the most moving

Pentathletes take aim at life-size targets during the shooting portion of their five-event program.

pageantry, the best facilities, the greatest public support, and some of the most exciting and memorable moments in the history of Olympic competition. In almost every way imaginable, it had been a sporting feast without compare.

What became of them all—the men and women who competed in Berlin in the summer of 1936? Some would go on to many more victories in international competitions. Some would quickly descend into obscurity. A few were guaranteed lifelong fame no matter what they did after the Games. Jesse Owens was one of those, but he had some rough times ahead.

Some of his problems would arise because of arrangements made earlier that summer by the Amateur Athletic Union, the governing body of American track and field. The AAU committed its Olympians to an exhibition tour of about a dozen European cities as soon as the Games were over. The reason was purely economic: Contributions for the Olympic effort had been scanty, and the AAU badly needed money to meet expenses. Neither Owens nor the other athletes thought much about it at the time; in any event, they were given no choice.

The exhibition tour proved exhausting, especially for Owens. Not only was the schedule relentless, but he was besieged by reporters and autograph hunters every step of the way. He also resented having to barnstorm around Europe when he could be back home looking after his own financial security. He was now enormously famous, and he figured that if he acted quickly, his fame could be transmuted into money—something he and his family had always lacked. Immediately after Owens' Olympic victories, American promoters had inundated him with tempting offers. The day after he won his fourth gold medal, for example, he got a telegram promising him $25,000 if he would appear with a California orchestra for two weeks.

By August 14, pausing in London between exhibition meets, he was fed up; he wanted to go home, and his coach agreed that he should. Owens was supposed to compete in Stockholm on the 16th, but the coach, acting on Owens' behalf, informed the Swedish promoters that the star attraction would be taking a ship for America instead. Soon afterward, an enraged AAU official called and said that Owens had to show up in Stockholm or risk suspension. The coach—fortified by knowledge of a new $40,000 offer to Owens from an agent representing American entertainer Eddie Cantor—declined. The official then called Avery Brundage, president of both the AAU and the American Olympic Committee. Brundage instantly made good on the suspension threat; he announced that Jesse Owens was banned from amateur track and field competition forever.

Germany's Gotthardt Handrick, a consistent performer, won the pentathlon gold medal, even though he failed to place first in any of the five disciplines.

Waving as he rides through the crowded streets of Manhattan, Jesse Owens is an honored guest in the victory parade for American Olympians. Owens' achievements were celebrated in New York, but in the American South he found less acclaim. Newspapers in Atlanta, for instance, wouldn't carry his picture.

Owens went back to America, sure that he had done the right thing. New York greeted him as a hero, Cleveland staged a huge parade in his honor, tributes poured in from all sides. Princely offers kept coming—but most of them, including the one from Eddie Cantor's agent, turned out to be illusory. Still, he managed to make money—quite a lot of it. Supporters of Republican presidential candidate Alf Landon quietly paid him $10,000 or so to stump for their man (who lost to Franklin D. Roosevelt in a landslide). Owens appeared at banquets and sport events for a fee. He went to Cuba and, at halftime during a soccer game, ran a 100-yard race against a horse. He was given a 40-yard head start and won handily, in the good time of 9.9 seconds. It was, no doubt, a diverting show. But there was an inescapable sadness in the spectacle of the greatest sports hero of his day becoming a sideshow attraction to keep himself financially afloat.

Owens would make money by running many more exhibition races, at county fairs and carnivals and sporting events, pitting his speed against anyone and anything, including cars and trucks. In 1937 he toured with a black musical band, singing a little and acting as an announcer. But he invested his earnings

unwisely—in a dry-cleaning business that failed and in some sports teams that didn't fare very well—and in 1939 he was forced to declare bankruptcy.

His life finally stabilized during World War II when he worked as the personnel director of black employees at Ford Motor Company. That job led him into public relations, which proved to be a natural calling for this gregarious and charming man. After the war he became a high-level representative for a number of corporations and institutions. "My business is primarily to be able and willing to talk to people from a motivating and inspirational standpoint," he once said. "I talk about people who have succeeded with a great deal of handicaps."

Owens was so effective that, beginning in the 1950s, the U.S. government sent him on world tours as a kind of unofficial ambassador. His athletic gifts were still intact: During a goodwill tour of India in 1956, Owens, then 43, ran 100 yards in 9.8 seconds. At home he continued to give hundreds of speeches a year, and he maintained his sprinter's pace as a spokesman for various organizations and causes until his health finally collapsed in his 66th year. For most of his life he had been a heavy smoker. On March 30,

1980, he died of lung cancer. At his funeral in Chicago, his casket was draped with a white silk flag adorned with the five-ring Olympic symbol.

For other stars of the Berlin Games, fate had many a card to play. Helen Stephens, America's other legendary sprinter, followed Jesse Owens' lead by running exhibition races after her return home. On several occasions she ran against him. She also toured as a professional basketball player. During the war she served with the Marines; later, she worked for the Defense Mapping Agency for many years.

Many Olympians did not survive the war. Lutz Long, who formed a bond with Jesse Owens when they competed in the long jump, died in the Battle of San Pietro in 1943. (Owens stayed in touch with his family after the war.) Toni Merkens, the German cyclist who was fined but not disqualified for a foul in the 100-meter sprint, was killed in action in Russia in 1944. Helene Mayer returned to Germany in 1952, married an engineer, and settled in Heidelberg. She died of cancer in Munich in 1953.

Jack Lovelock, the New Zealander who ran such a magnificent 1,500-meter race in Berlin, was thrown from a horse in 1940 and suffered a head injury; afterward, double vision and dizziness plagued him. He moved to New York and worked in a hospital, but the dizziness kept returning, and in late 1949, as he stood on a subway platform, the vertigo overcame him. He fell forward from the platform and a train hit him. He died instantly.

Kitei Son, the Korean marathoner who ran for

A 1948 exhibition at Bay Meadows raceway in San Mateo, California, pitted Jesse Owens against Ocean, a seven-year-old pacer. Owens' fortunes rose and fell throughout his life after the Olympic Games.

Japan, returned to his homeland after the Games and worked in a bank—carefully watched by the country's Japanese overlords because he had become a symbol of Korean liberation. With the defeat of Japan in the war, his dream of national restoration came true. He became a successful coach and a wealthy salesman. Son carried South Korea's national flag in the 1948 Games in London—his country's first Olympic appearance. In 1988, Son, then 76, would carry the Olympic torch into the stadium for the Games in Seoul.

Decathlon winner Glenn Morris was drafted by the Detroit Lions football team when he came home but chose instead to accept an offer to play Tarzan in a movie. Party-loving Eleanor Holm, the backstroker who ran afoul of Avery Brundage, was cast in the role of Jane. The picture was generally adjudged the worst of all the apeman epics. Little was heard of Morris after that. Holm never lost her celebrity status and never stopped partying: After finishing the Tarzan picture, she divorced her nightclub-singer husband and married Billy Rose, the famed Broadway impresario and producer of the Aquacades, the swimming extravaganza in which she starred. The marriage would be stormy and short.

Ria Mastenbroek, the best woman swimmer in the Games, married disastrously, divorced her husband, and thereafter worked 14 hours a day as a cleaning woman to support her children. Decades later, she said to a reporter, "I am forgotten. Sometimes I think, 'Oh dear, oh dear, how good I must have been, how really good.'"

Reichssportführer Tschammer und Osten died in a Berlin hospital in March of 1943. He had been suffering from chest pains.

For the other Nazi leaders who had staged the grand pageant as a way to demonstrate the dynamism of the Third Reich, calamity lay ahead—calamity for Germany, for the world, and for themselves. In 1945, with Germany in ruins and more than three million German soldiers and uncounted millions of civilians dead, propaganda chief Joseph Goebbels had his six children killed by lethal injection, then ordered a guard to shoot him and his wife, Magda, in the back of the neck. Air Marshal Hermann Göring was captured by the Allies and convicted of war crimes, but he escaped the noose by swallowing a concealed cyanide capsule. Adolf Hitler committed suicide in a bunker beneath Berlin as the city fell to the Soviets.

Then there was Lieutenant Konrad Freiherr von Wangenheim, so briefly a hero for his self-sacrificing dedication to Germany's Olympic equestrian team. In July of 1943 he was dispatched to the war's Eastern Front. Letters he wrote at the time indicate he feared the worst for his country. In July of 1944 he was captured by the Russians.

More than 20 million Soviets died in World War II. The nation had great cause for bitterness, and it treated its German prisoners accordingly. Wangenheim, because he was an officer, was targeted for special miseries. He was periodically tortured, physically and psychologically. He was beaten and kept in isolation. Like so many German soldiers, he was kept imprisoned long after the war ended.

The years passed, and Wangenheim was moved from camp to camp. Existence was always bleak, but he bore up. Indeed, he once again became a hero, though this time in a quiet and underground way. Those who knew him say that wherever he went, he was a leader among the prisoners, bolstering their spirits with tales of his equestrian days, doing what he could to protect them from the worst depredations of their Soviet jailers. Because his special status was obvious, he was often singled out for punishment.

The year 1950 found Wangenheim in a particularly brutal camp in Stalingrad. By then his health was failing, and it grew steadily worse under constant Soviet badgering; some of his comrades would relate later that he went through at

least 470 interrogations during his first two years in the Stalingrad camp, none of them gentle. Yet he wrote to his wife, "This life gave me much. It was so great and so beautiful. If it must end, I will go under with love, hope, and faith."

In January of 1953, after yet another spell in solitary confinement, Wangenheim was given some parcels that his family had sent. He passed the contents out to his comrades. "For me alone it will be too much," he explained. Then he went off alone and killed himself. Apparently, having endured as much as he could, he wanted to forestall any possibility of behaving badly or becoming a burden to the others. He was a Prussian officer. He did his duty.

The horrors to come were all but unimaginable, however, on August 16, 1936, when the curtain came down on the Games of the XI Olympiad. The closing moments were almost reverential, as though Berlin had truly been touched by the spirit of ancient Olympia. On the evening of that final day, the stadium was jammed beyond its listed capacity. Upwards of 100,000 people watched as the sunset blazed, grew pearly, then faded. Somewhere in the thickening darkness, a cannon sounded. The Olympic bell began to ring. Trumpets blew a fanfare, and spotlights surrounding the stadium were switched on, throwing their beams upward to a point of convergence far above and creating a magical roof of light.

Flag bearers on the hill stood quiet as IOC president Count Henri de Baillet-Latour thanked the German people for being such excellent hosts. More cannons fired. An orchestra and chorus performed a series of slow-paced works. The flag bearers lowered their national banners, and the great five-ring Olympic flag flying from a pole at one end of the infield slowly came down.

A silence descended on the stadium. All eyes turned to the brazier where the Olympic flame had burned in rippling glory for two weeks. The flame began to sink in its great bowl. Its light thinned and flickered, as though struggling.

Then it died.

Konrad von Wangenheim wears the winter uniform of a German officer on the Russian front in a 1942 photograph. Wangenheim's Olympic heroism didn't spare him from the horrors of World War II. He would survive the war but suffer great hardship in Russian prisoner of war camps.

Military spotlights focus on a point in the sky above the Olympic stadium in Berlin. The dramatic closing ceremony would be the last Olympic celebration for 12 years.

THE WAR YEARS

Baron Pierre de Coubertin did not fully exhibit the travails of his 74 years as he set forth on a favorite walk that gentle Geneva evening in the late summer of 1937. True, his once-rosy complexion had gone a bit sallow, and his sternly upright posture had given way to a slight stoop. Still, a contemporary photograph showed a man with remarkably few of the sags and creases that attend advancing age: Dark eyes set off by bushy brows gazed out forthrightly over a strong nose, the whole framed by a full head of white hair and set off by a splendid, snowy moustache. It was the face of a man still in command of his mind and of his courage and faith—not the visage of someone defeated and discarded by life. Yet Pierre de Coubertin, father and forever champion of the modern Olympic movement, might have been excused a bit of somber reflection as he commenced his usual brisk constitutional in the twilight of September 2.

As a visionary young aristocrat, Coubertin had seen his first Olympic Games in 1896 capture the imagination of people everywhere and blossom into the greatest pageant of sport the world had ever known. But he regarded the Games as infinitely more than a mere test of athletic caliber. The baron and his apostles knelt at the altar of Olympism, that immaculate state in which all prejudices—social, racial, religious, political—were laid aside in a celebration of pure and perfect sport, untrammeled sport, sport to celebrate and shape exuberant youth.

Peace and goodwill for all, Coubertin believed, would flow from this "adherence to an ideal of superior life, of the aspiration to perfection." In the same spirit, Carl Diem had written: "Sport is a kind of worship, provided it is practiced for the greater glory of omnipotent Nature, the human body and soul, and for the glory of Creation which surrounds us." Avery Brundage had added his paean to the transforming power of Olympism: "Where amateur sports with its high idealism flourishes, there civilization advances."

Baron Pierre de Coubertin, January 1, 1863-September 2, 1937

Yet from the first, the Olympic reality had fallen short of the dream. The baron's ideal of sport to educate, sport as one of the humanities, had been trampled by the onrush of sport for its own sake, sport merely for winning. And, from the first, there had been men who wanted to turn the Games to their own ends, men driven by narrow national pride or lust for personal power. Coubertin had stood against them—he and a few fellow idealists whom he loved and trusted. Now most members of that faithful cadre were dead: expansive, indefatigable Viktor Balck of Sweden; mystical Robert de Courcy-Laffan, the English clergyman who had so clearly understood and shared Coubertin's spiritual vision of Olympism; and—perhaps most sorely missed—William Milligan Sloane, the brilliant and principled American historian whose intellect had been a beacon and bulwark for Coubertin.

Friends gone. Family gone. Through the carelessness of Coubertin's mother-in-law, his son had suffered severe sunstroke as an infant and had been institutionalized since 1898 with irreparable brain damage. The baron's daughter, perhaps paying a price for parental guilt, was emotionally fragile. His marriage had long since descended into endless quarreling, often about money. (The money was gone, too. Coubertin had poured

Pierre de Coubertin, still active at 72, rows on Lake Leman in 1935. A lifelong advocate of the sport, Coubertin published a book in 1926 entitled *The Cure of Rowing*. During his life he authored 30 books on sport and on French history.

much of his considerable fortune into the Olympic cause and lost most of the rest in bad investments.) On his retirement in 1925 as president of the International Olympic Committee, he and his wife, Marie, had moved out of Mon Repos, the handsome mansion in Lausanne that served as both residence and headquarters for the president of the IOC. They had taken a small apartment in Lausanne, scraping to keep up a respectable front. Finally the marital wrangling became unbearable, and the baron moved to a one-room flat in Geneva, a flat near the park where he liked to walk in the evening.

Sometimes it must have seemed that the Games were gone as well—lost to Coubertin, at least, and not just because they so tantalizingly eluded the peacemaking, pedagogical role he had envisioned. Far from rising above politics, the Olympics had fallen victim to a great war—that ultimate expression of parochialism—which forced the cancellation of the Games of the VI Olympiad, whose host city in 1916 was to have been Berlin. When the Games resumed at Antwerp in 1920, rampant nationalism twisted them into a competition among countries, with endless medal counts and elaborate point scores to show which states were winning, which were losing.

Then, at Berlin 1936, Adolf Hitler had co-opted the Games of the XI Olympiad, making them a showcase for the Nazis' hollow facade of a new and better Germany. That fact had been too much for Pierre de Coubertin to encompass; he simply could not harbor the thought of his Olympics put to base purpose. "That is entirely false," he had snapped to a newsman who queried him about Nazi exploitation. "The imposing success of the Berlin Games has served the Olympic ideal magnificently."

In fact, though, few people cared anymore what Coubertin thought about the Berlin Games or anything else. By now he had become something of an anachronism in the Olympic movement, the revolutionary whose revolution had rolled over him. After his retirement he had gradually come to play a peripheral role in Olympic affairs and, increasingly, he was ignored by his successors. True, a few of his old friends in the IOC, along with some admiring heads of state (Hitler was one of them), had raised almost 47,000 Swiss francs and offered the sum to him in the guise of a grant for his work toward founding an Olympic museum. The baron, a proud man, did not touch the money. Before the Berlin Games, the IOC also paid homage to his half century of dedication by supporting his nomination for the Nobel Peace Prize. It would not be his. The 1935 prize went to a German journalist, the famed pacifist Carl von Ossietzky, who had been persecuted and interned by the Nazis and was seen as a prisoner of conscience.

If losing the prize was a disappointment, Coubertin never showed it. He was a gentleman, after all; besides, there had been so many disappointments. He had borne up under all of them, toiling on with his writing, his educational endeavors, growing a little weary, perhaps, but never losing his hope and pride in both his cause and himself. He was like an aging general who, having lost many comrades and many battles, could nevertheless not conceive of losing the war.

For this old campaigner, September 2, 1937, was like so many other days. He did his usual morning exercises, followed by long hours of writing and reading in his flat amid the souvenirs of his Olympic endeavors. Finally it was time for his evening promenade. The baron enjoyed strolling through Geneva's Parc de la Grange with its fine Roman ruins and lovely French gardens. Now, as the daylight dimmed, he paused in his walk and sat on a park bench to savor the breeze off Lake Leman. There, without warning, death reached out for Pierre de Coubertin: A massive stroke tore through his brain and quickly killed him.

He had long before arranged one last expression of his devotion to the Olympic cause: Coubertin's

Crown Prince Paul of Greece places an urn holding Coubertin's heart in a monument on the grounds of Olympia. Some historians believe Coubertin's inspiration for his unconventional burial came from the funeral of Evangelis Zappas, a Greek industrialist who sponsored an Olympic-type festival 37 years before the modern Games began. Zappas' head had been interred in the foyer of a public building he'd erected in Athens.

will provided that his body be buried in Lausanne, but he asked that his heart be removed and transported to the true hub of his universe—to the valley in the Peloponnesus where the Olympic Games had come into existence more than three millennia before.

It was done as he wished. On March 26, 1938, a satin-lined box containing the baron's heart was laid to rest beneath a commemorative stele. On the pillar were inscribed the words, "Here lies the heart of Pierre de Coubertin."

Count Henri de Baillet-Latour of Belgium, the baron's successor as IOC president, spoke briefly at the interment at Olympia. He eulogized Coubertin as "one of the great benefactors of humanity"—a man who "did more than all others for the cause of peace and good understanding between men of all races and all religions." Then the small party of mourners, most of them IOC members, walked somberly around the ruins of Olympia—across the site where 40,000 spectators had watched the ancient Games, through the remains of the peristyle where long-dead athletes had once practiced, past the broken columns of temples reared to lost gods, everything now overgrown with shrubs and trees and carpeted with wildflowers.

It was a beautiful, moving moment. But as everyone there well knew, Coubertin's passing signaled the death of the Olympic ideal as it had

been originally conceived. To survive and grow, the IOC would henceforth be forced into dubious compromise with much that was ugly in an increasingly complex world. Considering those realities, the movement had an appropriate leader in Henri de Baillet-Latour. Though he would be much reviled in later years, the Belgian count had already shown a talent for threading his way through political minefields.

Like Coubertin—and so many of their IOC colleagues—Baillet-Latour had been born to privilege, scion of the governor of Antwerp Province, where most of Belgium's wealth resided. He had grown up a chum of future king Albert I, had gone on to Leuven, one of Europe's most prestigious universities, and from there settled into the life of a diplomat and fervent equestrian. His connections won him a seat on the IOC in 1903 at the youthful age of 27. He distinguished himself in organizing the Olympic Congress in Brussels in 1905 and the 1920 Antwerp Games. In 1925 a majority of the IOC's members found the 49-year-old Baillet-Latour a logical replacement for the retiring Coubertin.

No one expected the new president to light any fires, for he had little of the baron's vision, and he probably knew it: Coubertin may have been an increasingly marginal figure to most IOC members in the years before his death, but Baillet-Latour had remained a steadfast admirer, often seeking his mentor's counsel. A large, ordinarily agreeable man, conservative in outlook and pragmatic in approach, Baillet-Latour saw himself as keeper of the Olympic flame, nothing more. He had opposed the inclusion of women's track and field events at Amsterdam 1928, arguing, as Coubertin had before him, that the fair sex had no place in strenuous athletics. But he had acceded with better grace than Coubertin would have mustered when the vote went against him. The proposed anti-Nazi boycott of the Berlin Games was something else altogether. In

the fierce debate, Baillet-Latour made it clear that he would have sided with the devil himself if it meant saving the Games. Some thought that he had done precisely that.

The count publicly and privately condemned Hitler's mistreatment of Jews. "I am not personally fond of Jews and of the Jewish influence, but I will not have them molested in any way whatsoever," he wrote Brundage. He had demonstrated as much at the Winter

IOC president Henri de Baillet-Latour takes a break from a hunt in the Soignies forest to speak with Victor Boin, a Belgian journalist and, in his youth, an Olympic medalist in three Games. This picture was taken only a few days before Baillet-Latour's death in 1942.

105

Games at Garmisch-Partenkirchen, demanding that the Nazis remove the anti-Semitic signs that festooned the town. Yet he was quite willing to accept the German government's transparently false promises of fair play at the Olympics and its pledge to invite a few athletes with Jewish blood onto the national squad. Most of the IOC supported his position. Sweden's Sigfrid Edström, destined to play a pivotal role in the years ahead, attributed Nazi racial policies to resentment: "Jews have taken a too prominent position in certain branches of life and have—as the Jews very often do when they get in the majority—misused their positions." While Edström did not approve of the persecutions (the worst of which were not yet even imagined by most of the world at the time), he professed understanding.

Not so Ernest Lee Jahncke, one of the IOC's three U.S. members. In November 1935, Jahncke wrote Baillet-Latour that the Nazis were defiling every norm of civilized behavior in their treatment of Jews, that Germany's motives in hosting the Games were blatantly political, and that athletes of the world must in all honor boycott Berlin. He repeated these passionate sentiments in a letter to Dr. Theodor Lewald, president of Berlin's Olympic organizing committee. And he gave copies of both letters to the press. To Baillet-Latour and many other IOC members, this public airing of grievances amounted to treason against the Olympic movement.

In most respects, Jahncke represented the sort of man who was taken onto the IOC for life. He was rich and important, with solid credentials as

Ernest Lee Jahncke, an American IOC member, was a civic leader and New Orleans socialite with a penchant for speaking his mind. His vocal opposition to the Berlin Games brought him afoul of the IOC leadership.

a sportsman. His father had emigrated from Germany to New Orleans in 1869 and made a great deal of money, mostly in shipbuilding and marine salvage. The son—tall, handsome, and intelligent—built on those successes, financially and socially. He became a leading light of New Orleans' beau monde and earned a reputation as one of America's premier yachtsmen, winning a number of national competitions. All this led to an invitation to join the American Olympic Committee in 1926. A year later, recommended by IOC member Charles Sherrill and endorsed by President Calvin Coolidge, he was elected to the all-powerful IOC itself.

As it turned out, sports administration interested Jahncke very little, nor did his new position's requirement of periodic trips away from his beloved New Orleans. He didn't bother to attend his IOC induction in Monte Carlo and absented himself from every committee meeting thereafter except one. Given his evident indifference to Olympic matters, his furious call for a general boycott of the Berlin Games came as a great surprise to fellow delegates. Apparently it was precipitated by Hitler's proclamation of the infamous Nuremberg Laws disenfranchising Jews. Considering his ancestry, Jahncke felt that he had no choice but to speak out. In his letter to Lewald he said, "As you know, I am of German descent. I love the Germany that was and which, I pray, will some day be again. It is as much because of my affection for that Germany as because of my devotion to the spirit of sport that I feel it my duty

as an American citizen to stand for fundamental principle in this matter."

"Let me urge upon you that you place your great talents and influence in the spirit of fair play and chivalry instead of the service of brutality, force, and power," Jahncke wrote to Baillet-Latour. "Let me beseech you to seize your opportunity to take your rightful place in the history of the Olympics alongside of de Coubertin instead of Hitler." These words stung the count, and when they appeared in the public prints the enraged Baillet-Latour wrote to Jahncke and demanded that he resign from the IOC. Jahncke replied that he had no intention of resigning; he was serving Coubertin's ideals, he said, while Baillet-Latour and the German authorities were betraying them. At that, the IOC Executive Board announced to the general membership that "Mr. Jahncke has seriously acted against the Statutes of the IOC." The infraction was grave, said the board, but Jahncke would be given a chance to apologize at the Berlin Session of the full IOC on the eve of the 1936 Games.

Jahncke ignored the summons. Thus when 50 IOC members met at Berlin's Hotel Adlon on July 30, one of their first actions was to banish the renegade. Every delegate save one voted for Jahncke's removal. That delegate was William May Garland, the only American present, since Charles Sherrill had died in June. Garland did not conceal his distaste for Jahncke's conduct but abstained rather than participate in the ouster of a countryman. Afterward, Baillet-Latour informed Jahncke that the IOC had expelled him "for the reason that by your attitude you have been a traitor to its interests." At that same Session, William Garland nominated and the IOC unanimously elected hard-working, foursquare Avery Brundage specifically to fill Jahncke's seat—a most pointed gesture, since Sherrill's seat was vacant too.

Brundage spoke his mind as readily as Ernest Lee Jahncke had, but what he had to say could hardly have been more different. After the Berlin Games, Brundage joined Coubertin in vehemently denying that the Nazis had in any way co-opted the Olympics or used them to score a propaganda coup. The 1936 Games, he insisted, had been "arranged and controlled entirely and exclusively by non-Nazis for the benefit of non-Nazis," and it was his firm opinion that they had furthered "international peace and harmony." In later speeches he quite openly cheered Germany's economic progress under Hitler and noted approvingly that "all enemies of the country" were being "deported or interned." The same sort of toughness, he suggested, might not be such a bad idea for the United States, leaving the impression that he would be delighted to conduct the national housecleaning personally and with a large broom.

For all his bellicose ways and black-and-white views, Brundage had strong assets—keen intelligence, phenomenal energy, and gifts of persuasion

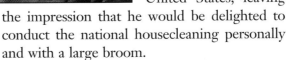

Avery Brundage ruled American amateur sport in 1936. President of both the American Olympic Committee and the American Olympic Association since 1930, he also became president of the Amateur Athletic Union in December 1935. He would be invited to join the IOC a few months later, following the ouster of Ernest Lee Jahncke.

A poster advertising the Tokyo 1940 Olympics depicts a samurai warrior with a dove perched on his fingertip. The Japanese had already completed many of the preparations for the Games—promotional materials, stadium layouts, and the program of events were already finalized—before withdrawing its bid in 1938.

that made him a natural leader. He differed from most of his IOC colleagues in that his was a real-life Horatio Alger story in which a young man had risen above humble birth and adverse circumstances by pluck and hard work. Brundage excelled in his studies, becoming a fine engineer and in time the multimillionaire head of a Chicago construction company that employed 10,000 people. He was also a good athlete, blessed with a big, strong, well-coordinated body and a tremendous determination that lifted him above his natural limits.

Track and field sports attracted Brundage because "they are a demonstration of individual skill and supremacy. The track athlete stands or falls on his own merits." The young man's specialty was the so-called all-around competition, a kind of hurry-up affair that allowed only five minutes of rest between each of 10 events. Brundage was good enough to compete in both the pentathlon and decathlon at Stockholm 1912, but the experience proved traumatic. He finished sixth in the pentathlon, far behind winner Jim Thorpe. The great American Indian athlete also won the decathlon, while Brundage didn't even complete the course. He had accumulated so few points by the time of the 1,500-meter run that he quit in disgust—and then was appalled at what he had done. "Failure to finish the competition was unforgivable," he said, and for years he flagellated himself over that character lapse. Indeed, his feelings of guilt may have had something to do with his zealot's approach to amateur sport ever after.

As Brundage saw it, the amateur athlete competed entirely on his own strengths and for the love of the contest. The Olympic movement carried this striving to the highest possible level, drawing the whole world into its embrace. Olympic athletes, Brundage wrote, were judged "solely on their merit, regardless of social position,

wealth, family connections, race, religion, color, or political affiliation. Here was no commercial connivery nor political chicanery. The rules were the same for everyone, respected by all and enforced impartially." It naturally followed that those rules must never be compromised—as the likes of an Eleanor Holm would discover. "I hold to the strict interpretation of the rules," Brundage said. "One deviation leads to another, and the first thing you know, all is hopeless confusion."

Given his boundless drive and his passion about amateur athletics, an involvement in sports administration was almost inevitable. Brundage was head of the Amateur Athletic Union by the time he was 41, in 1928, and he won the presidency of the American Olympic Association the following year. Tireless in his efforts to promote and protect the Olympic movement, he soon came to the attention of its international leaders. Be patient, they counseled; he would join them on the IOC as soon as a slot opened up in the American delegation. Once it did, Brundage immediately made himself indispensable. Barely a year after election to the IOC, he was elevated to the Executive Board, the seven men who shaped the agenda for the 70-member committee. Along with Baillet-Latour, Sigfrid Edström, and a few others, Avery Brundage was now at the very center of Olympic policymaking.

In every Olympiad, an important piece of IOC business is to chose among would-be hosts of future Games. While the decision made in Berlin appeared to be eminently correct—even laudable—it would prove disastrous, pointing up once again the Olympics' vulnerability to the world's political storms.

There was no dearth of applicants for the 1940 Games of the XII Olympiad. In the mid-1930s, Tokyo, Helsinki, London, and Rome had all applied for the honor. Tokyo had a unique attraction: If chosen, it would be the first Asian venue, and would thus underscore the internationalism

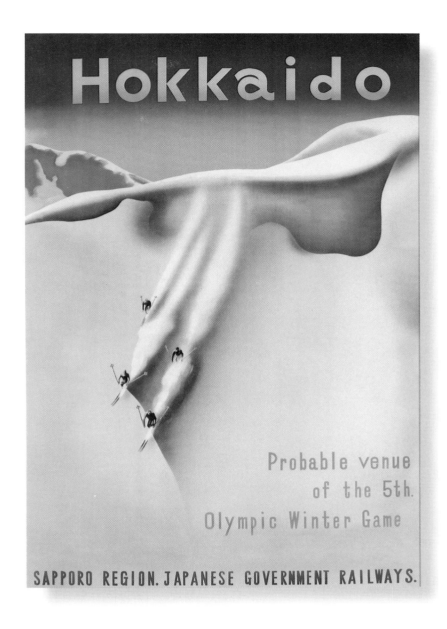

Hokkaido

Probable venue
of the 5th.
Olympic Winter Game

SAPPORO REGION. JAPANESE GOVERNMENT RAILWAYS.

of the Olympic movement. Japan had already demonstrated a commendable commitment to sport by thrice hosting the Far Eastern Games, the first of the regional sports festivals that sprang up under the IOC aegis.

But a shadow lay over Tokyo's candidacy. Early in the decade, as the Great Depression racked Japan, the government fell into the hands of ultranationalist groups supported by the military. Soon the policymakers came to see conquest as the solution to their island country's problems— overcrowding and a shortage of farmland and natural resources. In 1931, on the slimmest of pretexts, the Japanese army invaded Manchuria, then a part of China. Because China was in the throes of civil war, the invaders met no resistance. Manchuria was swiftly gobbled up, and Japan's leaders started planning the conquest of all East Asia. That would require a far larger military machine, so they bided their time while Japan's factories and shipyards went into high gear.

Any concerns IOC officials may have had over Japanese aggression didn't stop them from looking ever more favorably on Japan's candidacy for 1940. In no small measure, this was because of the efforts of Count Michimasa Soyeshima, an IOC member whose maneuverings reached well beyond the committee. Clever and personable, Soyeshima in 1935 talked Benito Mussolini into withdrawing Rome from the list of applicants; part of Soyeshima's pitch, well calculated to appeal to the dynastic pretensions of Il Duce, was that 1940 would commemorate the 2,600th year of Japan's imperial reign. Soyeshima also personally lobbied British Prime Minister Stanley Baldwin. After much internal discussion, the British Foreign Office thought it best to oblige the count: Great Britain had massive interests in East Asia and wished to remain on good terms with regional powers. An unofficial whisper to the British Olympic Committee took care of things.

Helsinki was the only remaining contender, but Baillet-Latour recommended Tokyo when the issue came to a vote in Berlin on July 30, 1936. In a recent trip to Japan, he said, he had found that "the sporting Olympic spirit has penetrated into all classes of the population. The youth not only take part in sport but appreciate the moral character that accompanies it." Tokyo was selected.

Under the Olympic Charter, Japan had the option of hosting the 1940 Winter Games as well as the summer festival. At first the Japanese delegates were not sure they had a suitable site, but eventually they decided that the Winter Games could be held at Sapporo, capital of Hokkaido, the northernmost island in the Japanese chain. When the IOC assembled in Warsaw in June

Skiers drop onto a snow-covered mountain on a poster promoting the Winter Games at Sapporo— the first of two 1940 Olympic festivals that would be aborted. After Tokyo won its bid for the Summer Games in July 1936, the Japanese spent a year searching for a city that had the right terrain and climate for winter sports. Sapporo wasn't confirmed as the Winter Games host city until June 1937.

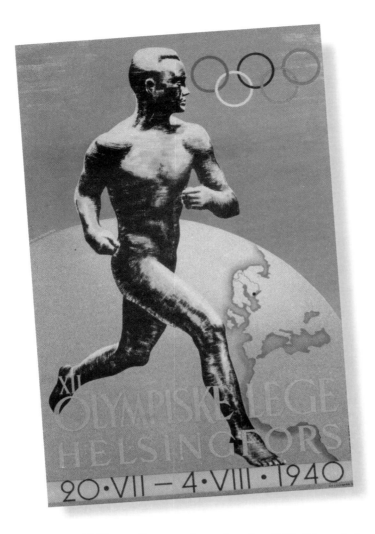

The poster for the canceled 1940 Games at Helsinki featured the image of Finland's living legend, Paavo Nurmi. The matchless Nurmi had won nine gold medals in track during the 1920s. The poster for Helsinki 1952 would adopt the same design with relatively few changes.

1937 to discuss plans for the XII Olympiad, Japan exercised its prerogative.

By then, preparations for the Tokyo Games were well under way. The Japanese had designed an Olympic complex that could stand comparison with what the Germans had created. The main stadium would seat 80,000 and have an ultrafast track. There would be large arenas for swimming, cycling, equestrian events, boxing, and other sports. Separate Olympic villages would be built for men and women, and special housing would be provided for visitors. Similarly ambitious plans were soon devised for Sapporo. The northern city would get capacious indoor and outdoor skating rinks, a superb new ski run, and the world's fastest bobsled course.

One knotty problem was how to convey the sacred flame from Olympia to Japan. The Japanese government proposed that it go by sea, but Carl Diem—inventor of the relay that had generated such excitement in 1936—had a better idea.

Diem was as active in the Olympic movement as ever. After the Berlin Games, he became the first director of the International Olympic Institute, founded by a grateful Reich at the suggestion of Coubertin. Located in Berlin, the institute established an Olympic archive and acted as a publishing and research arm of the IOC. Diem now argued that a maritime journey for the Olympic flame would be hopelessly dull; it must travel overland, and as usual, he was ready with specifics. He calculated the distance between Olympia and Tokyo to be 6,250 miles. Obviously, a major part of that immense span would have to be traversed on horseback, but runners could manage about 2,000 miles. Between runners and riders, said Diem, the flame could cross Europe and Asia and reach its destination in 25 days, even allowing for 120 local festivals along the way. Its only sea passage would be a brief hop from the Korean peninsula to Japan.

Diem commissioned a study of the idea from a famous explorer and writer, Sven Hedin, who had traveled widely in Asia (not to mention from pole to pole) and was a scholar of geography, anthropology, and ethnography. Not only did Hedin think the scheme viable, he wrote a vivid description of the torch's passage across mountains and valleys and rivers and streams, through towns and villages, traveling alongside oxcarts and caravans, exciting the admiration of both patrician and peasant all along the way.

This glorious vision—indeed the whole idea of a Tokyo Games—began to evaporate in 1937. That July, Japanese forces poured into China and seized Peking, Tientsin, and the Chinese Nationalist capital, Nanking, where the slaughter of 40,000 civilians horrified the world. Cries went up at once for an Olympic boycott.

But the IOC leaders turned a deaf ear. Avery Brundage was particularly outspoken in reminding the public that there was no connection between the Olympic movement and politics. He told the press: "If the International Olympic Committee

had to find a country whose present and past history was free from war and aggression in which to hold the Olympic Games, there would be no Games."

In early 1938, Count Soyeshima was still confident that the Tokyo Games would go forward, but his faith was shaken a few months later when Japan's government slowed construction work for the Olympics and redirected funds and materials to the military effort. Fearing that Japan would be unable to put on a good show in 1940, Soyeshima took his concerns to the prime minister and other high officials, advising them that the government should either support the Games properly or give them up. Accordingly, in mid-July of 1938 the Japanese cabinet canceled the Games. Moreover, the ministers forbade Japanese athletes to compete in any Olympic Games that might be held elsewhere.

Finland now stepped into the breach. One of its IOC delegates, Ernst Krogius, had already suggested that Helsinki could take over from Tokyo if the need arose, and his colleagues seized that option. A Finnish organizing committee immediately went to work. The Winter Games remained in limbo for another year.

Meanwhile, the IOC found itself embroiled yet again in the interminable controversy regarding amateurism. Over the years, "amateur" had been endlessly and often rancorously defined and redefined, both by the IOC and by the international federations that governed each sport and certified the amateurism of that sport's athletes. Unfortunately, the IOC and the federations weren't always in accord on the issue. At an IOC meeting held in Prague in 1925, delegates decreed that the international federations must deny amateur status to trainers, sports instructors and coaches, and athletes who gave exhibitions. The decree would invite rebellion.

The focus of the revolt would be Alpine skiing, a sport that would make its Olympic debut at the 1936 Winter Games at the German resort of Garmisch-Partenkirchen. In 1932 the Fédération Internationale de Ski, or FIS, decided that skiers who were compensated for coaching could be regarded as amateurs—the IOC dictum notwithstanding—and therefore were eligible for Olympic competition. But when the IOC met in Oslo in 1935, it reaffirmed its position that instructors were professionals, and Baillet-Latour effected an immediate ban on their participation

IOC members and their wives enjoy an outing during the 1935 Oslo Session. The eligibility of ski instructors was debated at length during the annual IOC meeting. Arguments over what constituted a professional in Alpine skiing would force a vote on whether to discontinue the Olympic Winter Games cycle.

A skier on a sleigh ride graced the St. Moritz poster promoting its 1940 Olympic Winter Games. St. Moritz took over as host city on September 3, 1938, but withdrew less than a year later.

competitions—had been a big hit at Garmisch. Skiing was the most beloved of all winter sports, and its cancellation would unquestionably have a dampening effect. But there was a principle to uphold. At a meeting in Cairo in March 1938, the IOC discussed three possible courses: abandon the Olympic Winter Games altogether, cancel the 1940 Winter Games while leaving open the possibility of reinstating winter festivals in future Olympiads, or hold the 1940 Winter Games without skiing. In the end, the committee voted to hold the Winter Games but scrap the skiing. The pages of the *Olympic Review*, official publication of the IOC, delivered a stern lecture: "Leaders of sporting federations who, lacking in foresight, are willing, as in the case of the skiing federation, to permit sport instructors to participate in amateur competition meet with the determined opposition of all the other sporting bodies, and their attitude will soon be a thing of the past."

Hardly.

A few months later, Japan gave up the 1940 Winter Games, and the IOC awarded them to St. Moritz, Switzerland—on condition that the Swiss Olympic Committee deal with the skiing problem. As it happened, however, the members of that committee strongly supported the FIS stance. More argument; further intransigence—until the IOC switched the 1940 Winter Games to Garmisch-Partenkirchen, where the facilities remained in ready-to-go condition. Carl Diem, the consummate organizer, began planning a five-country torch run on skis, to be capped off with an Alpine "Ski Day" that would serve in lieu of medal events. Ski Day would be a classic Diem production, with artillery salutes echoing off the slopes, choruses of hymns, and a spectacular mass descent by no fewer than 10,000 skiers—men, women, children, postal officials, customs inspectors, soldiers, policemen, and so forth. "We hope these plans will result in a festive event which will demonstrate

in the Games. Hardest hit were two of the great Alpine ski powers, Austria and Switzerland, whose top stars were expected to schuss away with many medals. Both countries boycotted the skiing events at Garmisch. Moreover, the IOC ban so angered the FIS that it threatened that no skiers, Alpine or Nordic, would show up for the 1940 Winter Games unless the IOC relented on the amateurism question.

Baillet-Latour and his colleagues were on the horns of a dilemma. Nordic skiing had always been hugely popular at the Winter Games, and the showier Alpine events—downhill and slalom cousins to the Nordic cross-country and jumping

Nazi symbols appear on an advertisement for an Olympic pageant. As host of the 1936 Winter Games, Garmisch-Partenkirchen made the perfect emergency candidate for the thrice-orphaned 1940 festival. Souvenir pins and the daily program were already created before the outbreak of war brought preparations to a halt.

V.OLYMPISCHE WINTERSPIELE
GARMISCH-PARTENKIRCHEN
2.–11.FEBRUAR 1940

skiing in all of its magnificence," wrote Diem.

It would doubtless have been a lollapalooza of a show. But the 1940 Winter Games would never take place. Nor would the 1944 summer and winter festivals, awarded respectively to London and to Italy's Cortina d'Ampezzo. Hitler's hour had come.

The world did not lack for warnings about Adolf Hitler's ambitions. He had repudiated the Treaty of Versailles, goose-stepped into the Rhineland, absorbed Austria, seized Czechoslovakia, and, in September 1939, joined the Soviet Union in crushing and carving up Poland. As a consequence of the blitzkrieg on Poland, Germany was at war with Great Britain and France. But now an eerie quiet reigned in Europe while the Führer prepared his ultimate aggressions. This calm before the cataclysm gave Olympians, all unknowing and praying desperately for the best, hope that the 1940 Games might yet be held.

The organizers of the Helsinki Games understood that Finland might be drawn into the war, but they continued with their preparations, as did Carl Diem in Germany. The Winter Games

were the first to go: In November, Germany opted out as host. Diem grieved that "the world of sport has been deprived of an event which would have been a festival of peace and joy." At the same time, devout believer that he was, Diem expressed confidence that his country's Olympic future remained bright; Germany, he said, was "completely imbued with the inner force of the Olympic concept."

Soviet dictator Joseph Stalin, meanwhile, was busy expanding his northwestern frontiers. The Baltic states of Latvia, Lithuania, and Estonia succumbed to Soviet intimidation. But the Communists had to fight for Finland. The unequal struggle bloodied the snows all through the winter of 1939-40, until the courageous Finns finally capitulated in March. Finland's national Olympic committee carried on a brief but stubborn resistance of its own. The members refused to write off the Helsinki Games until the beginning of May.

Now came Hitler's all-out assault, first sweeping west to overrun Norway, Denmark, Holland, Belgium, and finally France. Only the British fought on, but their days seemed numbered. And then, on June 22, 1940, the true extent of the

German dictator's grandiose dementia came clear when three million German soldiers exploded into the Soviet Union along a 2,000-mile front, driving irresistibly eastward until winter and a sea of Soviets halted the attack in Russia. The madness ratcheted up another dozen notches on December 7, 1941, when Japan took the war global by attacking the U.S. naval base at Pearl Harbor, Hawaii. In Berlin, Hitler announced that henceforth the Third Reich, too, would be at war with the United States. This "simplified things," he said. The Nazi despot was fatally correct, for in the end both Japan and Germany would be demolished by their assembled enemies, although it would take another four terrible years to bring that about.

As the war raged, the Olympic Games receded almost totally from public consciousness. How could it be otherwise? Even the stewards of Coubertin's creation wondered if the movement—or any of the old sporting pursuits, for that matter—had a recognizable future. Baillet-Latour got a personal first taste of the Nazis' New Order immediately after Wehrmacht tanks overran Belgium. Going from stable to stable, German Army quartermasters confiscated every thoroughbred in the country, including those of the IOC's president. To a lifelong horseman like Baillet-Latour, this was an outrage beyond comprehension. He complained in fury to German IOC member Karl Ritter von Halt, and in time Baillet-Latour, at least, got back his prized steeds.

Yet horse thievery was the least of it. If Hitler had his way, the Olympics themselves would become a possession of the Thousand-Year Reich. He reviewed grandiose plans for a 450,000-seat Deutsches Stadion in Nuremberg, where the Games would remain "for all time to come." The Nazis sent emissaries, including Carl Diem, to Brussels for discussions with Baillet-Latour on how they meant to "rejuvenate" the IOC. Committee members had always elected their own colleagues, but Hitler's messengers insisted that

Germany and her allies would henceforth appoint their own representatives—effectively stacking the IOC with a controlling number of pro-Nazis. The Germans asked Baillet-Latour to continue as president. These terms were included in a document written by Diem, who recorded in his diary that Baillet-Latour "approved my draft, he found it excellent."

This reported acquiescence to the Nazi takeover, coupled with displays of geniality toward the occupiers, led Belgians and others to mark Baillet-Latour as a collaborator. The count may have been flattered by the idea of remaining president; he may also have been grateful for the return of his beloved horses. He most certainly realized the utter impotence of his position. But what he refused to do, no doubt pleading wartime exigencies, was convene an IOC Session to ratify the Nazis' amendments to the Olympic Charter. That must await peace. In the meantime, the rules would remain as they were.

Nor did the Nazis succeed in seizing physical control of the movement, though they tried. At one point an unhappy Carl Diem appeared at the Lausanne headquarters and explained that he had been sent to take possession of the Olympic archives. But he was forestalled by Lydia Zanchi, the IOC's secretary since 1927. "I hid the most important documents in the cellar," she recalled, "and convinced the community that Diem was a spy." Then, she said, "I alerted Mr. Edström of Sweden."

Like Avery Brundage, big, bluff Sigfrid Edström had been a notable athlete (an 11-flat sprinter in the 100-meter dash—and that in the 1890s) and had gone on to accumulate a fortune at the helm of ASEA, the huge Swedish electrical combine. In 1913 he helped found one of the earliest and most powerful sports federations, the International Amateur Athletics Federation, which oversees track and field. Edström would preside over the IAAF for 33 years. He had also been an early leader in the Olympic movement, serving as chief organizer for Stockholm 1912

A prisoner in the Theresienstadt concentration camp used sheet-music paper to create a haunting portrait of Gustav Felix Flatow, a gold-medal gymnast for Germany at Athens 1896. Flatow's Olympic achievement wasn't enough to save him from the infamous camp. He died there.

OLYMPIANS TO THE DEATH

The Nazis' Final Solution threatened Jews in every territory controlled by the Germans—and Jewish Olympians were not exempt. Many of them immigrated from Europe to safety elsewhere. At least six Olympic medalists, however, were not so lucky. Cousins Alfred and Gustav Felix Flatow, who together won five gold medals in gymnastics for Germany at the Athens Games of 1896, starved to death at the Theresienstadt camp in German-occupied Czechoslovakia. Dr. Otto Herschmann, an Austrian swimmer at the Athens Games, perished in Izbica in Poland. Hungarian fencers Janos Garai and Oszkar Gerde were killed in Mauthausen in Germany, and countryman Attila Petschauer died in a Ukrainian labor camp. Another Hungarian, Ferenc Kemeny, a founding member of the IOC and a close friend of Pierre de Coubertin, killed himself in 1944 rather than face a concentration camp.

The camps, whether for prisoners of war or enemies of the Reich, were horrors. Yet the spirit of Olympism was some comfort to the internees at Woldenberg and Gross Born, two eastern German stalags for Polish soldiers. The commandants of both camps allowed prisoners to hold a version of the Olympic Games from late July through mid-August 1944. The celebrations strove for authenticity, featuring both athletic and cultural events. Grandstands were built and tickets printed. Prisoners even created a set of Olympic stamps and stationery to use in intracamp mail. Winners received paper medals. Sadly, the games would be a last respite for many of the prisoners. Both camps were closed in early 1945, and the inmates were sent on forced marches into the interior of Germany. Survivors were liberated in April by advancing American and Russian armies.

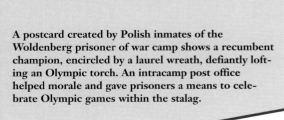

A postcard created by Polish inmates of the Woldenberg prisoner of war camp shows a recumbent champion, encircled by a laurel wreath, defiantly lofting an Olympic torch. An intracamp post office helped morale and gave prisoners a means to celebrate Olympic games within the stalag.

During the 1939 IOC Session in London, Count Henri de Baillet-Latour carries a wreath to place at Britain's Tomb of the Unknown Soldier. Sweden's Sigfrid Edström, IOC vice president, walks to his left. Chairing the London Session would be Baillet-Latour's last public duty as IOC president. After the count's death, Edström would maintain ties among IOC members during World War II.

and joining the IOC in 1920. Within a year he was invited onto the IOC Executive Board, and 16 years later he became vice president.

Edström was a man of old-fashioned opinions. He joined Baillet-Latour in opposing women's events in the Games, and he championed the cause of smaller cities against urban giants as Olympic hosts. All issues of play-for-pay drew his ire: He abhorred the growing practice among athletes of double-dipping from various organizers on travel expenses for meets, and the disputes over amateurism in skiing so irritated him that he once cast the only vote on the entire IOC for eliminating the Winter Games altogether.

But if the 70-year-old Edström was sometimes in the minority, he was nonetheless popular and well respected. And that, along with his being a citizen of a neutral country, enabled him to keep at least some channels of communication open among IOC members during the war. Only in Europe's handful of neutral countries could international mail be reliably sent or received. Beginning in 1940, Edström issued three or four "circular letters" every year to as many of the IOC's members as he could reach. Each letter was a lengthy compendium of news sent to him in Sweden by the other members, 60 of whom replied to his letters at one time or another.

"Bohemia-Moravia: Mr. Jiri Guth-Jarkovsky is in good health and sends warm regards to all," one letter reported. And in another: "Estonia: Mr. Joakim Puhk was imprisoned in Russia with two of his brothers; his youngest brother was able to flee to Helsinki and I am in contact with him. Unfortunately, he does not know where his brother Joakim is."

Edström related in hopeful detail the efforts of Avery Brundage to keep the flame of sports festivals alive by organizing what would come to be called the Pan-American Games. Brundage's plans progressed nicely for a while but were eventually thwarted by the war. The first Pan-American Games would not take place until 1951.

In early 1942, Edström had sad tidings for his colleagues: Count Henri de Baillet-Latour, a member of the IOC for 39 years and president for 17, had followed Coubertin to the grave: "Tuesday, January 6, Mr. Baillet-Latour was feeling fine, taking care of business as usual. In the afternoon, he presided over a meeting of the Belgian Olympic Committee, dined at home, then worked several more hours before going to sleep. The following morning, his valet found him lying in bed as usual, but lifeless."

The count had died of a stroke at age 66.

Because ordinary travel was nearly impossible in this war-torn world, only three IOC members were able to attend Baillet-Latour's memorial service. One was Belgian, another Dutch, and the third was Karl Ritter von Halt. Carl Diem came as representative of the International Olympic Institute in Berlin. He and uniformed functionaries brought wreaths, including one adorned with a big swastika and presented in the name of Adolf Hitler and the IOC—a rather incongruous pair. Hitler also sent condolences to Baillet-Latour's widow.

The tributes from Nazi leaders and the disproportionate presence of German mourners apparently perturbed the members of the Belgian Olympic Committee who attended. Diem

confided to his diary, "We sensed their concern that we were making ourselves too obvious and seeking to make some kind of propaganda."

Now Edström assumed the functions and prerogatives of IOC president. In 1944 he traveled to London and New York to consult with two fellow members of the IOC Executive Board, Lord Aberdare and Avery Brundage. Edström was 74 and beginning to worry about continuity in the IOC leadership. He found his successor in Brundage, and with a circular letter dated December 29, 1944, he nominated the American as second vice president. "M. Brundage belongs to the oldest members of the IOC," said Edström. "He collaborated with Pierre de Coubertin and M. de Baillet-Latour. He is an experienced sportsman and is very aware of the Olympic idea, the one defined by Pierre de Coubertin. I am sure that I will be able, if the case arises, to successfully deliver the presidency into his expert and sure hands. I would be much obliged, my dear friends and colleagues, if you could let me know your opinion."

In the next letter, on June 11, 1945, Edström announced that a majority of members had agreed to his recommendation. By then the war in Europe was over. The war in the Pacific would end less than two months later. The world began a long convalescence, rebuilding shattered cities, reknitting ruined economies, grieving for the tens of millions of soldiers and civilians who had died.

The Olympic movement, too, would recover only slowly. During the war the IOC lost about a third of its members for one reason or another, and there had been no possibility of replacing them while the fighting continued; reconstituting the movement's leadership would be a lengthy process. But Edström and Brundage were determined to get things going. In late August 1945 they met with their Executive Board colleague Lord Aberdare in London. Aberdare was dispirited. In a letter to Brundage he had questioned the worth of continuing the Olympic Games at all,

A gymnastics demonstration at Riponne Square at the University of Lausanne was part of the 50th anniversary celebration of the Olympic movement.

Swiss artist Henri von der Mühl created the classically inspired design for the poster promoting the IOC's birthday jubilee.

GOLDEN ANNIVERSARY

As 1944 began, IOC leaders realized that war would once again make it impossible to celebrate the Games. That indignity was all the more egregious since 1944 would mark the IOC's 50th year. The modern Olympic movement dates its origin to a meeting at the Sorbonne in Paris held on June 23, 1894. Even though the Games were impossible, such an important milestone had to be celebrated.

Sigfrid Edström put the Swiss Olympic Committee to the task of organizing a two-week commemorative ceremony to be held in Lausanne from June 16 through July 3. The neutral Swiss came through admirably, considering the constraints imposed by the war. Travel was difficult, so turnout was predictably low: Only two IOC members managed to attend—Karl Ritter von Halt, a German, and Stephan Tchaprachikov, a Bulgarian diplomat with Nazi connections. A majority of the other guests were either German or Swiss leaders of sports federations.

The festival was, by and large, a tribute to Pierre de Coubertin. There were speeches in honor of the Olympic founder, and a vigil was held at his grave. Organizers even played a recording of one of his speeches.

There were athletic demonstrations, too. The commemoration was local and low-key, but sufficient to make its point: Olympism endured.

wondering if the ideal of international brotherhood had not been damaged beyond repair. Brundage, with Edström's help, convinced him that the need was greater than ever.

The three men addressed the issue of selecting venues for the 1948 Games, those of the XIII Olympiad. Candidate sites included Baltimore, Los Angeles, Minneapolis, and Philadelphia in the United States, and Lausanne and London in Europe. The Executive Board recommended London, and later the full IOC approved this choice by postal vote. The Winter Games were awarded to St. Moritz in Switzerland, a country that had been spared the ravages of war. Finally, the three men set a time and place for the first postwar Session of the IOC—Lausanne in September of 1946.

The Lausanne gathering was attended by just 26 IOC members, nine of them new. Many of the absentees had been unable to get to the meeting in the early postwar confusion. Others had died during the war years. Nevertheless, the Executive Board had picked in Lausanne a perfect venue for rebuilding. In that shrine of Olympism, with the spirit of Baron Pierre de Coubertin almost palpably present, there was a feeling of momentum. Edström was elected IOC president by acclamation, and Avery Brundage— his heir apparent—was elected first vice president. The International Olympic Institute, its Berlin headquarters badly damaged by wartime bombing, was moved to Lausanne. (Its director, Carl Diem, would begin teaching physical culture at Berlin University and would soon set up a sports university in Cologne.) The selection of London and St. Moritz as host cities for 1948 was confirmed. And the old dispute about ski instructors was finally laid to rest. The IOC and the FIS compromised: For purposes of the St. Moritz Games, ski instructors would be considered amateurs if they took no pay for ski lessons after October 1946.

The Olympic movement was back on track, feeling its way forward in a much-altered world.

A smiling Avery Brundage *(left)* sits next to his mentor, Sigfrid Edström, during the 1946 IOC Session at Lausanne. During the meetings, Edström won election as the IOC's fourth president. Both he and Brundage would play pivotal roles in shepherding the Olympic movement through the difficult postwar period.

POSTWAR WAR

The 28 delegations that marched into the St. Moritz Olympic Ice Stadium (*left*) should have been in high spirits, considering that the Olympic Games were resuming after a 12-year hiatus. But the mood at St. Moritz 1948 was not particularly joyous. A fight over credentials for two rival U.S. hockey teams had soured the air, and on January 30, opening day, the *New York Times* reported that "the American squabble was catching." The Swedes were grumbling about accommodations; the British thought there was too much emphasis on teas and parties rather than on sporting events; and journalists were threatening a boycott unless organizers made better arrangements for the press.

Nevertheless, the opening ceremony began at 10 a.m. with relative serenity. Towering mountains, covered with a thick layer of fresh snow, formed a perfect backdrop to the colorful pageantry inside the Olympic stadium. Dr. Enrico Celio, the Swiss president, declared the Games open, and Riccardo "Bibi" Torriani, a Swiss hockey player, swore the athlete's oath. There was no elaborate torch relay, but organizers did have a cauldron ignited with a flame brought into the stadium by a series of cross-country skiers.

Peace reigned—but not for long: An American player took a swing at a Swiss competitor in the hockey game immediately following the ceremony, Canadian and Swedish hockey players got into a free-for-all in their opening-day game, and the fight between the IOC and the Swiss organizers over which American hockey team would compete continued to gather steam.

RENEWAL

When *Life* magazine took a photographic peek at goings-on in the Swiss resort of St. Moritz not long after World War II, the glamour-loving publication was dazzled. St. Moritz, it proclaimed, was "the most fashionable village in Europe."

That may have been an understatement; St. Moritz was arguably the most fashionable village in the world. For more than half a century, the rich and famous had been gathering there in glittering swarms. Initially, they were attracted by the flower-strewn Alpine summers and the reputed healing properties of local mineral springs. Soon, however, winter pleasures became the main allure. Said *Life*, "The exiled royalty, minor princes, beauties, near beauties, sportsmen, and bankers of the International Set consider St. Moritz the place to spend the winter holiday."

It was easy to see why. Perched on a lakeside terrace in a valley wending through the most majestic part of the Swiss Alps, St. Moritz was nothing less than a winter-sports paradise; it had endless miles of mountain trails, an array of ice rinks for skating and curling, a thrilling toboggan run, and magnificent ski slopes on a pair of mountains that reared 12,000 feet above the town (itself at 6,000 feet). Luxury hotels offered every imaginable comfort, and fine restaurants and lively nightspots kept visitors amused by night. Not even war could shut down the snowy playground: Vacationers—a thinned stream, to be sure—kept on coming even through the worst years of the conflict.

Early 1948 saw the arrival of another, very different elite—the world's best skiers, skaters, and sledders. Their stay would be brief. For 10 days, from January 30 to February 8, St. Moritz would host the Fifth Olympic Winter Games. It was not the first time the resort had been so honored; the Second Winter Games had been held there in 1928. But the upcoming festival was truly special, marking the rebirth of Olympic competition after a hiatus of 12 years.

Three members of the American Hockey Association team, practicing in New York prior to the St. Moritz Games

THE GAMES AT A GLANCE

	JANUARY 30	JANUARY 31	FEBRUARY 1	FEBRUARY 2	FEBRUARY 3	FEBRUARY 4	FEBRUARY 5	FEBRUARY 6	FEBRUARY 7	FEBRUARY 8
OPENING CEREMONY	■									
ALPINE SKIING				■		■	■			
BOBSLED	■	■						■	■	
FIGURE SKATING				■	■	■	■	■	■	
ICE HOCKEY	■	■	■	■	■	■		■	■	■
NORDIC SKIING		■	■		■		■			
SKELETON						■	■	■		
SKI JUMPING							■			
SPEED SKATING		■	■	■	■					
CLOSING CEREMONY										■
DEMONSTRATION SPORTS										
MILITARY PATROL										■
WINTER PENTATHLON		■	■	■	■	■				

Amid the Alpine scenery of soaring peaks and sun-spangled snowfields, the troubles of Europe seemed far away. In truth, of course, they were very close. On all sides of Switzerland, nations grieved and suffered. Italy, whose border lay just nine miles from St. Moritz, had been devastated by the war—its transportation system destroyed, its industrial production reduced to one fifth of prewar levels, its agricultural output halved. Millions of Italians had been left homeless and jobless by the conflict, and now the Italian Communist Party seemed to be on the verge of taking power. In Austria, on Switzerland's eastern border, the great city of Vienna had been severely damaged, and the country was now occupied by the victors in the war—Great Britain, France, the United States, and the Soviet Union. France, to the west, was racked by labor strife; the disruptions were led by local Communists, but, as in Italy, Moscow called the tune. Germany, to the north, was a nightmare vista of rubble, a blighted country fast heading for partition.

Farther afield, other national ordeals were in progress. Joseph Stalin was rapidly transforming a number of Eastern European countries into Soviet satellite states; he had already swallowed the Baltic lands of Lithuania, Latvia, and Estonia. Great Britain, mighty before the war, was impoverished. Greece, ancestral home of the Olympic Games, had endured agonies under German occupation and now was being ripped apart by a civil war that pitted Communist guerrillas against a wobbling government.

Although St. Moritz was well shielded from these storms, a few signs of Europe's distress could be detected as the Olympians gathered for the Winter Games. Money was in generally short supply, and the Swiss organizers were worried about making ends meet. Some entrant countries were so poor that their athletes arrived in St. Moritz without adequate equipment: The Austrians had to borrow skis from the U.S. team. Even the age of the participants was a reminder of what the world had gone through. On average, the

athletes were considerably older than in previous Games. War had interfered with the training and development of the generation behind them.

Still, they were there and glad of it. The only real threat to a successful resumption of the Games was the weather. January had brought unusually heavy snowfalls—good for the skiers but a problem for the skaters if it continued, since all of their competitions would be held on outdoor rinks. A potentially more serious problem was a warm south wind called the Föhn, which sometimes blew up the valley from Italy, raising temperatures and turning ice and snow to slush for a day or two. On opening day, however, there was neither Föhn nor snowstorm. The sky was a cloudless vault of blue. The air was cold and bracing.

A little after 9:30 a.m., officials and the athletes of 28 countries assembled in the center of the town and marched toward the 6,000-seat Olympic Ice Stadium, where the opening ceremonies would be held and the Olympic flame lighted. In the traditional Parade of Nations were some newcomers: Chile, Denmark, Iceland, Korea, and Lebanon were taking part in the Winter Games for the first time. There were also some conspicuous but understandable absences: Germany and Japan had been

Snow-capped Alps shelter the lovely Swiss village of St. Moritz. The town's mineral-rich springs have lured visitors for hundreds of years. Winter sports became an attraction around the turn of the 19th century.

WHERE THE GAMES WERE PLAYED

Olympic Ice Stadium

Olympic Ski Jump

Olympic Bobsled Run

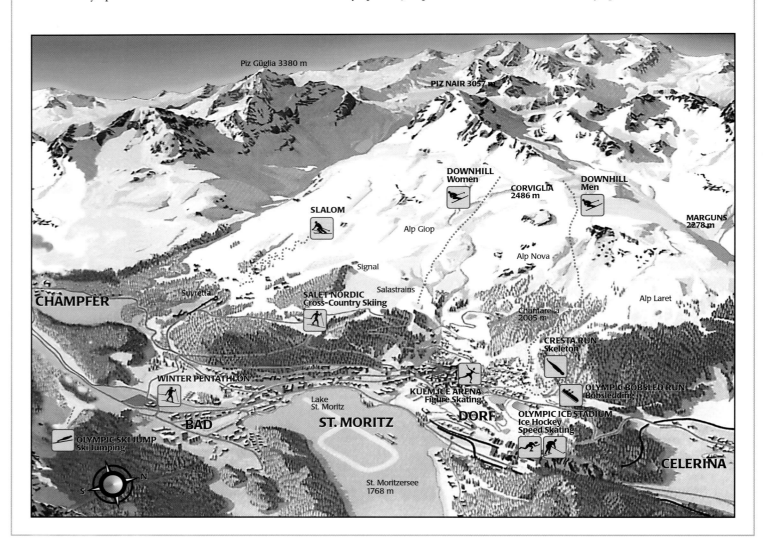

barred. Altogether, a total of 713 athletes had come to St. Moritz, 77 of them women. The USSR had sent no competitors, as usual, but a group of 10 Soviet observers had arrived with cameras and notebooks—a sign that their nation's policy of noninvolvement in the Games might be coming to an end.

All in all, it was a heartening moment, suggesting that the Olympic movement was making a strong comeback. The picture had, however, a peculiar little flaw: Marching with the American squad (110 strong, including support staff) was a hockey team that had entered the Winter Games under the auspices of the U.S. Olympic Committee; watching from the sidelines was a second American hockey team that had been declared eligible by the international federation that governed the sport. This was an Olympic first: Two teams from one nation had come to St. Moritz, both expecting to play.

The fact that one of the American teams now stood on the sidelines didn't indicate a defeat for its hopes. The IOC, faced with choosing between the two claimants, had offered something to both: One team could march in the Parade of Nations but could not take part in the Winter Games; the other team could take part in the Winter Games but could not march in the parade. This decision had the virtue of symmetry. In the opinion of practically everyone but the IOC, it was also utterly absurd.

Not surprisingly, the central issue of the hockey dispute was amateurism, that ever-shifting foundation stone of the Olympic movement. Nor was it surprising to anyone who followed Olympic affairs that the quarrel had been stirred up by the steely-eyed man seen striding along behind the American flag in the Parade of Nations: Avery Brundage. For decades, Brundage had warned that any relaxation of the standards of amateurism would destroy the Games; his views, if anything, had

hardened with time. Now he had made a stand.

In theory, Olympic regulations provided the tools to enforce the ideal of amateurism. All would-be competitors in the 1948 Games in both St. Moritz and London were required to sign the following oath, whose wording had been worked out the year before: "I, the undersigned, declare on my honor, that I am an amateur according to the rules of the International Federation governing my sport, that I have participated in sport solely for pleasure and for physical, mental or social benefits I derive therefrom; that sport to me is nothing more than a recreation without material gain of any kind, direct or indirect, and that I am eligible in all respects for participation in the Olympic Games." In practice, unfortunately, the oath did nothing to resolve jurisdictional disputes over amateurism, such as the hockey controversy.

The roots of the hockey problem could be traced back to 1930, when the AAU—the governing body of a number of amateur sports in the United States—became a member of the Ligue Internationale de Hockey sur Glace (LIHG), the federation that exercised international supervision over amateur hockey. Among other roles, the AAU was empowered to say who was an amateur in the United States and who was not. A tricky matter soon arose in hockey. During the 1930s, commercial rink owners began to put together teams that were ostensibly amateur in status but that sometimes fed players into the professional ranks; in addition, the players received modest stipends for games they played on the commercial rinks. The AAU, concluding that these were unacceptable taints, expelled such teams from its competitions.

The rink owners fought back. They formed an oversight group called the American Hockey Association (AHA), and this group applied to the LIHG to take the place of the AAU as the administrator of amateur hockey in the United States. In 1946 the LIHG granted the request,

The winners' diploma for St. Moritz 1948 features a snowflake and the Olympic rings.

The design for the winners' medals (*above*) at St. Moritz was a simple pattern of a hand-held torch with the Olympic rings against a background of snowflakes. Inscribed at the top is the Olympic motto: *CITIUS ALTIUS FORTIUS*. The reverse has more snowflakes, plus the inscription: V Winter Games—St. Moritz 1948. The Swiss jewelry firm of Huguenin Brothers minted the prizes.

The commemorative medals (*left*), also made by Huguenin, display a barefoot woman with her hair billowing in the wind and Alps in the background. The reverse has the Olympic rings with the inscription: V Winter Games—St. Moritz 1948.

on the grounds that the AAU represented many sports and the AHA just one. But the AAU had the support of Avery Brundage, who had once been its president and currently was president of the American Olympic Association (AOA, a precursor of the U.S. Olympic Committee). It was Brundage's position that only an AAU team could qualify for Olympic competition, no matter what the LIHG might say.

When the IOC met in Stockholm in 1947, one item on its agenda was to sort out differences between the AOA and the LIHG. Neither organization would budge. Said Brundage in his usual sententious style: "This is a battle in which the future of sport and the Olympic Games are at stake." The LIHG replied with an escalation that was more than rhetorical: Unless the AHA team represented the United States at St. Moritz, said the international federation, no other LIHG team would take part—which effectively meant that the Winter Games would have no hockey.

Brundage then lobbed a bomb of his own.

IOC members enjoy a sumptuous dinner in the Golden Hall of Stockholm's city hall in 1947. The Golden Hall is dominated by a mosaic of the Queen of Lake Mälaren, a mythic figure representing Sweden as a power lying between East and West. Despite the lavish setting, the banquet took place amid a controversy: The amateur question as it related to ice hockey was the subject of hot debate during the Stockholm Session.

Speaking as president of the AOA, he warned, "If the outlaw ice hockey team is permitted to compete, our teams are to be withdrawn from the Games." In other words, if he didn't get his way, no American athletes of any kind would go to Switzerland—no skiers, no skaters, no sledders, nobody at all.

Blackmail! cried Fritz Kraatz, the head of the LIHG, who refused to believe that Brundage would go through with his threat. "If he withdraws the Americans," Kraatz said, "he will be killing the Olympic idea."

To the St. Moritz organizers, the prospect of a U.S. pullout was dismaying, but the LIHG threat of withdrawal seemed even worse, since hockey was expected to sell more tickets than any other sport. Both the St. Moritz Olympic Organizing Committee and the Swiss Olympic Committee sided with the LIHG.

It was far from over, however. When the various officials convened in St. Moritz, the wrangling descended into farce. At the IOC Session just before the Games began, the rivals accused each other of making mistakes in the documents

that were required to enter a team. This pettiness led to loud arguments over whether the AHA team was or was not professional. (In fact, it was composed mostly of former college players who had no professional aspirations and whose "pay" consisted of barely adequate expense money. Recently the squad had toured Europe, each player receiving a pound a day in Britain and the equivalent of 33 cents a day in Czechoslovakia.)

At one point in the discussions, a highly agitated Sigfrid Edström tried to call the disputants to order by rapping a table with his cane. The table was topped with glass, which shattered into a thousand pieces. But the quarreling went on, and even the usually amicable IOC Executive Board was divided. Edström felt that neither the AAU team nor the AHA team should be allowed to participate. Great Britain's Lord Aberdare argued that there was no proof that the AHA players were professionals. Finally, the board came around to Edström's position and decided that both teams must be withdrawn. A press release to that effect was issued at 7 p.m.

The Swiss NOC would have none of it. The

WINTER WASHOUT

St. Moritz 1948 hosted a singular event: the first and last Olympic winter pentathlon. The modern pentathlon, a five-stage event with fencing, shooting, riding, swimming, and running, had been on the Summer Games program since Stockholm 1912. Swedish enthusiasts on the IOC lobbied for a winter version that would replace swimming and running with downhill and cross-country skiing. There wasn't enough support to add it to the Winter Games as a medal event, but organizers did win approval to make it a demonstration sport at St. Moritz. The event would never appear again, with either medal or demonstration status.

Fourteen competitors showed up, most of them from Sweden, Great Britain, and Switzerland, but the downhill ski race quickly whittled down the field. Switzerland's Josef Vollmeier crashed and had to be carried off the course on a sled. Sweden's Clas Engell crossed the finish line—then promptly fell and broke a leg. The equestrian event took out several more competitors when a soft and muddy track caused the horses to slip and tumble.

Sweden took the top three spots. Gustaf Lindh, a 21-year-old cadet with the Swedish Royal Army, took over the lead in the second event, shooting, and went on to become the first—and so far the only—person to win an Olympic winter pentathlon. Wille Grut, the second-place finisher, would go on to win the gold medal in the summer version of the pentathlon at London several months later.

Fencers duel in one leg of the winter pentathlon, held in St. Moritz for the first and only time.

Winter pentathletes take aim despite heavy snowfall during the shooting portion of their competition. Gustaf Lindh *(far left)*, who would become the all-around champion, was the best foul-weather marksman, scoring 194 points out of a possible 200.

committee openly defied the IOC, issuing its own press release at 7:40 p.m.: "The Swiss Olympic Committee has decided that, according to the Olympic rules, the Swiss, and only they, are responsible for the tournament. Only they can say which teams may play, and they want the AHA team, which is affiliated to the LIHG. They say that the International Olympic Committee has no right to give a decision. In this case the tournament will take place as organized with the AHA team playing."

The IOC then counterpunched powerfully, advising that the sport of hockey would be removed from the Olympic program at St. Moritz. There would be no hockey games. Moreover, said the IOC, the Swiss NOC would be censured and the LIHG would be stripped of Olympic recognition.

This pronouncement outraged the Swiss press. Soon the IOC found itself under heavy attack from local newspapers and radio stations. At the same time, Olympic leaders began to worry that the elimination of hockey might do serious financial harm to the Winter Games. After another long meeting that lasted deep into the night of January 29, the IOC decided that the AHA team would be allowed to play after all—but that only the AAU team could march with the American athletes in the opening day parade. Thus the surreal scene the following morning, with one group of U.S. hockey players taking part in the ceremonies and another watching, then going off to get dressed for a game.

It still wasn't quite over. The IOC, continuing its tortured deliberations even after competition began, announced that the hockey tournament in St. Moritz would not be recognized as an official Olympic event. Not so, declared the Swiss, who argued that hockey couldn't be removed from the Olympic program with the Games already under way. Finally, a face-saving formula for compromise was found. It was agreed that if the AHA team won a medal, the results would

not be officially recognized. If, however, the AHA team failed to gain a medal, the results would be deemed to have Olympic reality. With that, the IOC subsided into silence, looking more than a little foolish.

The players themselves were largely unaffected by all the jurisdictional quarreling—except in the first game. That contest was held immediately after the opening ceremonies and pitted the AHA team against Switzerland's entry. The AAU players were in the stands, and they expressed their sentiments by booing the AHA team and cheering the Swiss. Then, to underscore the point, they left the arena midway through the first period. The AHA players were understandably disturbed, since relations between the two teams had been friendly until then. Their play suffered, and Switzerland won 5-4.

In the games that followed, the American team did well, as did the teams from Switzerland, Canada, Czechoslovakia, and Sweden. Many other teams had the opposite experience; 17 of them didn't score a single goal in the course of the tournament. Most hapless of all were the Italians. Although they managed to put the puck in the net from time to time, they sustained some epic defeats. In their match with the Americans, for example, they were beaten 31-1. Throughout this debacle, however, they amazed the U.S. players with their civility. Whenever the Italians made a heavy body check, they immediately apologized and shook hands with the bemused player on the receiving end. And when one of them cut the face of an American with a high check, the whole Italian team rushed to the aid of the victim, lifted him tenderly from the ice, and helped patch him up.

The beleaguered hockey tournament was further beset by difficulties presented by its open-air rink. On clear days the players had to wear eye black and occasionally lost sight of the puck in the ice glare. On snowy days play sometimes broke down completely: "If it snowed and you lost the puck," remembered American player

A Canadian hockey player sprawls on the ice after losing the puck to a Swedish opponent. The Canadians, represented by Ottawa's Royal Canadian Air Force Flyers, would win the match 3-1. Canada and Czechoslovakia had identical records in the ice hockey tournament: seven wins, no losses, and one tie. Goal differentials gave the gold medal to the Canadian team, its fifth title in six Olympic tournaments.

Jack Riley, "they'd stop play until we found it." The worst weather problem of all was the warm Föhn; it blew on the day Canada played Switzerland, and the game amounted to a long, messy slog through slush.

That was the final match of the tournament. To win the gold medal, the Canadians needed to beat the Swiss by at least two goals. They managed the task handily, winning 3-0, despite the extreme partisanship of Swiss spectators, who threw snowballs at officials whose rulings they found objectionable. Czechoslovakia took the silver medal and Switzerland the bronze. The U.S. team finished fourth—a happy outcome as far as the IOC was concerned: The results received official

Olympic recognition because the Americans had failed to win a medal.

One of the best hockey players at St. Moritz was Jaroslav Drobny of Czechoslovakia, a remarkable all-around athlete whose sports career would soon take a drastic turn. Drobny, then 27, had earned a spot on the Czech national hockey team when he was only 15 and had led that squad to the world championship three times. Short, stocky, and exceedingly quick, he was a star in tennis as well as hockey, with a devastating left-handed serve and superb touch. In the postwar years he represented his country in Davis Cup competition, went to Wimbledon, and earned a reputation as the best tennis player in Europe. But Czechoslovakia's

Stalinist government and its captive press didn't always appreciate him. Communist athletes were expected to beat those from "decadent capitalist" nations, and they could expect heavy criticism if they failed. When Drobny was defeated at Wimbledon in the summer of 1948, a Prague newspaper called him "a lazy bourgeois who had adopted criminal capitalist habits."

Politics also dictated where Drobny could play. The following summer, when he was competing in a tennis tournament in Gstaad, Switzerland, the Czech government sent instructions that he must withdraw because "German and Spanish Fascists were taking part in it." For Drobny, that was the last straw. He defied the government and stayed in the tournament, then announced that he would not return home until Czechoslovakia was freed from Communist tyranny. Afterward,

he lived in Australia for a time and continued to perform at the highest levels. He made it to the finals of Wimbledon in 1949 and 1952 and finally won that most coveted of tennis titles by beating Ken Rosewall in 1954. He was then almost 33, a veritable tennis graybeard.

If a good geographical distribution of talent was evident in the hockey tournament at St. Moritz, the opposite was true of Nordic skiing. As the name implies, Nordic events were a Scandinavian specialty. Five contests were on the program: the 18-kilometer cross-country, the 50-kilometer cross-country, the 4 x 10-kilometer relay, the ski jump, and the Nordic combined, consisting of an 18-kilometer race plus a jumping competition. All were for men only.

Skiing had long been deeply embedded in

Sweden's Nils Täpp touches off to teammate Martin Lundström to start him on the final leg of the 4 x 10-kilometer relay. Lundström would finish first for Sweden, a feat he had already managed in the 18-kilometer individual race.

Finland's Heikki Hasu sails through the jumping phase of the Nordic combined. Though his countrymen have fared well in most Nordic skiing events over the years, Hasu remains the only Finn ever to win the Olympic Nordic combined.

Scandinavian culture. Once it was the principal way for people to get around in winter; with the coming of trains and automobiles, it was transformed from necessity to pastime—a hugely popular pastime. Sweden alone had more than 2,500 ski clubs, with some 25,000 members. The results at St. Moritz reflected this. In the 18-kilometer race, Swedish skiers Martin Lundström, Nils Östensson, and Gunnar Eriksson finished 1-2-3. In the 50-kilometer race, Sweden's Nils Karlsson, considered a titan among cross-country skiers, won the gold handily, even though he was bothered by the high altitude of St. Moritz. Another Swede earned the silver medal, and a Finn came in third. Swedish superiority was most pronounced in the relay: The four Swedish skiers beat the second-place Finns by about 9 minutes and the third-place Norwegians by 12.

Norway was generally expected to win the Nordic combined, having done so in all four previous Winter Olympics. But Heikki Hasu of Finland finished first, another Finn took second, and a Swede earned third place. Still, everyone was sure that Norwegians would dominate in the jump, as they had since the Winter Games began in 1924. The most famous of all Norwegian jumpers was Birger Ruud. He had won the gold medal at Lake Placid 1932 and again at Garmisch-Partenkirchen 1936. (In the 1936 Winter Games, he also had competed in the Alpine combined, winning the downhill and finishing fourth overall—a display of versatility that, together with his jumping feats, prompted some knowledgeable observers to call him the greatest skier the world had ever seen.)

After the German invasion of Norway at the start of World War II, Ruud was imprisoned in an internment camp, and he remained there until the war ended. Now he was in St. Moritz, but not to compete; he was serving as team captain. He changed his mind about his role after a thaw left the 80-meter jumping hill deeply rutted. Knowing the value of experience in such bad conditions, the 36-year-old Ruud took the name of the last team member off the entry list and substituted his own.

The winner of the event was his countryman Petter Hugsted, who put on a brilliant show in both distance and style—the double basis for scoring. Wrote an admiring reporter: "In the air his skis are carried as one—not an inch of air between them—and he seems as calm as a statue as he dives and floats down." In the final, Hugsted jumped 229 feet 7 inches (70 meters) and made a perfect landing; it was the longest jump of the day by a sizable margin. But Birger Ruud gained a share of glory. In a 1-2-3 Norwegian sweep, he took the silver medal—a worthy finish to a luminous Olympic career.

In terms of popularity, Nordic skiing had been overtaken by its steep-terrain cousin, Alpine skiing, introduced at the 1936 Games in Garmisch-Partenkirchen. Six Alpine events were held at St. Moritz, three each for men and women: the downhill, a single long run that was basically a test of speed; the special slalom, a two-run event that was shorter and tested control with a series of tight turns; and the Alpine combined, a test of versatility that called for a downhill run and a slalom run.

The men and women skiers had separate courses, laid out on the flank of the huge, open-slope mountain that loomed directly above St. Moritz. The view from the mountainside was spectacular—lakes, villages, and woods spread out below, and snow-clad peaks jabbing skyward all around. From a skier's point of view, however, this vista was anything but beautiful. The terrain presented a gauntlet of complex contours and rapid changes in steepness, and the surface was almost as hard as ice. (Earlier, a hose had been played on the snow base to freeze it solid, and subsequent snowfalls were tamped down to maintain the firmness.)

The men's downhill course, a 2 1/2-mile (4-kilometer) run with a drop of about 3,000 feet (914.4 meters), was especially challenging, with several abrupt turns right after steep pitches. A Frenchman, Henri Oreiller, was favored to win. Big and lean and powerful, Oreiller had exceptional balance. Commentator James Laughlin, who had watched him in earlier competitions, wrote in the *American Ski Journal*: "His racing style is no style at all. It is just his own perverse, acrobatic equilibrium. Going into bumps at full tilt, he seems to absorb them in those rubbery legs. Half the time he is on one ski or the other, and much of the time he is in the air, unwinding himself like a contortionist." Along with outstanding physical skills, Oreiller had a personality well suited for racing: He was easygoing, something of a clown, and supremely self-confident. Before the St. Moritz competitions he told other racers that they might as well withdraw because he was bound to win.

And win he did, although his headlong style almost cost him dearly in the downhill. At the bottom of a particularly steep section, traveling at full speed, Oreiller caught an edge. In plotting his run, he had planned to check his speed at that point, but now he had to go onto one ski and couldn't slow himself. Somehow he stayed

upright. Because of that unintended increment of speed, his margin of victory over the second-place Austrian was more than 4 seconds.

In the slalom, the skiers were required to weave through a series of closely placed gates—45 of them on the men's course—spaced along a vertical drop of about 720 feet (220 meters). Oreiller may not have been elegant, but he was highly effective. In the Alpine combined, his performance in the slalom was swift and sure, earning him first place with ease. His only disappointment came in the last Alpine event, the special slalom—two slalom runs along a course with a drop of 590 feet (180 meters), with the best

Carrying his skis after a thrilling downhill race, France's Henri Oreiller awaits the results of the remaining competitors. His winning run, adjudged edgy and out of control by reporters, led American ski writer James Laughlin to dub Oreiller "the original India Rubber Man."

Switzerland's Edi Reinalter dissects the slalom course on his way to a gold medal. Reinalter was only third after the first run, but his second effort bettered the time of the next-fastest skier by half a second.

combined time deciding the winner. He finished a mere third. It was rumored that he held himself back slightly to let a teammate win; if so, it was a serious error, since the teammate, James Couttet, could do no better than second, behind Switzerland's Edi Reinalter.

Henri Oreiller's love of speed later led him to take up car racing. In 1962, while driving a Ferrari in a national championship race not far from Paris, he crashed and was killed. He was in the lead at the time.

As in the men's Alpine program, the favored women skiers were European. But Canada harbored hopes for a daredevil twosome—identical twins Rhona and Rhoda Wurtele. In international skiing circles, the Wurteles were renowned for fearlessness. (An early manifestation occurred when they were 11 years old and one of their brothers dared them to try ski jumping at a resort in Canada, never dreaming they would do it. He changed his tune when he saw them head for the platform of the senior men's jump. Ignoring his cries of alarm, they skimmed down the incline and launched themselves into space, landing hard but intact.) Unfortunately, a chipped ankle prevented Rhoda from competing at St. Moritz. Rhona, battling illness, entered the downhill, but she was out of shape and took a

Henri Oreiller (right) raises his hands as he flashes across the finish of the slalom race, the final leg of the Alpine combined. The secret of his success was his use of the Allais technique, named for French skier Emile Allais. The method introduced the speedy parallel turn to Alpine skiing.

Below, Austria's Trude Beiser (right), gold medalist in the Alpine combined event and winner of the silver in the downhill, poses with Hedy Schlunegger. Beiser and her fellow Austrian women skiers were so strapped for cash at St. Moritz that they had to race in equipment borrowed from the Americans.

Hedy Schlunegger gets into a tuck during her downhill run. The Swiss speedster fell during the race, but she bobbed up quickly enough to win. France's Georgette Thiollière, expected to dominate the women's Alpine events, was off form and failed to win a single medal.

bad fall. She got up and managed to finish, even though she had a broken leg.

The winner of the downhill was Switzerland's Hedy Schlunegger, a careful, deliberate skier. She too fell—a kind of awkward sit-down at a gate that hadn't troubled other skiers—but she bounced back up and continued on with little loss of time.

A dark horse among the women skiers was Gretchen Fraser of the United States. The daughter of a Norwegian mother and German father, she grew up in the Pacific Northwest, began skiing at 16, and married the sports director for the ski resort of Sun Valley, Idaho. During the war years she won a number of national skiing titles, but when she arrived in St. Moritz at 28, she wasn't considered to be in a class with the best of the European women. Indeed, Americans in general weren't regarded as much of a factor

in international skiing: No male or female skier from the United States had ever finished higher than 11th in an Olympic skiing competition. Gretchen Fraser—calm and steady, if unspectacular—would change that.

Fraser's first event was the combined. Although she posted only a middling time in the downhill, her performance in the slalom run was so good that she finished second in the event with an overall score that was just 0.37 of a point behind Trude Beiser of Austria. A day later came the special slalom, requiring two runs down a course with 37 gates and a drop of 575 feet (175.3 meters). There were 31 entrants. At least eight of them enjoyed a higher competitive ranking than Gretchen Fraser, but she proved swifter than all of them on her first run, with a time of 59.7. Her margin was hardly secure, however. Four other skiers were within 1 second of her, and one was just 0.1 of a second slower.

Fraser's chance of victory seemed to waver when she learned that, by the luck of the draw, she would have to go off first on the next run— a mixed blessing: She would have the advantage of a fresh, unrutted course, but she wouldn't be able to pick up clues about the hill's idiosyncrasies by watching the other skiers perform. Nor was that her only problem. As she stood at

America's Gretchen Fraser charges the gates on the slalom course at St. Moritz. Fraser was the first American skiing medalist in Olympic history.

Italy's Nino Bibbia looks grimly determined as he steers his sled. Bibbia had been racing the Cresta Run for only a year before winning the Olympic gold medal in the skeleton race. His working-class upbringing contrasted with the privileged backgrounds of the typical skeleton racers of the day.

the starting gate, the telephone connecting the starter with officials at the bottom of the hill went dead. She had to wait in the gate for 17 minutes before the phone was fixed. But the delay apparently didn't faze her. She sped down the hill without an error, clocking 57.5 seconds. One after another, the European skiers tried to surpass her time, and one after another they came up short. At the end, spectators and reporters crowded around her. "How do you feel?" someone asked.

"I feel out of character," she replied.

If Alpine skiing was a rising star among winter sports, the opposite was true of the sledding event known as the skeleton. This was a St. Moritz specialty, held nowhere else. It was named for the distinctive sled used—heavy, four feet long, low-slung, and ridden headfirst, with the rider dragging his spiked boots or shifting his weight in order to steer. The course, tailor-made for that idiosyncratic vehicle, was the famous Cresta Run—a kind of tobogganing shrine that had been laid out by a group of sportsmen in 1884 and, in normal circumstances, was mainly used by members of the very exclusive St. Moritz Tobogganing Club.

Despite its posh associations, the Cresta Run posed many dangers. BBC commentator Max Robertson drew this vivid picture: "Streamlined is an overworked word, but it describes perfectly the

beautifully chiseled contours of the Cresta Run, which snakes down the mountain for exactly three-quarters of a mile, its five-foot-wide track of wicked ice glittering unsheathed in the sun like purest steel, and like finely forged steel the Cresta bends and twists into myriad pitfalls for the human ball of quicksilver as it hurtles its way down the intricate puzzle. A false move, an unsteady hand, an error of eye or timing and the ball is over the edge." With a vertical drop of 515 feet (157 meters), the Cresta Run could produce speeds of 80 miles per hour or higher at the bottom.

The Olympic format for the skeleton event called for three runs from a point about two-thirds of the way up the course and three runs from the top. Combined times would determine the winner. It was generally believed that only a rider who had extensive experience on the Cresta Run—two or three years, say—could hope to gain a medal. Only six countries entered.

Great Britain seemed well positioned for success; it had long supplied much of the membership of the St. Moritz Tobogganing Club. But, of the eight men chosen for its team, seven hadn't attempted the Cresta Run since before the war. In addition to being out of practice, they were well past their physical prime (one suffered from gout). The results reflected these deficiencies. The best of the British, John Crammond, finished third.

Nonetheless, experience proved decisive, as predicted. The winner was not a blue-blooded sportsman but a tough-looking young Italian named Nino Bibbia, who had grown up just across the border and whose father now ran a fruit-and-vegetable shop in St. Moritz. Bibbia had practiced extensively on the Cresta Run and knew every inch of it intimately. Inches counted. On one run, he went too high on a turn called Shuttlecock and barely managed to avoid disaster. Afterward, he said coolly, "I still had two fingers of space between the edge of the bank and the runner of my skeleton—that's just enough."

Second place went to an American, John

Heaton. He had often visited St. Moritz before the war and at 19 had won the silver medal in the only other Olympic skeleton event ever held, at St. Moritz 20 years earlier. (His brother, Jennison Heaton, had taken the gold in that event.)

In contrast to the skeleton, bobsledding was an Olympic fixture: There had been a four-man event ever since the first Winter Games, Chamonix 1924, and the five-man bobs were added at St. Moritz in 1928. The two-man event had been added at Lake Placid 1932. The United States was a traditional power in the sport, and at St. Moritz, American sledders would once again fare well, although not without some storm and stress. A crisis flared at the very outset, when it appeared that the American equipment had been sabotaged.

The story unfolded this way: At night the American sleds, like those of other teams, were kept in an official Olympic storage shed. On the morning of the first heats in the two-man event, the Americans went to retrieve their sleds and discovered they were damaged. Nuts were loose, and on one sled the pushers were broken and the bolt holding the steering wheel to the runners seemed to have been unscrewed. "When we lifted the sled," said Kurt Stevens, manager of the American bobsled team, "the steering wheel fell off. Had the bolt been unscrewed only part of the way, we might not have noticed. It could have come off during the run and badly injured our boys. We never dreamed it would be necessary to check such matters, but we will check every bolt and nut from here on." As a further

American bobsledders *(from left)* **Bud Washbond, Ed Rimkus, Tuffield Latour, and Leo Martin** ponder what to do about their broken sled. Some American reports linked the damage to the hockey controversy before discovering that an accident had caused the problem.

Switzerland's Felix Endrich (*driving*) and Friedrich Waller hurtle down the St. Moritz bobsled run in gold-medal style. Endrich would die tragically in 1953 when a four-man sled he was piloting flew off the infamous "dead man's curve" on the Garmisch-Partenkirchen bob course and slammed into a tree.

precaution, he said, armed guards would be posted outside the storage shed by night.

In truth, there had been no sabotage. The shed was also used for cars. In the darkness, a driver had backed in blindly and had hit a sled, knocking it over and sheering the steering-post bolt. Unaware that he had caused damage, the driver didn't bother to report the incident at first. He finally came forward when all of St. Moritz was abuzz with accusations of foul play. Tempers then quieted, and the Americans went on to take third place in the two-man bobsled event. Swiss teams won the gold and silver.

American bobsledders were doing well in the four-man contest when another controversy erupted. This time the cause was a broken water pipe that flooded the course shortly after one of the U.S. sleds had posted an excellent time in a heat. Officials closed the course for repairs and announced that the entire heat would be run again the following day. The pilot of the American sled, Francis Tyler, was furious. He insisted that his speedy descent in that heat should count, began to talk darkly of "injustice," and threatened to withdraw. Finally, his coach was able to calm him down. In the end, he and his sledmates from Lake Placid won the gold.

Speed skating was a Scandinavian story—as

usual. Swedes, Norwegians, and Finns took almost every medal in the four events: the 500 meters, the 1,500 meters, the 5,000 meters, and the 10,000 meters. The only exception occurred in the 500 meters, where an American somehow managed to make off with a silver medal. But an even bigger surprise was the order of finish in the 5,000 meters. One of the entrants in that race was Åke Seyffarth of Sweden, long considered a great talent among speed skaters. At St. Moritz he demonstrated his abilities by earning a gold medal in the 10,000 meters and a silver in the 1,500 meters. He had every reason to expect a medal in the 5,000 meters as well, since he held the world record of 8:13.7 in that event. What he didn't expect was that a photographer would jump out onto the ice on the final lap to take a picture of him sweeping to victory. Seyffarth bumped into him, lost precious time as he struggled to recover his balance, and finished seventh.

In figure skating, two North American stars seemed likely to outshine all others: Both were recent winners of the European championships. One was 19-year-old Barbara Ann Scott of Ottawa, Canada—doll-like in appearance but an extraordinarily disciplined athlete. Scott's strength lay in tracing the compulsory figures that counted for 60 percent of the score in the individual figure-skating event. The other was 18-year-old Dick Button of Englewood, New Jersey, a Harvard freshman who was in the process of revolutionizing his sport with a daring, acrobatic version of freestyle skating.

Barbara Ann Scott took up skating as a small child, encouraged by a father who had been an enthusiastic sportsman before being severely wounded in World War I. At the age of nine, Barbara Ann began skating full time (a private tutor handled her education), and soon she was winning one championship after another. Her secret was endless practice, particularly in the so-called school figures: circles, loops, and other variations on the figure eight that skaters were

required to trace, first on one foot, then the other. She practiced eight hours a day for years. The precision of the task greatly appealed to her. "I like detail," she said. "I like everything to be neat and tidy and symmetrical. I enjoyed trying to get as near perfect a circle as possible. It just interested me." She showed the same perfectionism in free skating, although her performances tended to be conservative. Like Sonja Henie before her, she believed that it was wiser to execute a single jump well than to attempt a double jump and miss it.

In 1947, Scott crossed the Atlantic to compete

The hefty American four-man bobsled team—it averaged almost 225 pounds per man—propels its sled downhill. Weight, rather than sled design and driving skill, was often a deciding factor in bobsled races of the era. Rule changes in 1952 set weight limits on teams.

in the European and world championships, winning both. She returned a national heroine. Ottawa schoolchildren were given a half-day off for a parade in her honor, and the mayor expressed the country's appreciation by handing her the keys to a yellow Buick convertible. Unfortunately, this gift came to the attention of Avery Brundage, who informed the IOC that her acceptance of the car jeopardized her amateur status. To the fury of practically all Canadians, the skating star was forced to return the gift.

In early 1948, Scott traveled to Prague for the European championships. There, as fans admired her blond, blue-eyed loveliness and local newspapers published her picture 17 times in the space of three days, she cruised to victory. Then it was on to the Winter Games.

At St. Moritz the only problem Scott encountered was the rutted condition of the outdoor ice. But it hardly seemed to affect her. Picture perfect in a white, fur-trimmed costume, she executed both her figures and her freestyle jumps with supreme poise. Gushed one newspaper, "Canada's superb ballerina of the ice won the Olympic crown with a dazzling exhibition of grace and beauty that left her rivals nowhere." Later that year she turned professional, thus rendering Avery Brundage irrelevant. Another car was offered by Ottawa's mayor. She kept it.

Dick Button's career had started more slowly than Barbara Ann Scott's. Not until he was 12 did he show any real interest in figure skating, and his first instructor

Norway's Reidar Liaklev takes the gold in the 5,000-meter speed-skating race. Liaklev's title was one of three for Norway in speed skating at St. Moritz.

Judges watch patiently while Canada's Barbara Ann Scott performs her compulsory exercises. Her figures placed her first among 25 competitors.

Flawless jumps in her free-skate routine made Barbara Ann Scott the top choice of seven of the nine judges; the two dissenting panelists voted for their compatriots. Fellow gold medalist Dick Button called Scott "delicate, precise, exact, meticulous—simply perfect."

was less than supportive. Looking at the chubby and rather uncoordinated boy, the teacher said, "You'll never learn to skate—not until hell freezes over." Within four years, Button had become national champion for the first of seven times.

Like Barbara Ann Scott, Button loved skating and practiced hard, spending 15 or 20 hours a week on the ice, all that he could spare from school. "Luckily for me," he said, "I've always been able to study best when I'm competing in figure-skating championships." Competition never seemed to make him nervous: "When you really like something," he explained, "you don't get nervous about it." Still, he worried at times, especially when he was trying to push the boundaries of the possible. One jump that seemed beyond his abilities in his early years was the double axel, which required two complete revolutions and then another half-turn to land going backward.

Today the jump is part of every world-class skater's repertoire, but in the days of Button's ascendancy, no one had ever performed it in a major competition. He wanted to be the first. He thought about trying the double axel at the European championships in Prague before the St. Moritz Games, but because he couldn't seem to get the landing right in practice sessions, he left it out of his routine. His standard assortment of leaps was nevertheless dazzling enough for him to become the first non-European ever to win the European title.

When Button arrived at St. Moritz, he assumed that he would again bypass the double axel. That decision seemed particularly sensible after he built up a big lead in the compulsory figures—enough so that he was almost assured of a gold medal if he gave his usual performance in the free skating. Yet he continued to practice the jump, and one day he made the clean landing he had

Micheline Lannoy and Pierre Baugniet begin a spiral pivot, one of the moves that won them a gold medal at St. Moritz. The dramatic maneuver, introduced to pairs skating by the Belgian couple, was a forerunner of the death spiral.

America's Dick Button performs a toe loop during his free skate. Button once said that if his coach Gustave Lussi told him to jump out a window, he would, but not before checking to see that his toe was pointed and his head held in the right position.

sought so long. Astonished, he tried again and again. Each time he landed perfectly.

The moment of truth came late in the Winter Games. Spectators had jammed the stadium for the ever-popular men's freestyle skating. Nature, however, had not been very cooperative: The ice had been softened by the Föhn and deeply gouged by previous skaters, and now the ruts were frozen solid. Button, as was his custom, did a minimal warm-up, saving his energy for the real thing. When his turn to skate finally came, he found himself breathing hard in the thin mountain air.

"The music crescendoed into a long sweeping movement and I approached the steps that led into my double axel," Button would recall later. "At the start of the program I had faltered momentarily—should I risk my chances doing it? I had practiced it correctly only a dozen or so times, and despite the fact that once I had 'found' the jump there had been no error in its execution, I disliked being so unprepared. But the cravenness of backing away from something because of the pressure of an Olympic Games repulsed me and, once I had made up my mind, I could not divert the steps that culminated in the double axel."

He leaped, spun, landed perfectly, and continued on through the flips, double-Salchow combinations, jump camels, and other moves in his uniquely bold repertoire. When the judges raised their cards to indicate their scoring of the performance, all of the marks were high, and one was a 6, signifying perfection. Button had won America's first Olympic gold medal in figure skating. He would be a force in the sport for many years to come.

Figure skaters Dick Button and Barbara Ann Scott, Alpine skiers Gretchen Fraser and Henri Oreiller, ski jumper Petter Hugsted, speed skater Åke Seyffarth—these were brilliant athletes, capable of performances that could lift the human heart. No less than the champions who had preceded them, they stirred a kind of deep and joyful awareness of human potential, and that, after all, was the essence of Olympic magic. True, the St. Moritz Games seemed a little tattered at times, and Olympic dreams of universal brotherhood hardly jibed with the condition of Europe outside this mountain fastness. But by the time the winter festival drew to an end, IOC president Sigfrid Edström was thoroughly pleased. "I think the Games have been a wonderful success," he said. No doubt he was also gratified by how his own country's athletes had done. The Swedish squad took four gold medals, three silvers, and three bronzes, a haul equaled only by Norway.

A number of thoughts about winners and losers were aired as the Winter Games wound down. The Soviet delegates who had come to observe Olympic procedures announced to reporters that if their athletes had competed, they would have won practically all of the events. *New York Times* sports columnist Arthur Daley had another observation. Harking back to the hockey controversy, he wrote that the biggest Olympic winners were the Swiss organizers, who "threw so many curve balls at the International Olympic Committee that the IOC struck out ignominiously."

Perhaps so, but the leaders of the Olympic movement were nonetheless in a cheerful mood at the closing ceremonies on the afternoon of February 8, 1948. In the Ice Stadium a small military band played as the Olympic flag was lowered. Next the flag of Switzerland came down, then the flag of Great Britain, since London would be the next Olympic host. Over a rasping public-address system, winners of the various competitions were called forward to receive their medals. Finally, the sacred flame—a modest, two-foot-high flame atop a smallish tower—was extinguished.

By that time, velvety snow was falling soft and thick. Winter still ruled in pretty St. Moritz. But from an Olympic point of view, spring was in the air at last.

Flagbearers hold their national standards as snow falls during the closing ceremony at St. Moritz. Sweden, Switzerland, and Norway were the kings of winter sport with 10 medals apiece at the Games.

◎◎◎◎◎ APPENDIX

CALENDAR OF THE XI OLYMPIAD

AUGUST 1, 1936 — JULY 19, 1940

1936

JULY 26 & AUGUST 8	25th IOC Executive Board meeting at Berlin
JULY 30, 31, & AUGUST 15	36th Session of the IOC at Berlin
AUGUST 1-16	**BERLIN 1936** 10th Olympic Games
DECEMBER 17	26th IOC Executive Board meeting at Lausanne

1937

JUNE 8-11	**37th Session of the IOC at Warsaw**
AUGUST 21-29	7th World University Games at Paris
SEPTEMBER 2	*Baron Pierre de Coubertin dies of a heart attack at age 74 in Geneva.*

NOVEMBER 17	5th USOC Quadrennial meeting at the Willard Hotel, Washington, DC

1938

FEBRUARY 5-12	3rd Commonwealth Games at Sydney
FEBRAURY 5-24	4th Central American and Caribbean Games at Panama
MARCH 13-18	**38th Session of the IOC at Cairo and on the Nile**
MARCH 22-25	*Funeral service for Baron Pierre de Coubertin's heart at Olympia, Greece*
MARCH 17-18, 20	27th IOC Executive Board meeting at Cario
MAY 17	28th IOC Executive Board meeting at Brussels
SEPTEMBER 3	29th IOC Executive Board meeting at Brussels

1939

JUNE 6	30th IOC Executive Board meeting at London
JUNE 6-9	**39th Session of the IOC at London**
AUGUST 24-27	5th Summer Games for the Deaf at Stockholm
AUGUST 28-29	8th World University Games at Monaco

1940

FEBRUARY 2-11	**GARMISCH-PARTENKIRCHEN 1940** Canceled
FEBRUARY 3-11	**ST. MORITZ 1940** Canceled
FEBRUARY 3-14	**SAPPORO 1940** Canceled

CALENDAR OF THE XII OLYMPIAD

JULY 20, 1940 — JULY 19, 1944

1940

JULY 20-AUGUST 4	**HELSINKI 1940** Canceled
SEPTEMBER 21-OCTOBER 6	**TOKYO 1940** Canceled

1941

NOVEMBER 19	6th USOC Quadrennial meeting at the New York Athletic Club, New York, New York

1942

JANUARY 6	*Count Henri de Baillet-Latour dies of a stroke in Brussels. Johannes Sigfrid Edström becomes acting president of the IOC.*

1944

NO SET DATES	**CORTINA D'AMPEZZO 1944** Canceled
JUNE 16-JULY 3	IOC 50th anniversary celebration of the 1st Olympic Congress at Lausanne

CALENDAR OF THE XIII OLYMPIAD

JULY 20, 1944 — JULY 28, 1948

1944

NO SET DATES	**LONDON 1944** Canceled

1945

MAY 7	End of WWII in Europe
JUNE 26	United Nations Charter signed at San Francisco
AUGUST 14	End of WWII in the Pacific
AUGUST 21-24	31st IOC Executive Board meeting at London
DECEMBER 10	7th USOC Quadrennial meeting at the New York Athletic Club, New York, New York

1946

SEPTEMBER 1-6	32nd IOC Executive Board meeting at Lausanne
SEPTEMBER 2-3	6th IOC Executive Board with IFs at Lausanne
SEPTEMBER 4	Johannes Sigfrid Edström elected 4th IOC President
SEPTEMBER 4-6	**40th Session of the IOC at Lausanne**
DECEMBER 8-28	5th Central American and Caribbean Games at Barranquilla

1947

JUNE 15	33rd IOC Executive Board meeting at Stockholm

JUNE 16-17	7th IOC Executive Board with IFs at Stockholm
JUNE 19-21	**41st Session of the IOC at Stockholm**
AUGUST 24-31	9th World University Games at Paris

1948

JANUARY 27,28, & FEBRUARY 7	34th IOC Executive Board meeting at St. Moritz
JANUARY 29-31, & FEBRUARY 2, 4-8	**42nd Session of the IOC at St. Moritz**
JANUARY 30-FEBRUARY 8	**ST. MORITZ 1948** **5th Olympic Winter Games**

Saturday, AUGUST 1

PM	EVENT	VENUE
4:00	OPENING CEREMONY	Olympic Stadium

Sunday, AUGUST 2

AM	EVENT	VENUE
9:00	MODERN PENTATHLON	Döberitz
	equestrian cross-country	
9:00	FENCING	The Gymnasium and Cupola Hall
	team foil, qualification	
10:30	ATHLETICS	Olympic Stadium
	• 100 meters, preliminaries	
	• high jump, qualification	
	• women's javelin, preliminaries	
11:00	FREESTYLE WRESTLING	Deutschland Hall
	preliminaries	
11:30	ATHLETICS	Olympic Stadium
	shot put, qualification	

PM	EVENT	VENUE
3:00	ATHLETICS	Olympic Stadium
	• high jump, final	
	• 100 meters, intermediate round	
	• women's javelin, final	
3:00	FENCING	The Gymnasium and Cupola Hall
	team foil, preliminaries, 2nd round	
4:00	ATHLETICS	
	800 meters, preliminaries	
5:30	ATHLETICS	
	• shot put, preliminaries and final	
	• 10,000 meters, final	
6:00	FREESTYLE WRESTLING	Deutschland Hall
	preliminaries	
8:00	WEIGHT LIFTING	Deutschland Hall
	• featherweight, final	
	• lightweight, final	
8:00	FENCING	The Gymnasium and Cupola Hall
	team foil, 3rd round	

Monday, AUGUST 3

AM	EVENT	VENUE
9:00	MODERN PENTATHLON	Tennis Stadium
	épée fencing	
10:00	FREESTYLE WRESTLING	Deutschland Hall
	intermediate round	
11:00	ATHLETICS	Olympic Stadium
	hammer throw, qualifications	

PM	EVENT	VENUE
2:00	POLO	Mayfield
	qualification round	
3:00	ATHLETICS	Olympic Stadium
	• 400-meter hurdles, preliminaries	
	• hammer throw, preliminaries and final	
3:30	ATHLETICS	
	men's 100 meters, semifinals	
4:00	ATHLETICS	Olympic Stadium
	women's 100 meters, preliminaries	
5:00	ATHLETICS	Olympic Stadium
	men's 100 meters, final	
5:15	ATHLETICS	Olympic Stadium
	800 meters, intermediate heats	

5:30	ATHLETICS	Olympic Stadium
	women's 100 meters, intermediate heats	
5:30	SOCCER	Post Stadium & Mommsen Athletic Field
	elimination matches	
6:00	ATHLETICS	Olympic Stadium
	3,000-meter steeplechase, preliminaries	
6:00	FREESTYLE WRESTLING	Deutschland Hall
	intermediate round	
6:20	GYMNASTICS	Olympic Stadium
	demonstration by Denmark	
8:00	WEIGHT LIFTING	Deutschland Hall
	light heavyweight, final	

Tuesday, AUGUST 4

AM	EVENT	VENUE
9:00	MODERN PENTATHLON	Ruhleben Shooting Range
	shooting	
9:00	FENCING	The Gymnasium and Cupola Hall
	• women's foil, preliminaries	
	• foil, team, 3rd round	
9:30	YACHTING	Kiel Bay
10:00	FREESTYLE WRESTLING	Deutschland Hall
	preliminaries	
10:30	ATHLETICS	Olympic Stadium
	• long jump, qualification	
	• women's discus, qualification	
	• 200 meters, preliminaries	
11:00	GLIDING EXHIBITION	Staaken Aerodrome (near Berlin)

PM	EVENT	VENUE
1:00	FENCING	The Gymnasium and Cupola Hall
	women's foil, 2nd round	
2:00	POLO	Mayfield
	qualification round	
3:00	ATHLETICS	Olympic Stadium
	400-meter hurdles, intermediate heat	
3:00	FENCING	The Gymnasium and Cupola Hall
	team foil, final	
3:15	ATHLETICS	Olympic Stadium
	discus, women, preliminaries and final	
3:30	ATHLETICS	Olympic Stadium
	200 meters, intermediate heat	
4:00	ATHLETICS	Olympic Stadium
	women's 100 meters, final	
4:30	ATHLETICS	Olympic Stadium
	long jump, preliminaries and final	
4:30	FIELD HOCKEY	Hockey Stadium
	qualification round	
5:30	SOCCER	Post Stadium & Hertha Field
	elimination matches	
5:30	ATHLETICS	Olympic Stadium
	400-meter hurdles, final	
5:45	ATHLETICS	Olympic Stadium
	800 meters, final	
6:00	ATHLETICS	Olympic Stadium
	5,000 meters, preliminaries	
6:10	GYMNASTICS	Olympic Stadium
	demonstration by Norway	
7:00	FREESTYLE WRESTLING	Deutschland Hall
	final	
8:00	FENCING	The Gymnasium and Cupola Hall
	foil, women, 3rd round	

Wednesday, AUGUST 5

AM	EVENT	VENUE
9:00	MODERN PENTATHLON	Olympic Swim Stadium
	swimming	
9:00	FENCING	The Gymnasium and Cupola Hall
	individual foil, preliminaries	
9:30	YACHTING	Kiel Bay
10:30	ATHLETICS	Olympic Stadium
	• pole vault, qualification	
	• discus, qualification	

PM	EVENT	VENUE
1:30	ATHLETICS	Olympic Stadium
	50,000-meter walk (start)	
2:00	POLO	Mayfield
	qualification round	
3:00	ATHLETICS	Olympic Stadium
	• 200 meters, semifinals	
	• discus, preliminaries and final	
3:00	FENCING	The Gymnasium and Cupola Hall
	individual foil, 2nd and 3rd round	
3:30	ATHLETICS	Olympic Stadium
	women's 80-meter hurdles, preliminaries	
4:00	ATHLETICS	Olympic Stadium
	pole vault, final	
4:30	ATHLETICS	Olympic Stadium
	110-meter hurdles, preliminaries	
4:30	FIELD HOCKEY	Hockey Stadium
	qualification round (2 games)	
5:00	ATHLETICS	Olympic Stadium
	1,500 meters, preliminaries	
5:00	FENCING	The Gymnasium and Cupola Hall
	women's foil, final	
5:30	ATHLETICS	Olympic Stadium
	women's 80-meter hurdles, intermediate heats	
5:30	SOCCER	Post Stadium & Mommsen Athletic Field
	elimination matches	
6:00	ATHLETICS	Olympic Stadium
	200 meters, final	
6:00	WEIGHT LIFTING	Deutschland Hall
	middleweight & heavyweight, final	
6:10	ATHLETICS	Olympic Stadium
	50,000-meter walk (finish)	
6:30	CHINESE BOXING	Olympic Stadium
	demonstration	
8:00	FENCING	The Gymnasium and Cupola Hall
	individual foil, 3rd round	

Thursday, AUGUST 6

AM	EVENT	VENUE
8:30	SHOOTING	Wannsee Shooting Range
	rapid-fire pistol	
9:00	MODERN PENTATHLON	Wannsee Golf Course
	cross-country run	
9:00	FENCING	The Gymnasium and Cupola Hall
	individual foil, final	
9:30	YACHTING	Kiel Bay
10:30	ATHLETICS	Olympic Stadium
	• 400 meters, preliminaries	
	• triple jump, qualification	
	• javelin, qualification	

11:00	GRECO-ROMAN WRESTLING	Deutschland Hall
	preliminaries	

PM	EVENT	VENUE
2:00	POLO	Mayfield
	qualifying matches	
3:00	SHOOTING	Wannsee Shooting Range
	rapid-fire pistol	
3:00	FENCING	The Gymnasium and Cupola Hall
	individual foil, 3rd round	
3:00	ATHLETICS	Olympic Stadium
	110-meter hurdles, intermediate heats	
3:15	ATHLETICS	
	• 400 meters, intermediate heats	
	• javelin, preliminaries and final	
4:15	ATHLETICS	Olympic Stadium
	1,500 meters, final	
4:30	FIELD HOCKEY	Hockey Stadium
	qualifying matches (2 games)	
4:30	ATHLETICS	Olympic Stadium
	triple jump, preliminaries and final	
5:15	TEAM HANDBALL	Police Stadium & Hohenzollern-Damm Sports Ground
	elimination rounds	
5:30	SOCCER	Mommsen Athletic Field & Hertha Field
	elimination matches	
5:30	ATHLETICS	Olympic Stadium
	women's 80-meter hurdles, final	
5:45	ATHLETICS	Olympic Stadium
	110-meter hurdles, final	
6:00	CYCLING	Olympic Velodrome
	• 1-kilometer time trial, preliminaries	
	• 4-kilometer pursuit, preliminaries	
	CYCLING DEMONSTRATION	
	• German champion 6-man	
	• bicycling acrobatics team	
	CYCLING DEMONSTRATION	
	• German champion 2-man	
	• bicycling acrobatics team	
6:30	GYMNASTICS	Olympic Stadium
	demonstration by Finland	
7:00	GRECO-ROMAN WRESTLING	Deutschland Hall
	semifinals	

Friday, AUGUST 7

AM	EVENT	VENUE
8:30	SHOOTING	Wannsee Shooting Range
	free pistol	
9:00	FENCING	Tennis Stadium & Courts
	team épée, 1st round	
9:30	YACHTING	Kiel Bay
10:00	ATHLETICS	Olympic Stadium
	decathlon (100 meters)	
10:00	GRECO-ROMAN WRESTLING	Deutschland Hall
	intermediate round	
11:30	ATHLETICS	Olympic Stadium
	decathlon (long jump)	

PM	EVENT	VENUE
2:00	POLO	Mayfield
	qualifying matches	

Time	Event	Venue
3:00	ATHLETICS • 400 meters, semifinals • decathlon (shot put)	Olympic Stadium
3:00	FENCING team épée, 2nd round	Tennis Stadium & Courts
3:00	SHOOTING free pistol	Wannsee Shooting Range
3:15	ATHLETICS 5,000 meters, final	Olympic Stadium
4:00	ATHLETICS decathlon (high jump)	Olympic Stadium
4:00	BASKETBALL qualification	Tennis Courts
4:30	FIELD HOCKEY qualifying matches (2 games)	Hockey Stadium
4:30	CANOEING pairs kayak	Grünau Regatta Course
4:50	CANOEING pairs folding	Grünau Regatta Course
5:10	CANOEING single kayak	Grünau Regatta Course
5:15	TEAM HANDBALL elimination rounds	Police Stadium & Hohenzollern-Damm Sports Ground
5:30	CANOEING single folding	Grünau Regatta Course
5:30	ATHLETICS 400 meters, final	Olympic Stadium
5:30	SOCCER intermediate round (2 games)	Post Stadium & Mommsen Athletic Field
5:45	ATHLETICS decathlon (400 meter)	Olympic Stadium
6:00	CANOEING Canadian doubles	Grünau Regatta Course
6:00	GYMNASTICS demonstration by Hungary	Olympic Stadium
6:00	CYCLING • 1,000-meter time trial, semifinals & final • 4,000-meter pursuit, qualifying rounds • 2,000-meter tandem, qualifications and preliminaries	Olympic Velodrome
	CYCLING DEMONSTRATION • German champion 8-man • cycling acrobatic team	
	CYCLING DEMONSTRATION • German champion individual • cycling acrobatics	
6:00	GRECO-ROMAN WRESTLING intermediate round	Deutschland Hall

Saturday, AUGUST 8

AM	EVENT	VENUE
8:30	SHOOTING small bore	Wannsee Shooting Range
9:00	SWIMMING • 100-meter freestyle, preliminaries • women's 200-meter breaststroke, preliminaries	Olympic Swim Stadium
9:00	WATER POLO	Olympic Swim Stadium

Time	Event	Venue
9:00	FENCING épée team, 3rd round	Tennis Stadium & Courts
9:30	CANOEING regatta, short race, preliminaries	Grünau Regatta Course
9:30	YACHTING	Kiel Bay
10:00	GRECO-ROMAN WRESTLING preliminaries	Deutschland Hall
10:00	ATHLETICS decathlon (110-meter hurdles)	Olympic Stadium
11:00	ATHLETICS decathlon (discus)	Olympic Stadium

PM	EVENT	VENUE
2:00	POLO final round	Mayfield
3:00	ATHLETICS • decathlon (pole vault) • 4 x 100-meter relay, preliminaries	Olympic Stadium
3:00	SWIMMING • women's 100-meter freestyle, preliminaries • men's 100-meter freestyle, intermediate heats	Olympic Swim Stadium
3:00	WATER POLO	Olympic Swim Stadium
3:00	SHOOTING small caliber	Wannsee Shooting Range
3:00	CANOEING single kayak	Grünau Regatta Course
3:00	FENCING team épée, final	Tennis Stadium & Courts
3:30	ATHLETICS • women's 4 x 100-meter relay, preliminaries	Olympic Stadium
3:30	CANOEING Canadian doubles	Grünau Regatta Course
4:00	ATHLETICS 3,000-meter steeplechase, final	Olympic Stadium
4:00	BASKETBALL qualifying matches	Tennis Courts
4:00	CYCLING • 4-kilometer pursuit, semifinals & final • 2-kilometer tandem, semifinals & final • 1-kilometer time trial	Olympic Velodrome
	DOUBLE CYCLE BALL demonstration match	
4:30	FIELD HOCKEY qualifying matches (2 games)	Hockey Stadium
4:30	CANOEING kayak, doubles	Grünau Regatta Course
4:30	ATHLETICS • 4 x 400-meter relay, preliminaries • decathlon (javelin)	Olympic Stadium
5:00	CANOEING Canadian singles	Grünau Regatta Course
5:15	TEAM HANDBALL elimination rounds	Police Stadium & Hohenzollern-Damm Sports Ground
5:30	ATHLETICS decathlon (1,500 meters)	Olympic Stadium
5:30	CANOEING kayak, four	Grünau Regatta Course

Time	Event	Venue
5:30	SOCCER intermediate round (2 games)	Post Stadium & Hertha Field
6:00	GRECO-ROMAN WRESTLING preliminaries	Deutschland Hall
6:15	GYMNASTICS demonstration by Sweden	Olympic Stadium

Sunday, AUGUST 9

AM	EVENT	VENUE
9:00	FENCING épée, individual, 1st round	Tennis Stadium & Courts
9:30	YACHTING	Kiel Bay
10:00	SWIMMING women's 200-meter breaststroke, semifinals	Olympic Swim Stadium
10:00	WATER POLO	Olympic Swim Stadium
10:00	GRECO-ROMAN WRESTLING final	Deutschland Hall

PM	EVENT	VENUE
2:00	BERLIN SCHOOL CHILDREN'S SONG & GYMNASTIC DISPLAY	Mayfield
3:00	ATHLETICS • marathon • women's high jump, final	Olympic Stadium
3:00	SWIMMING • women's 100-meter freestyle, intermediate heats • men's 100-meter freestyle, final	Olympic Swim Stadium
3:00	WATER POLO	Olympic Swim Stadium
3:15	ATHLETICS men's 4 x 100-meter relay, final	Olympic Stadium
3:30	ATHLETICS women's 4 x 100-meter relay, final	Olympic Stadium
3:45	ATHLETICS 4 x 400-meter relay, final	Olympic Stadium
4:00	BASKETBALL qualifying matches	Tennis Courts
4:30	GYMNASTICS demonstration by Germany	Olympic Stadium
4:30	FIELD HOCKEY qualifying matches (2 games)	Hockey Stadium
5:30	ATHLETICS marathon (finish)	Olympic Stadium
6:00	GRECO-ROMAN WRESTLING final	Deutschland Hall
8:00	FENCING individual épée, qualification	Tennis Stadium & Courts

Monday, AUGUST 10

AM	EVENT	VENUE
7:00	GYMNASTICS men's compulsory exercises	Dietrich Eckart Open-Air Theater
8:00	SWIMMING 4 x 200-meter relay, preliminaries	Olympic Swim Stadium
8:00	DIVING springboard, final	Olympic Swim Stadium
8:00	WATER POLO	Olympic Swim Stadium
8:00	CYCLING 100 kilometers	Starting in Avus

Time	Event	Venue
9:00	FENCING épée, individual, 2nd round qualifications	Tennis Stadium & Courts
9:30	YACHTING	Kiel Bay
11:00	TEAM HANDBALL elimination rounds (match for 5th/6th places)	Police Stadium & Hohenzollern-Damm Sports Ground

PM	EVENT	VENUE
2:00	GYMNASTICS men's compulsory exercises	Dietrich Eckart Open-Air Theater
3:00	SWIMMING • women's 100-meter freestyle, final • 400-meter freestyle, preliminaries	Olympic Swim Stadium
3:00	WATER POLO	Olympic Swim Stadium
3:00	FENCING épée, individual, 3rd round	Tennis Stadium & Courts
3:00	BOXING qualifying matches	Deutschland Hall
4:00	BASKETBALL qualifying matches	Tennis Courts
4:30	FIELD HOCKEY qualifying matches	Reichssportfeld
5:00	SOCCER semifinals	Olympic Stadium
5:15	TEAM HANDBALL elimination	Handball Field Police Station
8:30	BOXING qualifying matches	Deutschland Hall
9:00	DEMONSTRATION "Strength Through Joy"	

Tuesday, AUGUST 11

AM	EVENT	VENUE
7:00	GYMNASTICS men's free exercises	Dietrich Eckart Open-Air Theater
8:00	DIVING springboard, free diving	Olympic Swim Stadium
8:00	SWIMMING • 400-meter freestyle, intermediate heats • women's 100-meter backstroke, preliminaries	Olympic Swim Stadium
11:15	WATER POLO	Olympic Swim Stadium

PM	EVENT	VENUE
2:00	ROWING preliminaries	Grünau Regatta Course
3:00	DIVING springboard, show diving	Olympic Swim Stadium
3:00	SWIMMING • 4 x 200-meter relays, final • women's 200-meter breaststroke, final	Olympic Swim Stadium
3:00	GYMNASTICS men's, final	Dietrich Eckart Open-Air Theater
3:00	BOXING qualifying matches	Deutschland Hall
3:00	FENCING individual épée, final	Tennis Stadium & Courts
4:00	BASKETBALL qualification matches	Tennis Courts
4:25	WATER POLO	Olympic Swim Stadium
4:30	FIELD HOCKEY consolation games	Hockey Stadium

5:00 **SOCCER** ....*Olympic Stadium*
1 game
7:30 **CHINESE BOXING** ....*Dietrich Eckart Open-Air Theater*
demonstration
8:30 **BOXING** ....*Deutschland Hall*
qualifying matches

Wednesday, AUGUST 12

AM	EVENT	VENUE
7:00	**GYMNASTICS** ....*Dietrich Eckart Open-Air Theater* women's competition	
7:00	**EQUESTRIAN** ....*Mayfield* dressage	
8:00	**DIVING** ......*Olympic Swim Stadium* women's springboard, final	
8:00	**SWIMMING** .*Olympic Swim Stadium* • 100-meter backstroke, preliminaries • women's 4 x 100-meter relay, preliminaries	
9:00	**FENCING** ....*The Gymnasium and Cupola Hall* team saber, qualifications	

PM	EVENT	VENUE
12:05	**WATER POLO** ....*Olympic Swim Stadium*	
2:00	**GYMNASTICS** ....*Dietrich Eckart Open-Air Theater* women's competition	
2:00	**EQUESTRIAN** ....*Mayfield* dressage	
3:00	**ROWING** .....*Grünau Regatta Course* preliminaries and repechage	
3:00	**SWIMMING** .*Olympic Swim Stadium* • 400-meter freestyle, final • women's 100-meter backstroke, semifinals	
3:00	**DIVING** ......*Olympic Swim Stadium* • women's springboard • diving demonstration	
3:00	**BOXING** ....*Deutschland Hall* qualifying matches	
3:00	**FENCING** ....*The Gymnasium and Cupola Hall* team saber, qualifications	
3:00	**TEAM HANDBALL** ....*Olympic Stadium* Austria vs. Hungary	

4:00 **BASKETBALL** ....*Tennis Stadium*
qualifying matches
4:20 **TEAM HANDBALL** ....*Olympic Stadium*
Germany vs. Switzerland
4:25 **WATER POLO** ....*Olympic Swim Stadium*
4:30 **FIELD HOCKEY** ....*Hockey Stadium*
Semi-final
8:00 **BASEBALL** ....*Olympic Stadium*
with demonstration and concert
8:00 **FENCING** ....*The Gymnasium and Cupola Hall*
team saber, intermediate round
8:30 **BOXING** ....*Deutschland Hall*
qualifying matches

Thursday, AUGUST 13

AM	EVENT	VENUE
7:00	**EQUESTRIAN** ....*Mayfield* dressage test	
8:30	**DIVING** ......*Olympic Swim Stadium* women's high dive, final	
8:30	**SWIMMING** .*Olympic Swim Stadium* • women's 400-meter freestyle, preliminaries • 1,500-meter freestyle, preliminaries	
8:30	**WATER POLO** ....*Olympic Swim Stadium*	
9:00	**FENCING** ....*The Gymnasium and Cupola Hall* team saber, semifinals	

PM	EVENT	VENUE
2:00	**EQUESTRIAN** ....*Mayfield* combined dressage test	
2:00	**ROWING** .....*Grünau Regatta Course*	
3:00	**SWIMMING** .*Olympic Swim Stadium* • 1,500-meter freestyle, preliminaries • 200-meter breaststroke, preliminaries • 100-meter backstroke, semifinals • women's 100-meter backstroke, final	
3:00	**WATER POLO** ....*Olympic Swim Stadium*	
3:00	**BOXING** ....*Deutschland Hall*	
3:00	**FENCING** ....*The Gymnasium and Cupola Hall* team saber, final	

Friday, AUGUST 14

AM	EVENT	VENUE
7:00	**EQUESTRIAN** ....*Mayfield* three-day event, dressage	
9:00	**FENCING** ....*The Gymnasium and Cupola Hall* saber, singles, preliminaries	
9:00	**DIVING** ......*Olympic Swim Stadium* women's high dive, final	
9:00	**SWIMMING** .*Olympic Swim Stadium* women's 400-meter freestyle, semifinals	
9:00	**WATER POLO** ....*Olympic Swim Stadium*	

PM	EVENT	VENUE
2:00	**EQUESTRIAN** ....*Mayfield* dressage test	
2:30	**ROWING** .....*Grünau Regatta Course* four-oared shell with coxswain, final	
3:00	**ROWING** .....*Grünau Regatta Course* pair-oared shell without coxswain, final	
3:00	**FENCING** ....*The Gymnasium and Cupola Hall* Saber	
3:00	**SWIMMING** .*Olympic Swim Stadium* • 200-meter breaststroke, semifinals • 1,500-meter freestyle, semifinals • 100-meter backstroke, final	
3:00	**WATER POLO** ....*Olympic Swim Stadium*	
3:00	**TEAM HANDBALL** ....*Olympic Stadium* final	
3:00	**BOXING** ....*Deutschland Hall* semifinals	
3:00	**BASKETBALL** ....*Tennis Stadium* final	
3:30	**ROWING** .....*Grünau Regatta Course* single sculls, final	

4:00 **SOCCER** ....*Olympic Stadium*
final round (3rd and 4th places)
4:00 **BASKETBALL** ....*Tennis Stadium*
preliminaries
4:30 **FIELD HOCKEY** ....*Hockey Stadium*
8:30 **BOXING** ....*Deutschland Hall*

4:00 **ROWING** .....*Grünau Regatta Course*
pair-oared shell
with coxswain, final
4:30 **FIELD HOCKEY** ....*Hockey Stadium*
final
5:30 **ROWING** .....*Grünau Regatta Course*
four-oared shell without coxswain
6:00 **ROWING** .....*Grünau Regatta Course*
double sculls, final
6:30 **ROWING** .....*Grünau Regatta Course*
eight-oared shell with coxswain
8:00 **BOXING** ....*Deutschland Hall*
semifinals

Saturday, AUGUST 15

AM	EVENT	VENUE
8:00	**EQUESTRIAN** ....*Döberitz* three-day event, cross-country	
10:00	**DIVING** ......*Olympic Swim Stadium* high dive, final	
11:00	**FIELD HOCKEY** ....*Hockey Stadium* final, India vs. Germany	

PM	EVENT	VENUE
3:00	**FENCING** ....*The Gymnasium and Cupola Hall* saber, individual, final	
3:00	**SWIMMING** .*Olympic Swim Stadium* • 200-meter breaststroke, final • women's 400-meter freestyle, final • 1,500-meter freestyle, final	
3:00	**WATER POLO** ....*Olympic Swim Stadium*	
3:00	**DIVING** ......*Olympic Swim Stadium* high diving demonstration	
4:00	**SOCCER** ....*Olympic Stadium* final, Italy vs. Austria	
8:30	**BOXING** ....*Deutschland Hall* final	

Sunday, AUGUST 16

AM	EVENT	VENUE
10:00	**EQUESTRIAN** ....*Olympic Stadium* three-day event, jumping	

PM	EVENT	VENUE
6:00	**CLOSING CEREMONY** ....*Olympic Stadium*	

BERLIN 1936
10TH OLYMPIC SUMMER GAMES

ATHLETICS (TRACK & FIELD)

Event	Gold	Silver	Bronze	4th / 5th / 6th		
100 METERS	USA 10.3 — JESSE OWENS	USA 10.4 — RALPH METCALFE	NED 10.5 — MARTINUS OSENDARP	4. USA Frank Wykoff / 5. GER Erich Borchmeyer / 6. SWE Lennart Strandberg		10.6 / 10.7 / 10.9
200 METERS	USA 20.7 — JESSE OWENS	USA 21.1 — MATTHEW ROBINSON	NED 21.3 — MARTINUS OSENDARP	4. SUI Paul Hänni / 5. CAN Lee Orr / 6. NED Wijnand van Beveren		21.6 / 21.6 / 21.9
400 METERS	USA 46.5 — ARCHIE WILLIAMS	GBR 46.7 — A. GODFREY BROWN	USA 46.8 — JAMES LUVALLE	4. GBR William Roberts / 5. CAN William Fritz / 6. CAN John Loaring		46.8 / 47.8 / 48.2
800 METERS	USA 1:52.9 — JOHN WOODRUFF	ITA 1:53.3 — MARIO LANZI	CAN 1:53.6 — PHILIP EDWARDS	4. POL Kazimierz Kucharski / 5. USA Charles Hornbostel / 6. USA Harry Williamson		1:53.8 / 1:54.6 / 1:55.8
1,500 METERS	NZL 3:47.8 — JOHN LOVELOCK	USA 3:48.4 — GLENN CUNNINGHAM	ITA 3:49.2 — LUIGI BECCALI	4. USA Archie San Romani / 5. CAN Philip Edwards / 6. GBR John Cornes		3:50.0 / 3:50.4 / 3:51.4
5,000 METERS	FIN 14:22.2 — GUNNAR HÖCKERT	FIN 14:25.8 — LAURI LEHTINEN	SWE 14:29.0 — HENRY JONSSON	4. JPN Kohei Murakoso / 5. POL Józef Noji / 6. FIN Ilmari Salminen		14:30.0 / 14:33.4 / 14:39.8
10,000 METERS	FIN 30:15.4 — ILMARI SALMINEN	FIN 30:15.6 — ARVO ASKOLA	FIN 30:20.2 — VOLMARI ISO-HOLLO	4. JPN Kohei Murakoso / 5. GBR James Burns / 6. ARG Juan Carlos Zabala		30:25.0 / 30:58.2 / 31:22.0
MARATHON	KOR 2:29:19.2 — KEE-CHUNG SOHN	GBR 2:31:23.2 — ERNEST HARPER	KOR 2:31:42.0 — SEUNG-YONG NAM	4. FIN Erkki Tamila / 5. FIN Väino Muinonen / 6. RSA Johannes Coleman		2:32:45.0 / 2:33:46.0 / 2:36:17.0
110-METER HURDLES	USA 14.2 — FORREST TOWNS	GBR 14.4 — DONALD FINLAY	USA 14.4 — FREDERICK POLLARD	4. SWE Håkan Lidman / 5. GBR John Thornton / 6. CAN Lawrence O'Connor		14.4 / 14.7 / 15.0
400-METER HURDLES	USA 52.4 — GLENN HARDIN	CAN 52.7 — JOHN LOARING	PHI 52.8 — MIGUEL WHITE	4. USA Joseph Patterson / 5. BRA S. de Magalhães Padilha / 6. GRE Christos Mantikas		53.0 / 54.0 / 54.2
3,000-METER STEEPLECHASE	FIN 9:03.8 — VOLMARI ISO-HOLLO	FIN 9:06.8 — KAARLO TUOMINEN	GER 9:07.2 — ALFRED DOMPERT	4. FIN Martti Matilainen / 5. USA Harold Manning / 6. SWE Lars Larsson		9:09.0 / 9:11.2 / 9:16.6
4 x 100-METER RELAY	USA 39.8 — JESSE OWENS, RALPH METCALFE, FOY DRAPER, FRANK WYKOFF	ITA 41.1 — ORAZIO MARIANI, GIANNI CALDANA, ELIO RAGNI, TULLIO GONNELLI	GER 41.2 — WILHELM LEICHUM, ERICH BORCHMEYER, ERWIN GILLMEISTER, GERD HORNBERGER	4. ARG Lavenas/Sande/Hofmeister/Beswick / 5. CAN Richardson/Humber/Orr/McPhee / NED Boersma/Berger/van Beveren/Osendarp		42.2 / 42.7 / DQ
4 x 400-METER RELAY	GBR 3:09.0 — FREDERICK WOLFF, GODFREY RAMPLING, WILLIAM ROBERTS, ARTHUR GODFREY BROWN	USA 3:11.0 — HAROLD CAGLE, ROBERT YOUNG, EDWARD O'BRIEN, ALFRED FITCH	GER 3:11.8 — HELMUT HAMANN, F. VON STÜLPNAGEL, HARRY VOIGT, RUDOLF HARBIG	4. CAN Limon/Edwards/Fritz/Loaring / 5. SWE Strömberg/Edfeldt/Danielsson/von Wachenfeldt / 6. HUN Ribényi/Zsitavi/Vadas/Kovacs		3:11.8 / 3:13.0 / 3:14.8
50,000-METER WALK	GBR 4:30:41.4 — HAROLD WHITLOCK	SUI 4:32:09.2 — ARTHUR SCHWAB	LAT 4:32:42.2 — ADALBERTS BUBENKO	4. TCH Jaroslav Štork / 5. NOR Edgar Bruun / 6. GER Fritz Bleiweiss		4:34:00.2 / 4:34:53.2 / 4:36:48.4
HIGH JUMP	USA 2.03 — CORNELIUS JOHNSON	USA 2.00 — DAVID ALBRITTON	USA 2.00 — DELOS THURBER	4. FIN Kalevi Kotkas / 5. JPN Kimio Yada / 6. four-way tie		2.00 / 1.97 / 1.94
POLE VAULT	USA 4.35 — EARLE MEADOWS	JPN 4.25 — SHUHEI NISHIDA	JPN 4.25 — SUEO OE	4. USA William Sefton / 5. USA William Graber / 6. eleven-way tie		4.25 / 4.15 / 4.00
LONG JUMP	USA 8.06 — JESSE OWENS	GER 7.87 — LUTZ LONG	JPN 7.74 — NAOTO TAJIMA	4. GER Wilhelm Leichum / 5. ITA Arturo Maffei / 6. USA Robert Clark		7.73 / 7.73 / 7.67

Event	1st	2nd	3rd	4th / 5th / 6th
TRIPLE JUMP	JPN 16.00 Naoto Tajima	JPN 15.66 Masao Harada	AUS 15.50 John Metcalfe	4. GER Heinz Wöllner 15.27 / 5. USA Rolland Romero 15.08 / 6. JPN Kenkichi Oshima 15.07
SHOT PUT	GER 16.20 Hans Woellke	FIN 16.12 Sulo Bärlund	GER 15.66 Gerhard Stöck	4. USA Samuel Francis 15.45 / 5. USA Jack Torrance 15.38 / 6. USA Dimitri Zaitz 15.32
DISCUS THROW	USA 50.48 Kenneth Carpenter	USA 49.36 Gordon Dunn	ITA 49.23 Giorgio Oberweger	4. NOR Reidar Sorlie 48.77 / 5. GER Willy Schröder 47.93 / 6. GRE Nikolaos Syllas 47.75
JAVELIN THROW	GER 71.84 Gerhard Stöck	FIN 70.77 Yrjö Nikkanen	FIN 70.72 K. Kalervo Toivonen	4. SWE Lennart Attervall 69.20 / 5. FIN Matti Järvinen 69.18 / 6. USA Alton Terry 67.15
HAMMER THROW	GER 56.49 Karl Hein	GER 55.04 Erwin Blask	SWE 54.83 Fred Warngård	4. FIN Gustaf Alfons Koutonen 51.90 / 5. USA William Rowe 51.66 / 6. USA Donald Favor 51.01
DECATHLON	USA 7,900 Glenn Morris	USA 7,601 Robert Clark	USA 7,275 Jack Parker	4. GER Erwin Huber 7,087 / 5. NED Reindert Brasser 7,046 / 6. SUI Armin Guhl 7,033
100 METERS	USA 11.5 Helen Stephens	POL 11.7 S. Walasiewiczówna	GER 11.9 Käthe Krauss	4. GER Marie Dollinger 12.0 / 5. USA Annette Rogers 12.2 / 6. GER Emmy Albus 12.3
80-METER HURDLES	ITA 11.7 Trebisonda Valla	GER 11.7 Anni Steuer	CAN 11.7 Elizabeth Taylor	4. ITA Claudia Testoni 11.7 / 5. NED Catharina ter Braake 11.8 / 6. GER Doris Eckert 12.0
4 x 100-METER RELAY	USA 46.9 Harriet Bland, Annette Rogers, Elizabeth Robinson, Helen Stephens	GBR 47.6 Eileen Hiscock, Violet Olney, Audrey Brown, Barbara Burke	CAN 47.8 Dorothy Brookshaw, Mildred Dolson, Hilda Cameron, Aileen Meagher	4. ITA Bongiovanni/Valla/Bullano/Testoni 48.7 / 5. NED ter Braake/Koen/de Vries/Koning 48.8 / GER Albus/Krauss/Dollinger/Dörffeldt DQ
HIGH JUMP	HUN 1.60 Ibolya Csák	GBR 1.60 Dorothy Odam	GER 1.60 Elfriede Kaun	4. GER Dora Ratjen 1.58 / 5. FRA Marguerite Nicolas 1.58 / 6. three-way tie
DISCUS THROW	GER 47.63 Gisela Mauermayer	POL 46.22 Jadwiga Wajs	GER 39.80 Paula Mollenhauer	4. JPN Ko Nakamura 38.24 / 5. JPN Hide Mineshima 37.35 / 6. SWE Birgit Lundström 35.92
JAVELIN THROW	GER 45.18 Tilly Fleischer	GER 43.29 Luise Krüger	POL 41.80 Maria Kwaśniewska	4. AUT Herma Bauma 41.66 / 5. JPN Sadako Yamamoto 41.45 / 6. GER Lydia Eberhardt 41.37

BASKETBALL

	1st	2nd	3rd	4th / 5th / 6th
FINAL STANDINGS	USA	CAN	MEX	4. POL / 5. PHI / 6. URU

BOXING

Event	1st	2nd	3rd	4th / 5th
FLYWEIGHT 112.5 lbs. (51 kg)	GER Willi Kaiser	ITA Gavino Matta	USA Louis Daniel Laurie	4. ARG Alfredo Carlomagno / 5. four-way tie
BANTAMWEIGHT 119.5 lbs. (54 kg)	ITA Ulderico Sergo	USA Jack Wilson	MEX Fidel Ortiz	4. SWE Stig Cederberg / 5. four-way tie
FEATHERWEIGHT 126 lbs. (57 kg)	ARG Oscar Casanovas	RSA Charles Catterall	GER Josef Miner	4. HUN Dezsö Frigyes / 5. four-way tie
LIGHTWEIGHT 132 lbs. (60 kg)	HUN Imre Harangi	EST Nikolai Stepulov	SWE Erik Ågren	4. DEN Poul Kops / 5. four-way tie
WELTERWEIGHT 148 lbs. (67 kg)	FIN Sten Suvio	GER Michael Murach	DEN Gerhard Petersen	4. FRA Roger Tritz / 5. four-way tie
MIDDLEWEIGHT 165.5 lbs. (75 kg)	FRA Jean Despeaux	NOR Henry Tiller	ARG Raúl Villareal	4. POL Henryk Chmielewski / 5. four-way tie

LIGHT HEAVYWEIGHT 179.5 lbs. (81 kg)	FRA ROGER MICHELOT	GER RICHARD VOGT	ARG FRANCISCO RISIGLIONE	4. RSA 5.	Sydney Leibbrandt four-way tie	
HEAVYWEIGHT >179.5 lbs. (>91 kg)	GER HERBERT RUNGE	ARG GUILLERMO LOVELL	NOR ERLING NILSEN	4. HUN 5.	Ferenc Nagy four-way tie	

CANOEING

KAYAK SINGLES 1,000 METERS	AUT 4:22.9 GREGOR HRADETZKY	GER 4:25.6 HELMUT CÄMMERER	NED 4:35.1 JACOBUS KRAAIER	4. USA 5. SWE 6. FRA	Ernest Riedel Joel Rahmqvist Henri Eberhardt	4:38.1 4:39.5 4:41.2
KAYAK SINGLES 10,000 METERS	GER 46:01.6 ERNST KREBS	AUT 46:14.7 FRITZ LANDERTINGER	USA 47:23.9 ERNEST RIEDL	4. NED 5. FIN 6. TCH	Jacobus van Tongeren Evert Johansson František Brzák-Felix	47:31.0 47:35.5 47:36.8
KAYAK PAIRS 1,000 METERS	AUT 4:03.8 ADOLF KAINZ ALFONS DORFNER	GER 4:08.9 EWALD TILKER FRITZ BONDROIT	NED 4:12.2 NICOLAAS TATES WILLEM VAN DER KROFT	4. TCH 5. SUI 6. CAN	Brzák-Felix/Dusil Vilim/Klingelfuss Deir/Willis	4:15.2 4:22.8 4:24.5
KAYAK PAIRS 10,000 METERS	GER 41:45.0 PAUL WEVERS LUDWIG LANDEN	AUT 42:05.4 VIKTOR KALISCH KARL STEINHUBER	SWE 43:06.1 TAGE FAHLBORG HELGE LARSSON	4. DEN 5. NED 6. SUI	Lövgreen/Svendsen Starreveld/Siderius Zimmermann/Bach	44:39.8 45:12.5 45:14.6
FOLDING KAYAK SINGLES 10,000 METERS	AUT 50:01.2 GREGOR HRADETZKY	FRA 50:04.2 HENRI EBERHARDT	GER 50:06.5 XAVER HÖRMANN	4. SWE 5. TCH 6. SWE	Lennart Dozzi František Svoboda Hans Mooser	51:23.8 51:52.5 52:43.8
FOLDING KAYAK PAIRS 10,000 METERS	SWE 45:48.9 SVEN JOHANSSON ERIK BLADSTRÖM	GER 45:49.2 WILLI HORN ERICH HANISCH	NED 46:12.4 PIETER WIJDEKOP CORNELIS WIJDEKOP	4. AUT 5. TCH 6. SUI	Kainz/Dorfner Kouba/Klima Knoblauch/Bottlang	46:26.1 47:46.2 47:54.4
CANADIAN SINGLES 1,000 METERS	CAN 5:32.1 FRANCIS AMYOT	TCH 5:36.9 BOHUSLAV KARLIK	GER 5:39.0 ERICH KOSCHIK	4. AUT 5. USA 6. LUX	Otto Neumüller Joseph Hasenfus Joe Treinen	5:47.0 6:02.6 7:39.5
CANADIAN PAIRS 1,000 METERS	TCH 4:50.1 VLADIMIR SYROVÁTKA JAN BRZÁK-FELIX	AUT 4:53.8 RUPERT WEINSTABL KARL PROISL	CAN 4:56.7 FRANK SAKER HARVEY CHARTERS	4. GER 5. USA	Wedemann/Sack McNutt/Graf	5:00.2 5:14.0
CANADIAN PAIRS 10,000 METERS	TCH 50:33.5 VÁCLAV MOTTL ŽDENEK ŠKRDLANT	CAN 51:15.8 FRANK SAKER HARVEY CHARTERS	AUT 51:28.0 RUPERT WEINSTABL KARL PROISL	4. GER 5. USA	Schuur/Holzenberg Hasenfus/Hasenfus	52:35.6 57:06.2

CYCLING

1,000-METER SPRINT	GER 2-0 TONI MERKENS	NED ARIE VAN VLIET	FRA LOUIS CHAILLOT	4. ITA 5.	Benedetto Pola four-way tie	
TANDEM SPRINT 2,000 METERS	GER 2-0 ERNST IHBE CARL LORENZ	NED BERNHARD LEENE HENDRIK OOMS	FRA PIERRE GEORGET GEORGES MATON	4. ITA 5.	Legutti/Loatti four-way tie	
1,000-METER TIME TRIAL	NED 1:12.0 ARIE VAN VLIET	FRA 1:12.8 PIERRE GEORGET	GER 1:13.2 RUDOLF KARSCH	4. ITA 5. DEN 5. HUN	Benedetto Pola Arne Pedersen László Orczán	1:13.6 1:14.0 1:14.0
4,000-METER TEAM PURSUIT	FRA 4:45.0 ROBERT CHARPENTIER JEAN GOUJAN GUY LAPÉBIE ROGER LE NIZERHY	ITA 4:51.0 BIANCO BIANCHI MARIO GENTILI ARMANDO LATINI SEVERINO RIGONI	GBR 4:53.6 HARRY HILL ERNEST JOHNSON CHARLES KING ERNEST MILLS	4. GER 5.	Arndt/Hasselberg/ Hoffman/Klockner four-way tie	4:55.0
ROAD RACE, INDIVIDUAL 100 KILOMETERS	FRA 2:33:05.0 ROBERT CHARPENTIER	FRA 2:33:05.2 GUY LAPÉBIE	SUI 2:33:05.8 ERNST NIEVERGELT	4. GER 4. GBR 4. FRA	Fritz Scheller Charles Holland Robert Dorgebray	2:33:06.0 2:33:06.0 2:33:06.0

ROAD RACE, TEAM 100 KILOMETERS		FRA 7:39:16.2 ROBERT CHARPENTIER GUY LAPÉBIE ROBERT DORGEBRAY		SUI 7:39:20.4 ERNST NIEVERGELT EDGAR BUCHWALDER KURT OTT		BEL 7:39:21.0 AUGUSTE GARREBEEK ARMAND PUTZEYS FRANCOIS VANDERMETTE	4. ITA Favalli/ 7:39:22.0 Servadei/Ardizzoni 5. AUT Altmann/ 7:39:24.0 Höfner/Schnalek

EQUESTRIAN

THREE-DAY EVENT, INDIVIDUAL		GER -37.7 LUDWIG STUBBENDORFF		USA -99.9 EARL THOMSON		DEN -102.2 H. MATHIESEN-LUNDING	4. DEN Vincens Grandjean -104.9 5. HUN Agoston Endrödy -105.7 6. GER Rudolf Lippert -111.6
THREE-DAY EVENT, TEAM		GER -676.65 LUDWIG STUBBENDORFF RUDOLF LIPPERT K.FREIHERR VON WANGENHEIM		POL -991.70 HENRYK ROJCEWICZ ZDZISLAW KAWECKI SEWERYN KULESZA		GBR -9,195.50 ALEC SCOTT EDWARD HOWARD-VYSE RICHARD FANSHAWE	4. TCH Procházka/ -18,952.70 Dobes/Bureš
DRESSAGE, INDIVIDUAL		GER 1,760.0 HEINZ POLLAY		GER 1,745.5 FRIEDRICH GERHARD		AUT 1,721.5 ALOIS PODHAJSKY	4. SWE Gregor Adlecreutz 1,675.0 5. FRA André Jousseaume 1,642.5 6. FRA Gérard de Ballore 1,634.0
DRESSAGE, TEAM		GER 5,074.0 HEINZ POLLAY FRIEDRICH GERHARD H. VON OPPELN-BRONIKOWSKI		FRA 4,846.0 ANDRÉ JOUSSEAUME GÉRARD DE BALLORRE DANIEL GILLOIS		SWE 4,660.5 GREGOR ADLERCREUTZ SVEN COLLIANDER FOLKE SANDSTRÖM	4. AUT Podhajsky/Dolleschall/4,672.5 von Pongracz 5. NED Versteegh/Le Heux/ 4,382.0 Camerling-Helmolt 6. HUN von Pados/Keméry/ 4,090.0 von Magasházy
JUMPING, INDIVIDUAL		GER 59.2 KURT HASSE		ROM 1:12.8 HENRI RANG		HUN 1:02.6 JÓZSEF VON PLATTHY	4. BEL G. Ganshof van der Meersch 5. USA Carl Raguse 6. five-way tie
JUMPING, TEAM		GER 44.0 KURT HASSE MARTEN VON BARNEKOW HEINZ BRANDT		NED 51.5 JOHAN JACOB GRETER JAN ADRIANUS DE BRUINE HENRI LOUIS VAN SCHAIK		POR 56.0 JOSÉ BELTRÃO L. MARQUÉZ DO FUNCHAL LUIS MENA E SILVA	4. USA Raguse/Bradford/ 72.5 Jadwin 5. SUI Mettler/Fehr/Iklé 74.5 6. JPN Iwahashi/Nishi/ 75.0 Inanami

FENCING

ÉPÉE, INDIVIDUAL		ITA FRANCO RICCARDI		ITA SAVERIO RAGNO		ITA G. CORNAGGIA-MEDICI	4. SWE Hans Drakenberg 5. BEL Charles Debeur 6. POR Henrique da Silveira
ÉPÉE, TEAM		ITA		SWE		FRA	4. GER 5. four-way tie
FOIL, INDIVIDUAL		ITA GIULIO GAUDINI		FRA EDWARD GARDÈRE		ITA GIORGIO BOCCHINO	4. GER Erwin Casmir 5. ITA Gioacchino Guaragna 6. BEL Raymond Bru
FOIL, TEAM		HUN		ITA		GER	4. POL 5. two-way tie
SABER, INDIVIDUAL		HUN ENDRE KABOS		ITA GUSTAVO MARZI		HUN ALADÁR GEREVICH	4. HUN László Rajcsányi 5. ITA Vincenzo Pinton 6. ITA Giulio Gaudini
SABER, TEAM		HUN		ITA		GER	4. POL 5. four-way tie
FOIL, INDIVIDUAL		HUN ILONA ELEK SCHACHERER		GER HELENE MAYER		AUT ELLEN PREIS	4. GER Hedwig Hass 5. DEN Karen Lachmann 6. BEL Jenny Addams

FIELD HOCKEY

FINAL STANDINGS		IND		GER		NED	4. FRA

FOOTBALL (SOCCER)

FINAL STANDINGS	⬤ ITA	⬤ AUS	⬤ NOR	4. POL 5. four-way tie	

GYMNASTICS

| ALL-AROUND, INDIVIDUAL | ⬤ GER 113.100
ALFRED SCHWARZMANN | ⬤ SUI 112.334
EUGEN MACK | ⬤ GER 111.532
KONRAD FREY | 4. TCH Alois Hudec
5. FIN Martti Uosikkinen
5. SUI Michael Reusch | 111.199
110.700
110.700 |

| ALL-AROUND, TEAM | ⬤ GER 657.430 | ⬤ SUI 654.802 | ⬤ FIN 638.468 | 4. TCH
5. ITA
6. YUG | 625.763
615.133
598.366 |

| FLOOR EXERCISES | ⬤ SUI 18.666
GEORGES MIEZ | ⬤ SUI 18.500
JOSEF WALTER | ⬤ SUI 18.466
EUGEN MACK

GER 18.466
KONRAD FREY | 5. GER Matthias Volz
6. two-way tie | 18.366
18.300 |

| HORIZONTAL BAR | ⬤ FIN 19.367
ALEKSANTERI SAARVALA | ⬤ GER 19.267
KONRAD FREY | ⬤ GER 19.233
ALFRED SCHWARZMANN | 4. GER Innozenz Stangl
5. FIN Heikki Savolainen
6. FIN Veikko Pakarinen | 19.167
19.133
19.067 |

| HORSE VAULT | ⬤ GER 19.200
ALFRED SCHWARZMANN | ⬤ SUI 18.967
EUGEN MACK | ⬤ GER 18.467
MATTHIAS VOLZ | 4. SUI Walter Bach
5. SUI Walter Beck
6. FIN Martti Uosikkinen | 18.400
18.367
18.300 |

| PARALLEL BARS | ⬤ GER 19.067
KONRAD FREY | ⬤ SUI 19.034
MICHAEL REUSCH | ⬤ GER 18.967
ALFRED SCHWARZMANN | 4. TCH Alois Hudec
5. SUI Eugen Mack
6. SUI Walter Bach | 18.966
18.834
18.733 |

| POMMELED HORSE | ⬤ GER 19.333
KONRAD FREY | ⬤ SUI 19.167
EUGEN MACK | ⬤ SUI 19.067
ALBERT BACHMANN | 4. FIN Martti Uosikkinen
5. GER Walter Steffens
5. SUI Walter Bach | 19.066
19.033
19.033 |

| RINGS | ⬤ TCH 19.433
ALOIS HUDEC | ⬤ YUG 18.867
LEON ŠTUKELJ | ⬤ GER 18.667
MATTHIAS VOLZ | 4. GER Alfred Schwarzmann
5. GER Franz Beckert
6. SUI Michael Reusch | 18.534
18.533
18.434 |

| ALL-AROUND, TEAM | ⬤ GER 506.5 | ⬤ TCH 503.6 | ⬤ HUN 499.0 | 4. YUG
5. USA
6. POL | 485.6
471.6
470.3 |

MODERN PENTATHLON

| INDIVIDUAL | ⬤ GER 31.5
GOTTHARDT HANDRICK | ⬤ USA 39.5
CHARLES LEONARD | ⬤ ITA 45.5
SILVANO ABBA | 4. SWE Sven Thofelt
5. HUN Nándor von Orbán
6. GER Hermann Lemp | 47
55.5
67.5 |

POLO

| FINAL STANDINGS | ⬤ ARG | ⬤ GBR | ⬤ MEX | 4. HUN
5. GER | |

ROWING

| SINGLE SCULLS | ⬤ GER 8:21.5
GUSTAV SCHÄFER | ⬤ AUT 8:25.8
JOSEF HASENÖHRL | ⬤ USA 8:28.0
DANIEL BARROW | 4. CAN Charles Campbell
5. SUI Ernst Rufli
6. ARG Pascual José Giorgio | 8:35.0
8:38.9
8:57.5 |

| DOUBLE SCULLS | ⬤ GBR 7:20.8
JACK BERESFORD
LESLIE SOUTHWOOD | ⬤ GER 7:26.2
WILLY KAIDEL
JOACHIM PIRSCH | ⬤ POL 7:36.2
ROGER VEREY
JERZY USTUPSKI | 4. FRA Giriat/Jacquet
5. USA Houser/Dugan
6. AUS Dixon/Turner | 7:42.3
7:44.8
7:45.1 |

| PAIR-OARED SHELL
WITHOUT COXSWAIN | ⬤ GER 8:16.1
WILLI EICHHORN
HUGO STRAUSS | ⬤ DEN 8:19.2
RICHARD OLSEN
HARRY LARSEN | ⬤ ARG 8:23.0
HORACIO PODESTÁ
JULIO CURATELLA | 4. HUN Györy/Magosy
5. SUI Klopfer/Müller
6. POL Borzuchowski/
Kobyliński | 8:25.7
8:33.0
8:41.9 |

Event	Gold	Silver	Bronze	4th–6th
PAIR-OARED SHELL WITH COXSWAIN	GER 8:36.9 GERHARD GUSTMANN, HERBERT ADAMSKI, DIETER AREND (COX)	ITA 8:49.7 ALMIRO BERGAMO, GUIDO SANTIN, LUCIANO NEGRINI (COX)	FRA 8:54.0 GEORGES TAPIE, MARCEAU FOURCADE, NÖEL VANDERNOTTE (COX)	4. DEN Larsen/Berner/Jensen/ 8:55.8 5. SUI Gschwind/Spring/ 9:10.9 Appenzeller 6. YUG Fabris/Mrduljaš/ 9:19.4 Ljubičič
FOUR-OARED SHELL WITHOUT COXSWAIN	GER 7:01.8 RUDOLF ECKSTEIN, ANTON ROM, MARTIN KARL, WILHELM MENNE	GBR 7:06.5 THOMAS BRISTOW, ALAN BARRETT, PETER JACKSON, JOHN DUNCAN STURROCK	SUI 7:10.6 HERMANN BETSCHART, HANS HOMBERGER, ALEX HOMBERGER, KARL SCHMID	4. ITA Ghiardello/Luscardo/ 7:12.4 Pellizzoni/Pittaluga 5. AUT Höpfler/Winkler/ 7:20.5 Pichler/Binder 6. DEN Olsen/Karise/ 7:26.3 Dröyer/Jensen
FOUR-OARED SHELL WITH COXSWAIN	GER 7:16.2	SUI 7:24.3	FRA 7:33.3	4. NED 7:34.7 5. HUN 7:35.6 6. DEN 7:40.4
EIGHT-OARED SHELL WITH COXSWAIN	USA 6:25.4	ITA 6:26.0	GER 6:26.4	4. GBR 6:30.1 5. HUN 6:30.3 6. SUI 6:35.8

SHOOTING

Event	Gold	Silver	Bronze	4th–6th
RAPID FIRE	GER 30/6 CORNELIUS VAN OYEN	GER 30/5 HEINZ HAX	SWE 30/4/4 TORSTEN ULLMAN	4. GRE Angelos Papadimas 30/4/1 5. SWE Helge Meuller 30/3 6. ITA Walter Boninsegni 29/6/3
SMALL-BORE RIFLE PRONE	NOR 300 WILLY RÖGEBERG	HUN 296 RALPH BERZSENYI	POL 296 WLADYSLAW KARAŚ	4. PHI Martin Gison 296 5. BRA José Trindade Mello 296 6. FRA Jacques Mazoyer 296
FREE PISTOL	SWE 559 TORSTEN ULLMAN	GER 544 ERICH KREMPEL	FRA 540 CHARLES DES JAMMONIÈRES	4. FRA Marcel Bonin 538 5. FIN Tapio Vartiovaara 537 6. USA Elliott Jones 536

SWIMMING

Event	Gold	Silver	Bronze	4th–6th
100-METER FREESTYLE	HUN 57.6 FERENC CSÍK	JPN 57.9 MASANORI YUSA	JPN 58.0 SHIGEO ARAI	4. JPN Masaharu Taguchi 58.1 5. GER Helmut Fischer 59.3 6. USA Peter Fick 59.7
400-METER FREESTYLE	USA 4:44.5 JACK MEDICA	JPN 4:45.6 SHUMPEI UTO	JPN 4:48.1 SHOZO MAKINO	4. USA Ralph Flanagan 4:52.7 5. JPN Hiroshi Negami 4:53.6 6. FRA Jean Taris 4:53.8
1,500-METER FREESTYLE	JPN 19:13.7 NOBORU TERADA	USA 19:34.0 JACK MEDICA	JPN 19:34.5 SHUMPEI UTO	4. JPN Sunao Ishiharada 19:48.5 5. USA Ralph Flanagan 19:54.8 6. GBR Robert Leivers 19:57.4
100-METER BACKSTROKE	USA 1:05.9 ADOLF KIEFER	USA 1:07.7 ALBERT VANDEWEGHE	JPN 1:08.4 MASAJI KIYOKAWA	4. USA Taylor Drysdale 1:09.4 5. JPN Kiichi Yoshida 1:09.7 6. JPN Yasuhiko Kojima 1:10.4
200-METER BREASTSTROKE	JPN 2:41.5 TETSUO HAMURO	GER 2:42.9 ERWIN SIETAS	JPN 2:44.2 REIZO KOIKE	4. USA John Herbert Higgins 2:45.2 5. JPN Saburo Ito 2:47.6 6. GER Joachim Balke 2:47.8
4 x 200-METER FREESTYLE RELAY	JPN 8:51.5 MASANORI YUSA, SHIGEO SUGIURA, MASAHARU TAGUCHI, SHIGEO ARAI	USA 9:03.0 RALPH FLANAGAN, JOHN MACIONIS, PAUL WOLF, JACK MEDICA	HUN 9:12.3 ÁRPÁD LENGYEL, OSZKÁR ABAY-NEMES, ÖDÖN GRÓF, FERENC CSÍK	4. FRA Nakache/Talli/ 9:18.2 Cavalero/Taris 5. GER Plath/Heimlich/ 9:19.0 Heibel/Fischer 6. GBR French-Williams/ 9:21.5 Gabrielson/Leivers/ Wainright
PLATFORM DIVING	USA 113.58 MARSHALL WAYNE	USA 110.60 ELBERT ROOT	GER 110.31 HERMANN STORK	4. GER Erhard Weiss 110.15 5. USA Frank Kurtz 108.61 6. JPN Tsuneo Shibahara 107.40
SPRINGBOARD DIVING	USA 163.57 RICHARD DEGENER	USA 159.56 MARSHALL WAYNE	USA 146.29 ALBERT GREENE	4. JPN Tsuneo Shibahara 144.92 5. GER Erhard Weiss 141.24 6. GER Leo Esser 137.99
WATER POLO	HUN	GER	BEL	4. FRA 5. NED 6. AUT
100-METER FREESTYLE	NED 1:05.9 HENDRIKA MASTENBROEK	ARG 1:06.4 JEANNETTE CAMPBELL	GER 1:06.6 GISELA ARENDT	4. NED Willemijntje den Ouden 1:07.6 5. NED Catherina Wagner 1:08.1 6. USA Olive McKean 1:08.4

400-METER FREESTYLE	NED 5:26.4 Hendrika Mastenbroek	DEN 5:27.5 Ragnhild Hveger	USA 5:29.0 Lenore Kight-Wingard	4. USA Mary Lou Petty 5:32.2 / 5. BRA P. Coutinho Azevedo 5:35.2 / 6. JPN Kazue Koijma 5:43.1

100-METER BACKSTROKE	NED 1:18.9 Dina Senff	NED 1:19.2 H. Mastenbroek	USA 1:19.4 Alice Bridges	4. USA Edith Motridge 1:19.6 / 5. DEN Tove Bruunström 1:20.4 / 6. GBR Lorna Frampton 1:20.6

200-METER BREASTSTROKE	JPN 3:03.6 Hideko Maehata	GER 3:04.2 Martha Genenger	DEN 3:07.8 Inge Sörensen	4. GER Johanna Hölzner 3:09.5 / 5. NED Johanna Waalberg 3:09.5 / 6. GBR Doris Storey 3:09.7

4 x 100-METER FREESTYLE RELAY	NED 4:36.0 Johanna Selbach, Catherina Wagner, Willemijntje den Ouden, Hendrika Mastenbroek	GER 4:36.8 Ruth Halbsguth, Leni Lohmar, Ingeborg Schmitz, Gisela Arendt	USA 4:40.2 Katherine Rawls, Bernice Lapp, Mavis Freeman, Olive McKean	4. HUN Ács/Biró/Lenkei/Harsányi 4:48.0 / 4. CAN McConkey/Stone/Milton-Pirie/Dewar 4:48.0 / 6. GBR Jeffery/Grant/Hughes/Wadham 4:51.0

PLATFORM DIVING	USA 33.93 Dorothy Poynton Hill	USA 33.63 Velma Dunn	GER 33.43 Käthe Köhler	4. JPN Reiko Osawa 32.53 / 5. USA Cornelia Gilissen 30.47 / 6. JPN Fusako Kono 30.24

SPRINGBOARD DIVING	USA 89.27 Marjorie Gestring	USA 88.35 Katherine Rawls	USA 82.36 Dorothy Poynton Hill	4. GER Gerda Daumerlang 78.27 / 5. GER Olga Jentsch-Jordan 77.98 / 6. JPN Masayo Osawa 73.94

TEAM HANDBALL

FINAL STANDINGS	GER	AUT	SUI	4. HUN / 5. ROM / 6. USA

WEIGHT LIFTING

FEATHERWEIGHT 132 lbs. (60 kg)	USA 312.5 Anthony Terlazzo	EGY 305.0 S. Mohammed Soliman	EGY 300.0 Ibrahim Hassan Shams	4. AUT Anton Richter 297.5 / 5. GER Georg Liebsch 290.0 / 6. ITA Attilio Bescapè 287.5

LIGHTWEIGHT 148.75 lbs. (67.5 kg)	EGY 342.5 A. Mohammed Mesbah	AUT 342.5 Robert Fein	GER 327.5 Karl Jansen	4. GER Karl Schwitalle 322.5 / 5. USA John Terpak 322.5 / 6. EGY E. Sayed Ibrahim Masoud 322.5

MIDDLEWEIGHT 165 lbs. (75 kg)	EGY 387.5 Khadr Sayed El Touni	GER 352.5 Rudolf Ismayr	GER 352.5 Adolf Wagner	4. AUT Anton Hangel 342.5 / 5. USA Stanley Kratkowski 337.5 / 6. AUT Hans Valla 335.0

LIGHT HEAVYWEIGHT 181.5 lbs. (82.5 kg)	FRA 372.5 Louis Hostin	GER 365.0 Eugen Deutsch	EGY 360.0 Ibrahim Wasif	4. GER Helmut Opschruf 355.0 / 5. LUX Nicolas Scheitler 350.0 / 6. AUT Fritz Hala 350.0

SUPER HEAVYWEIGHT unlimited weight	GER 410.0 Josef Manger	TCH 402.5 Václav Pšenička	EST 400.0 Arnold Luhäär	4. GBR Ronald Walker 397.5 / 5. EGY Hussein Mokhtar 395.0 / 6. AUT Josef Zemann 387.5

WRESTLING, FREESTYLE

BANTAMWEIGHT 125.5 lbs. (56 kg)	HUN Ödön Zombori	USA Ross Flood	GER Johannes Herbert	4. SWE Herman Tuvesson / 5. FIN Aatos Jaskari / 6. TUR Ahmet Çakiryildiz

FEATHERWEIGHT 136.5 lbs. (61 kg)	FIN Kustaa Pihlajamäki	USA Francis Millard	SWE Gösta Jönsson	4. CAN John Vernon Pettigrew / 5. HUN Ferenc Tóth / 6. JPN Mitsuzo Mizutani

LIGHTWEIGHT 149.5 lbs. (66 kg)	HUN Károly Kárpáti	GER Wolfgang Ehrl	FIN Hermanni Pihlajamäki	4. FRA Charles Delporte / 5. USA Harley Dewitt Strong / 6. ITA Paride Romagnoli

WELTERWEIGHT 163 lbs. (72 kg)	USA Frank Lewis	SWE Ture Andersson	CAN Joseph Schleimer	4. FRA Jean Jourlin / 5. SUI Willy Angst / 6. GER Josef Paar

MIDDLEWEIGHT 181 lbs. (79 kg)	FRA Emile Poilvé	USA Richard Voliva	TUR Ahmet Kireççi	4. SUI Ernst Krebs / 5. TCH Jaroslav Sysel / 6. FIN Kyösti Luukko

LIGHT HEAVYWEIGHT 198.5 lbs. (87 kg)	⬤ SWE Knut Fridell	⬤ EST August Neo	⬤ GER Erich Siebert	4. SUI Paul Dätwyler 5. USA Ray Clemons 6. AUS Eddie Scarf
HEAVYWEIGHT >195.5 lbs. (>87 kg)	⬤ EST Kristjan Palusalu	⬤ TCH Josef Klapuch	⬤ FIN Hjalmar Nyström	4. SWE Nils Åkerlindh 5. FRA Robert Herland 6. SUI Werner Bürki

WRESTLING, GRECO-ROMAN

BANTAMWEIGHT 125.5 lbs. (56 kg)	⬤ HUN Márton Lörincz	⬤ SWE Egon Svensson	⬤ GER Jakob Brendel	4. FIN Väinö Perttunen 5. ROM Iosef Tojar 6. EST Evald Sikk
FEATHERWEIGHT 136.5 lbs. (61 kg)	⬤ TUR Yaşar Erkan	⬤ FIN Aarne Reini	⬤ SWE Einar Karlsson	4. GER Sebastian Hering 5. LAT Krishjanis Kundsinsh 6. ITA Valentino Borgia
LIGHTWEIGHT 149.5 lbs. (66 kg)	⬤ FIN Lauri Koskela	⬤ TCH Josef Herda	⬤ EST Voldemar Väli	4. SWE Herbert Olofsson 5. ITA Alberto Molfino 6. NOR Arild Dahl
WELTERWEIGHT 163 lbs. (72 kg)	⬤ SWE Rudolf Svedberg	⬤ GER Fritz Schäfer	⬤ FIN Eino Virtanen	4. EST Edgar Puusepp 5. ITA Silvio Tozzi 6. TUR Nurettin Boytorun
MIDDLEWEIGHT 181 lbs. (79 kg)	⬤ SWE Ivar Johansson	⬤ GER Ludwig Schweikert	⬤ HUN József Palotás	4. FIN Väinö Kokkinen 5. EGY Ibrahim Erabi 6. ITA Ercole Gallegati
LIGHT HEAVYWEIGHT 198.5 lbs. (87 kg)	⬤ SWE Axel Cadier	⬤ LAT Edwins Bietags	⬤ EST August Neo	4. GER Werner Seelenbinder 5. ITA Umberto Silvestri 6. NOR Olaf Knutsen
HEAVYWEIGHT >198.5 lbs. (>87 kg)	⬤ EST Kristjan Palusalu	⬤ SWE John Nyman	⬤ GER Kurt Hornfische	4. TUR Mehmet Çoban 5. FIN Hjalmar Eemil Nyström 6. ITA Aleardo Donati

YACHTING

6-METER CLASS	⬤ GBR 67	⬤ NOR 66	⬤ SWE 62	4. ARG 52 5. ITA 50 6. GER 49
8-METER CLASS	⬤ ITA 55	⬤ NOR 53	⬤ GER 53	4. SWE 51 5. FIN 37 6. GBR 36
FINN MONOTYPYE	⬤ NED 163 Daniel Kagchelland	⬤ GER 150 Werner Krogmann	⬤ GBR 131 Peter Scott	4. CHI Erich Wichmann-Harbeck 130 5. ITA Giuseppe Fago 115 6. FRA Jacques Lebrun 109
STAR CLASS	⬤ GER 80 Peter Bischoff Hans-Joachim Weise	⬤ SWE 64 Arvid Laurin Uno Wallentin	⬤ NED 63 Willem de Vries-Lentsch Adriaan Maas	4. GBR Grogono/Welply 56 5. USA Waterhouse/Metcalf 51 6. NOR Christensen/Herbern 44

NATIONAL MEDAL COUNT

COMPETITORS   COUNTRIES: 50   ATHLETES: 4,700   MEN: 4,340   WOMEN: 360

	GOLD	SILVER	BRONZE	TOTAL		GOLD	SILVER	BRONZE	TOTAL		GOLD	SILVER	BRONZE	TOTAL		GOLD	SILVER	BRONZE	TOTAL
GER	38	37	32	107	SUI	1	9	5	15	EGY	2	1	2	5	ROM		1		1
USA	24	20	12	56	GBR	4	7	3	14	DEN		2	3	5	RSA		1		1
ITA	8	9	5	22	AUT	4	6	3	13	MEX			3	3	YUG		1		1
SWE	6	5	9	20	CAN	1	3	5	9	JPN	1		1	2	POR			1	1
FIN	7	6	6	19	TCH	3	5		8	TUR	1		1	2	PHI			1	1
FRA	7	6	6	19	EST	2	2	3	7	LAT	1	1		2	AUS			1	1
NED	6	4	7	17	ARG	2	2	3	7	BEL		2		2					
HUN	10	1	5	16	NOR	1	3	2	6	IND	1			1					
JPN	5	4	7	16	POL		3	3	6	NZL	1			1					

ST. MORITZ 1948 PROGRAM OF EVENTS

Friday, JANUARY 30

AM	EVENT	VENUE
10:00	OPENING CEREMONY	Olympic Ice Stadium
11:00	HOCKEY	Olympic Ice Stadium

PM	EVENT	VENUE
2:00	BOBSLED	Olympic Bob Sled Run two-man, 1st & 2nd runs
2:00	HOCKEY	Olympic Ice Stadium
2:00	HOCKEY	Palace
2:00	HOCKEY	Suvretta

Saturday, JANUARY 31

AM	EVENT	VENUE
10:00	SKIING, NORDIC	Salet 18-kilometer ski (special & combined)
10:30	SPEED SKATING	Olympic Ice Stadium 500 meter
10:30	HOCKEY	Palace
11:45	WINTER PENTATHLON	Salet 10-kilometer ski

PM	EVENT	VENUE
2:00	HOCKEY	Palace
2:00	HOCKEY	Olympic Ice Stadium
2:00	HOCKEY	Suvretta
2:00	BOBSLED	Olympic Bob Run two-man, 3rd & 4th runs

Sunday, FEBRUARY 1

AM	EVENT	VENUE
8:45	SPEED SKATING	Olympic Ice Stadium 5,000 meter
10:00	HOCKEY	Palace
10:00	HOCKEY	Suvretta
11:00	WINTER PENTATHLON	Stahlbad/ Eglise Française shooting

PM	EVENT	VENUE
2:30	SKIING, NORDIC	Olympic Ski Jump combined

3:00	HOCKEY	Palace
3:00	HOCKEY	Suvretta

Monday, FEBRUARY 2

AM	EVENT	VENUE
9:30	SPEED SKATING	Olympic Ice Stadium 1,500 meter
9:30	FIGURE SKATING	Kulm Ice Rink men's and women's compulsory figures
10:00	HOCKEY	Palace
10:00	SKIING, ALPINE	Mt. Piz Nair men's downhill and combined

PM	EVENT	VENUE
2:30	SKIING, ALPINE	Mt. Giop women's downhill and combined
3:00	HOCKEY	Palace
3:30	WINTER PENTATHLON	Corviglia downhill

Tuesday, FEBRUARY 3

AM	EVENT	VENUE
9:00	SKELETON	Cresta Run 1st runs
9:00	SKIING, CROSS COUNTRY	Salet 4 x 10 kilometer relay
9:00	FIGURE SKATING	Kulm women's compulsory figures
10:00	HOCKEY	Palace
10:00	HOCKEY	Suvretta
10:00	WINTER PENTATHLON	Tennis Palace fencing
10:00	SPEED SKATING	Olympic Ice Stadium 10,000 meter

PM	EVENT	VENUE
3:00	HOCKEY	Olympic Ice Stadium

Wednesday, FEBRUARY 4

AM	EVENT	VENUE
7:00	FIGURE SKATING	Kulm women's compulsory figures
8:00	HOCKEY	Palace
8:00	HOCKEY	Suvretta
8:00	HOCKEY	Olympic Ice Stadium
9:00	SKIING, ALPINE	Mt. Piz Nair men's combined slalom
9:00	SKELETON	Cresta Run 2nd runs
10:00	HOCKEY	Olympic Ice Stadium
10:00	SKIING, ALPINE	Mt. Piz Nair women's combined slalom
10:45	WINTER PENTATHLON	Near Bad, Catholic Church riding

PM	EVENT	VENUE
3:00	FIGURE SKATING	Kulm men's freestyle

Thursday, FEBRUARY 5

AM	EVENT	VENUE
7:30	FIGURE SKATING	Kulm women's figures
8:30	SKELETON	Cresta Run
9:00	SKIING, ALPINE	Mt. Piz Nair men's slalom
10:00	SKIING, ALPINE	Mt. Piz Nair women's slalom

PM	EVENT	VENUE
2:45	FIGURE SKATING	Olympic Ice Stadium men's freestyle

Friday, FEBRUARY 6

AM	EVENT	VENUE
8:00	HOCKEY	Olympic Ice Stadium
8:00	HOCKEY	Suvretta
8:00	HOCKEY	Palace
9:00	BOBSLED	Olympic Bob Run four-man, 1st & 2nd runs
10:00	SKIING, CROSS-COUNTRY	Salet 50 kilometers

PM	EVENT	VENUE
2:00	FIGURE SKATING	Olympic Ice Stadium women's freestyle

Saturday, FEBRUARY 7

AM	EVENT	VENUE
9:00	BOBSLED	Olympic Bob Run four-man, 3rd & 4th runs
10:00	HOCKEY	Olympic Ice Stadium
10:00	HOCKEY	Palace
10:00	HOCKEY	Suvretta

PM	EVENT	VENUE
2:00	FIGURE SKATING	Olympic Ice Stadium pairs
2:00	SKI JUMP	Olympic Ski Jump
3:00	HOCKEY	Suvretta

Sunday, FEBRUARY 8

AM	EVENT	VENUE
8:00	MILITARY PATROL	Corviglia to Salet demonstration sport
10:00	HOCKEY	Olympic Ice Stadium
10:00	HOCKEY	Suvretta
10:00	HOCKEY	Palace

PM	EVENT	VENUE
1:45	HOCKEY	Olympic Ice Stadium
4:00	CLOSING CEREMONIES	Olympic Ice Stadium

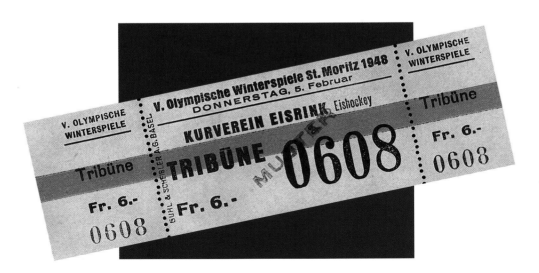

ST. MORITZ 1948
5TH OLYMPIC WINTER GAMES

BOBSLED

TWO-MAN	SUI 5:29.2 FELIX ENDRICH FRIEDRICH WALLER	SUI 5:30.4 FRITZ FEIERABEND PAUL HANS EBERHARD	USA 5:35.3 FREDERICK FORTUNE SCHUYLER CARRON	4. BEL Houben/Mouvet 5:37.5 5. GBR Coles/Collings 5:37.9 6. ITA Vitali/Poggi 5:39.0
FOUR-MAN	USA 5:20.1 FRANCIS TYLER PATRICK MARTIN EDWARD RIMKUS WILLIAM D'AMICO	BEL 5:21.3 MAX HOUBEN FREDDY MANSVELD LOUIS-GEORGES NIELS JACQUES MOUVET	USA 5:21.5 JAMES BICKFORD THOMAS HICKS DONALD DUPREE WILLIAM DUPREE	4. SUI Feierabend/Waller/ Endrich/Angst 5:22.1 5. NOR Holst/Johansen/ Berg/Large 5:22.5 6. ITA Bibbia/ Ronchetti/ Campadese/Cavalieri 5:23.0

FIGURE SKATING

SINGLES	USA 10 RICHARD BUTTON	SUI 23 HANS GERSCHWILER	AUT 33 EDI RADA	4. USA John Lettengarver 36 5. HUN Ede Király 42 6. USA James Grogan 62
SINGLES	CAN 11 BARBARA ANN SCOTT	AUT 24 EVA PAWLIK	GBR 28 JEANETTE ALTWEGG	4. TCH Jirina Nekolová 34 5. TCH Alena Vrzánová 44 6. USA Yvonne Sherman 62
PAIRS	BEL 17.5 MICHELINE LANNOY PIERRE BAUGNIET	HUN 26 ANDREA KÉKESSY EDE KIRÁLY	CAN 31 SUZANNE MORROW WALLACE DIESTELMEYER	4. USA Sherman/Swenning 53 5. GBR Silverthorne/ Silverthorne 53 6. USA Kennedy/Kennedy 59.5

ICE HOCKEY

FINAL STANDINGS	CAN	TCH	SUI	4. SWE 5. GBR 6. POL

SKELETON

SINGLE	ITA 5:23.2 NINO BIBBIA	USA 5:24.6 JOHN HEATON	GBR 5:25.1 JOHN CRAMMOND	4. USA William Martin 5:28.0 5. SUI Gottfried Kägi 5:29.9 6. GBR Richard Bott 5:30.4

SKIING, ALPINE

DOWNHILL	FRA 2:55.0 HENRI OREILLER	AUT 2:59.1 FRANZ GABL	SUI 3:00.3 KARL MOLITOR / SUI 3:00.3 ROLF OLINGER	5. AUT Egon Schöpf 3:01.2 6. two-way tie 3:02.4
SLALOM	SUI 2:10.3 EDI REINALTER	FRA 2:10.8 JAMES COUTTET	FRA 2:12.8 HENRI OREILLER	4. ITA Silvio Alverà 2:13.2 5. SWE Olle Dalman 2:13.6 6. AUT Egon Schöpf 2:14.2
COMBINED	FRA 3.27 HENRI OREILLER	SUI 6.44 KARL MOLITOR	FRA 6.95 JAMES COUTTET	4. AUT Edi Mall 8.54 5. ITA Silvio Alverà 8.71 6. SWE Hans Hansson 9.31
DOWNHILL	SUI 2:28.3 HEDY SCHLUNEGGER	AUT 2:29.1 TRUDE BEISER	AUT 2:30.2 RESI HAMMERER	4. ITA Celina Seghi 2:31.1 5. SUI Lina Mittner 2:31.2 6. FRA Suzanne Thiollière 2:31.4

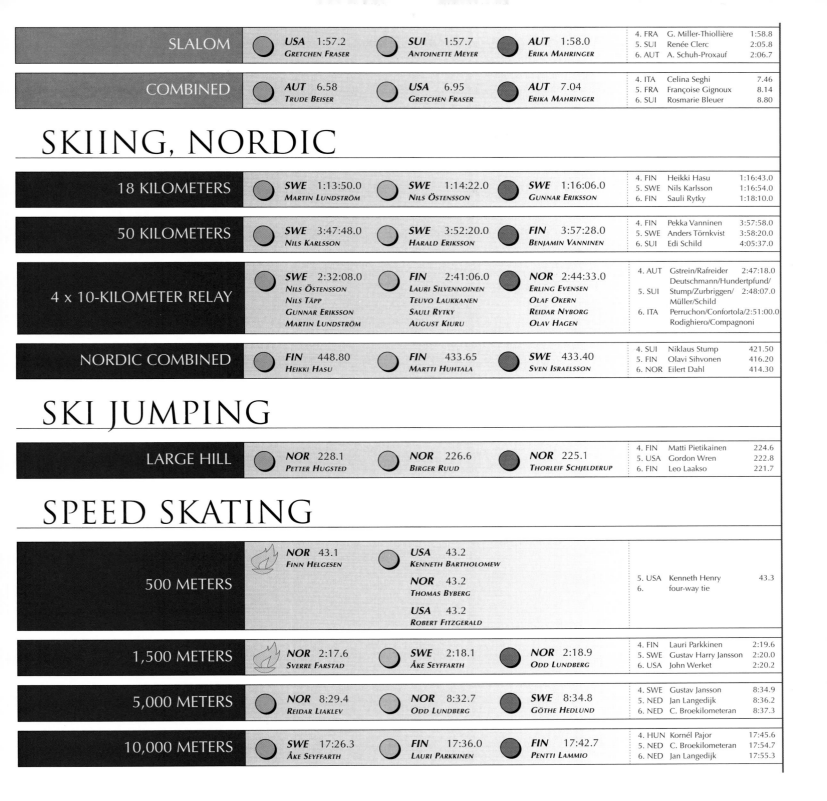

SLALOM	USA 1:57.2 GRETCHEN FRASER	SUI 1:57.7 ANTOINETTE MEYER	AUT 1:58.0 ERIKA MAHRINGER	4. FRA G. Miller-Thiollière 1:58.8 5. SUI Renée Clerc 2:05.8 6. AUT A. Schuh-Proxauf 2:06.7
COMBINED	AUT 6.58 TRUDE BEISER	USA 6.95 GRETCHEN FRASER	AUT 7.04 ERIKA MAHRINGER	4. ITA Celina Seghi 7.46 5. FRA Françoise Gignoux 8.14 6. SUI Rosmarie Bleuer 8.80

SKIING, NORDIC

18 KILOMETERS	SWE 1:13:50.0 MARTIN LUNDSTRÖM	SWE 1:14:22.0 NILS ÖSTENSSON	SWE 1:16:06.0 GUNNAR ERIKSSON	4. FIN Heikki Hasu 1:16:43.0 5. SWE Nils Karlsson 1:16:54.0 6. FIN Sauli Rytky 1:18:10.0
50 KILOMETERS	SWE 3:47:48.0 NILS KARLSSON	SWE 3:52:20.0 HARALD ERIKSSON	FIN 3:57:28.0 BENJAMIN VANNINEN	4. FIN Pekka Vanninen 3:57:58.0 5. SWE Anders Törnkvist 3:58:20.0 6. SUI Edi Schild 4:05:37.0
4 x 10-KILOMETER RELAY	SWE 2:32:08.0 NILS ÖSTENSSON NILS TÄPP GUNNAR ERIKSSON MARTIN LUNDSTRÖM	FIN 2:41:06.0 LAURI SILVENNOINEN TEUVO LAUKKANEN SAULI RYTKY AUGUST KIURU	NOR 2:44:33.0 ERLING EVENSEN OLAF OKERN REIDAR NYBORG OLAV HAGEN	4. AUT Gstrein/Rafreider 2:47:18.0 5. SUI Deutschmann/Hundertpfund/ Stump/Zurbriggen/ 2:48:07.0 Müller/Schild 6. ITA Perruchon/Confortola/2:51:00.0 Rodighiero/Compagnoni
NORDIC COMBINED	FIN 448.80 HEIKKI HASU	FIN 433.65 MARTTI HUHTALA	SWE 433.40 SVEN ISRAELSSON	4. SUI Niklaus Stump 421.50 5. FIN Olavi Sihvonen 416.20 6. NOR Eilert Dahl 414.30

SKI JUMPING

LARGE HILL	NOR 228.1 PETTER HUGSTED	NOR 226.6 BIRGER RUUD	NOR 225.1 THORLEIF SCHJELDERUP	4. FIN Matti Pietikainen 224.6 5. USA Gordon Wren 222.8 6. FIN Leo Laakso 221.7

SPEED SKATING

500 METERS	NOR 43.1 FINN HELGESEN	USA 43.2 KENNETH BARTHOLOMEW NOR 43.2 THOMAS BYBERG USA 43.2 ROBERT FITZGERALD		5. USA Kenneth Henry 43.3 6. four-way tie
1,500 METERS	NOR 2:17.6 SVERRE FARSTAD	SWE 2:18.1 ÅKE SEYFFARTH	NOR 2:18.9 ODD LUNDBERG	4. FIN Lauri Parkkinen 2:19.6 5. SWE Gustav Harry Jansson 2:20.0 6. USA John Werket 2:20.2
5,000 METERS	NOR 8:29.4 REIDAR LIAKLEV	NOR 8:32.7 ODD LUNDBERG	SWE 8:34.8 GÖTHE HEDLUND	4. SWE Gustav Jansson 8:34.9 5. NED Jan Langedijk 8:36.2 6. NED C. Broekilometeran 8:37.3
10,000 METERS	SWE 17:26.3 ÅKE SEYFFARTH	FIN 17:36.0 LAURI PARKKINEN	FIN 17:42.7 PENTTI LAMMIO	4. HUN Kornél Pajor 17:45.6 5. NED C. Broekilometeran 17:54.7 6. NED Jan Langedijk 17:55.3

NATIONAL MEDAL COUNT

COMPETITORS   COUNTRIES: 28   ATHLETES: 669   MEN: 592   WOMEN: 77

	GOLD	SILVER	BRONZE	TOTAL		GOLD	SILVER	BRONZE	TOTAL		GOLD	SILVER	BRONZE	TOTAL		GOLD	SILVER	BRONZE	TOTAL
SWE	4	3	3	10	AUT	1	3	4	8	BEL	1	1		2	HUN		1		1
NOR	4	3	3	10	FIN	1	3	2	6	GBR		2		2					
SUI	3	4	3	10	FRA	2	1	2	5	ITA	1			1					
USA	3	4	2	9	CAN	2		1	3	TCH	1			1					

OFFICERS OF THE INTERNATIONAL OLYMPIC COMMITTEE

XI OLYMPIAD

Count Henri de Baillet-Latour	President
Baron Godefroy de Blonay	Vice President
Lieutenant-Colonel A. G. Berdez	General Secretary
Werner Klingenberg	Technical Expert

Other Executive Members:
Marquis Melchoir de Polignac
J. Sigfrid Edström
Dr. Theodor Lewald
Lord Clarence Aberdare
Count Alfredo Bonacossa
Lydia Zanchi*

XII OLYMPIAD

Count Henri de Baillet-Latour	President
J. Sigfrid Edström[1]	Vice President

Other Executive Members:
Marquis Melchoir de Polignac
Lord Clarence Aberdare
Count Alfredo Bonacossa
Karl Ritter von Holt
Lydia Zanchi[2]

XIII OLYMPIAD

J. Sigfrid Edström	President
Avery Brundage	Vice President

Other Executive Members:
Marquis Melchoir de Polignac
Lord Clarence Aberdare
Count Alfredo Bonacossa
Karl Ritter von Holt
Lydia Zanchi

[1] Upon the death of Baillet-Latour on January 6, 1942, Edström was reluctant to assume the title of president until the IOC membership could meet in full session. On September 4, 1946, Edström was elected president by a vote of the full membership of the IOC during the 40th Session in Lausanne.

[2] As secretary, Zanchi also handled many of the tasks of the vacant position of executive director.

INTERNATIONAL OLYMPIC COMMITTEE MEMBERSHIP DURING THE XI, XII, & XIII OLYMPIADS

ARRIVALS: 40

— 1936 —

July 30	Avery Brundage	United States
	Franz Joseph	Liechtenstein
	Joakim Pukh	Estonia
	Prince Iesato Tokugawa	Japan
	Jorge B. Vargas	Philippines

— 1937 —

June 8	Frederic Coudert	United States
	Henry Guisan	Switzerland
	Joaquim Serratosa Cibils	Uruguay

— 1938 —

January	Walther von Reichenau	Germany
	Miguel A. Moenck	Cuba
March 13	Antonio Prado, Jr.	Brazil
September 15	Johan W. Rangell	Finland

— 1939 —

June 6	Gaston de Trannoy	Belgium
	Xiang Xi Kong	China
	Giorgio Vaccaro	Italy
	Masuzo Nagai	Japan
	Shingoro Takaishi	Japan
	Albert Victor Lindbergh	South Africa
	Miklos Horthy Jr.	Hungary

— 1946 —

September 4	Hugh Richard Weir	Australia
	Rodolphe W. Seeldrayers	Belgium
	John Coleridge Patteson	Canada
	Josef Gruss	Czechoslovakia
	Armand Massard	France
	Charles Pahud de Mortanges	Netherlands
	Benedikt G. Waage	Iceland
	Archduke Jean	Luxembourg
	José Joaquim Pontes	Portugal
	Sydney Dowsett	South Africa
	Reginald Honey	South Africa
	Albert Mayer	Switzerland
	Ioannie Ketseas	Greece

— 1947 —

July 19	Manfred Mautner-Markhof	Austria
	Sidney Dawes	Canada
	Yi-tung Sho	China
	Bhalendra Singh	India

— 1948 —

January 29	Bo Ekelund	Sweden
	Jerzy Loth	Poland
	Stanko Bloudek	Yugoslavia
	Ferenc Mezö	Hungary

DEPARTURES: 38

— 1936 —

July 30	Jotaro Sugimura	Japan
	Ernest Lee Jahncke+	United States
November 10	Francisco Ghigliani	Uruguay

— 1937 —

February 14	Godefroy de Blonay*	Switzerland
November	Porfirio Franca	Cuba

— 1938 —

January 13	Dimitri Tzokov*	Bulgaria
	Raul de Rio Branco	Brazil
March 13	Theodore Lewald	Germany
May 4	Jigoro Kano*	Japan
August 29	Geza Andrassy*	Hungary
November 25	Edouard de Laveley*	Belgium

— 1939 —

	Theodor Schmidt	Austria
June 2	Carlo Montu	Italy
June 6	Prince Iesato Tokugawa	Japan
June 8	José Matte Gormaz**	Chile
June 28	George McLaren-Brown*	Canada
October 18	Albert Gautier-Vignal*	Monaco
November	Henry Guisan	Switzerland
November 12	Albert Victor Lindbergh*	South Africa

— 1940 —

May 17	José de Penha-Garcia*	Portugal
August 30	P.J. de Matheu*	Central America

— 1942 —

January 7	Henry de Baillet-Latour*	Belgium
January 17	Walther von Reichenau*	Germany
May 13	Joakim Pukh*	Estonia
October 6	Henry Nourse*	South Africa

— 1943 —

January 8	Jiri Guth-Jarkovski*	Bohemia
April 30	Schimmelpenninck v.d. Oye*	Netherlands

— 1944 —

	Albert Glandaz*	France
	Stefan Tchapratchikov*	Bulgaria
	James Taylor*	Australia

— 1945 —

August 13	Stanislas Rouppert*	Poland

— 1946 —

February 23	Jules de Musza*	Hungary
April	James Merrick*	Canada
August 3	Ignace Matuszewski*	Poland
December 26	Franjo Bucar*	Yugoslavia

— 1947 —

March	Janis Dikilometeranis	Latvia

— 1948 —

January 29	Clarence von Rosen	Sweden
February 7	Miklos Horthy, Jr.*	Hungary

* Died in office; all others resigned
** Expelled

Net increase in the IOC membership: 1

Total IOC membership by the end of the XI, XII, & XIII OLYMPIADS: 69

OFFICERS OF THE UNITED STATES OLYMPIC COMMITTEE

On November 22, 1922, the USOC, then known as the American Olympic Association (AOA), adopted its first constitution, which called for a quadrennial meeting to elect officers to four year terms. The new constitution also mandated the creation of a second, temporary organization to be known as the American Olympic Committee, or AOC. Junior to the permanent AOA, the AOC was to become active a year before each Games to raise money for fielding an American team. The AOC was also to have its own President. The two-committee structure was destined to cause the AOA problems

4th USOC Quadrennial - November 22, 1933 to November 16, 1937

4th USOC quadrennial meeting was held November 22, 1933, at the Willard Hotel in Washington, D.C.

Avery Brundage
Brundage was elected AOA president for a second term on November 22, 1933. His second term spanned the X and XI Olympiads. On June 30, 1936, at the 36th Session of the IOC in Berlin, Brundage was also elected as the 12th IOC member in the United States. The chair he assumed had previously been held by Ernest Lee Jahncke of New Orleans, who had been expelled from the IOC moments before Brundage was elected.

Other elected officers were:

Dr. Joseph E. Raycroft	Vice president
Frederick W. Rubien	Secretary
Gustavus T. Kirby	Treasurer
James F. Simms	Assistant secretary
Asa Bushnell	Assistant treasurer
H. Jamison Swarts	Assistant treasurer
A.C. Gilbert, chairman	Administrative committee

5th USOC Quadrennial - November 17, 1937, to November 19, 1941

5th USOC quadrennial meeting was held November 17, 1937 at the Willard Hotel in Washington, DC.

Avery Brundage
IOC member Brundage was elected AOA president for a third term on November 17, 1937. This term spanned the XI and XII Olympiads. The AOA membership voted to change the AOA to the United States of America Sports Federation (USASF), thus retiring the American Olympic Association name forever. The membership felt this change reflected the increased emphasis the USASF was beginning to place on Pan-American relations and the growing possibility of participating in Pan-American regional games and other international athletic events. Using the words United States to replace America in the organizational name served to soothe the considerable resentment felt by other New World nations that traditionally considered themselves to also be Americans.

Other elected officers were:

Dr. Joseph E. Raycroft	Vice president
Frederick W. Rubien	Secretary
Gustavus T. Kirby	Treasurer
Dr. Graeme M. Hammond	President emeritus
James F. Simms	Assistant secretary
Asa Bushnell	Assistant treasurer
H. Jamison Swarts	Assistant treasurer
A.C. Gilbert, chairman	Administrative committee

6th USOC Quadrennial - November 19, 1941, to December 10, 1945

6th USOC quadrennial meeting was held November 19, 1941, at the New York Athletic Club in New York City.

Avery Brundage
Brundage was elected USASF president for a fourth term on November 19, 1941. This term spanned the XII and XIII Olympiads.

Other elected officers were:

Dr. Joseph E. Raycroft	Vice president
Frederick W. Rubien	Secretary
Gustavus T. Kirby,	Treasurer
Dr. Graeme M. Hammond (Died October 30, 1944)	President emeritus
James F. Simms	Assistant secretary
Asa Bushnell	Assistant treasurer
H. Jamison Swarts	Assistant treasurer
A.C. Gilbert, chairman	Administrative committee

7th USOC Quadrennial - December 10, 1945, to January 9, 1950

7th USOC quadrennial meeting was held December 10, 1945, at the New York Athletic Club in New York City.

Avery Brundage
Brundage was elected USOA president for a fifth term on December 10, 1945. His term spanned the XIII and XIV Olympiads. During this meeting, the membership voted to change its name from the United States of America Sports Federation (USASF) to the United States Olympic Association (USOA) in preparation for a public law, which would not be granted until 1950.

Other elected officers were:

Kenneth L. Wilson	Vice president
Asa Bushnell	Secretary
Owen VanCamp	Treasurer
Gustavus T. Kirby	President emeritus

HONORARY PRESIDENTS OF THE UNITED STATES OLYMPIC COMMITTEE

Starting with President Grover Cleveland, who accepted the then-honorary presidency of what was the American Olympic Association in 1895, every United States president has agreed to serve in this capacity. During the XI, XII and XIII Olympiads, President Franklin D. Roosevelt was the honorary president of the AOA and USASF. Shortly after his death on April 12, 1945, President Harry S. Truman became the honorary president of the USOA. Honorary vice presidents during the XII Olympiad and part of the XIII were Secretary of State Cordell Hull, Secretary of War Henry L. Stimson, and Secretary of the Navy Colonel Frank L. Knox. As these U.S. cabinet members left office, the new secretary of state, George C. Marshall, and the new secretary of defense, James Forrestal, became honorary vice presidents for the remainder of the XIII Olympiad.

OLYMPIC AWARDS

THE OLYMPIC CUP

Beginning in 1906, the Olympic Cup was awarded annually to a person, institution, or association that had contributed significantly to sport or to the development of the Olympic movement. The Olympic Cup was kept at the IOC; honorees received a reproduction. The award was originally conceived by Baron Pierre de Coubertin.

RECIPIENTS

S.E.G.A.S.: Union of Hellenic Gymnastics and Athletics Associations, Athens, awarded February 28, 1935, for the year 1936.

Austrian Skating Federation, awarded July 31, 1936, for the year 1937.

Hungarian Royal Academy of Physical Education awarded June 10, 1937, for the year 1938.

Strengh Through Joy, Germany, awarded March 18, 1938, for the year 1939.

Swedish National Sports Association, awarded June 9, 1939, for the year 1940.

National Olympic Committee of Finland, awarded September 5, 1946, for the year 1941.

William May Garland, Los Angeles, awarded September 5, 1946, for the year 1942.

National Olympic Committee of Argentina awarded September 5, 1946, for the year 1943.

The City of Lausanne, awarded September 5, 1946, for the year 1944.

The Norwegian Track and Field Association awarded September 5, 1946, for the year 1945.

National Olympic Committee of Colombia awarded September 5, 1946, for the year 1946.

J. Sigfrid Edström, Stockholm awarded June 21, 1947, for the year 1947.

The Central Council of Physical Recreation in London, awarded July 29, 1948, for the year 1948.

OLYMPIC DIPLOMA OF MERIT

The Olympic Diploma of Merit, created in 1905 during the III Olympic Congress in Brussels, was awarded to an individual who had been active in the service of sport and/or had contributed substantially to the Olympic Movement.

RECIPIENTS

1939	Louis Hostin	France
	Leni Riefenstahl	Germany

OFFICIAL PUBLICATIONS OF THE INTERNATIONAL OLYMPIC COMMITTEE

XI OLYMPIAD

OLYMPIC CHARTER

The Olympic Charter provides the official rules, procedures, and protocols of the IOC, which are periodically updated by vote of the Membership at an IOC Session. Two editions were issued during the XI Olympiad.

Edition 6.4   Issued July 1936 (In German)
Edition 6.5   Issued March 1938 (In French, English, Spanish, and German)

International Olympic Committee Official Bulletin (Bulletin Officiel du Comité International Olympique) - After Baron Pierre de Coubertin left the IOC presidency in 1925, the new president, Count Henri de Baillet-Latour, started the *International Olympic Committee Official Bulletin* which is considered the seventh version of the *Olympic Review*. Published in Brussels, the *International Olympic Committee Official Bulletin* was printed in French, English, German, and Spanish and started its own sequential numbering system. The first issue appeared in January 1926.

#32	September 1936
#33	November 1936
#34	May 1937
#35	July 1937
#36	January 1938

Olympic Review (Olympische Rundschau) - Starting in April 1938, Carl Diem began publishing *Olympische Rundschau* which is acknowledged as the eighth version of the *Olympic Review*. Published by the International Olympic Institute in Berlin, *Olympische Rundschau* was written in German with articles in French and English. The *International Olympic Committee Official Bulletin* continued to appear as a special insert in Diem's publication. The German periodical maintained its own numbering system. The bulletin's numbering system was unaffected by the piggy-back arrangement.

#37	April 1938
#37a	July 1938
#38	October 1938
#39	January 1939
#40	April 1939
#41	July 1939
#42	October 1939
#43	January 1940
#44	April 1940

XII OLYMPIAD

THE OLYMPIC CHARTER

There were no new editions during the XII Olympiad.

Olympic Review (Olympische Rundschau) - Carl Diem continued to publish *Olympische Rundschau* during the XII Olympiad. The war, however, made it impossible to produce on a regular basis and the *Olympic committee Official Bulliten* did not appear in every issue.

#45	July 1940
*	October 1940
#46	January 1941
#47	April 1941
#48	July 1941
#49	October 1941
*	January 1942
#50	April 1942
*	July 1942
#51	October 1942
*	January 1943
#52	April 1943
*	July 1943/January 1944
#53	April 1944

* Olympic Review not published

XIII OLYMPIAD

THE OLYMPIC CHARTER

The seventh edition of the Olympic Charter was published in September 1946 in French and English.

THE OLYMPIC REVIEW

As the war raged on, the lack of available printing paper, difficult postal delivery, and a general unwillingness to receive any publication coming out of Germany put an end to *Olympische Rundschau*. There was one edition published in the 13th Olympiad.

#54	October 1944

THE EDSTRÖM CIRCULAR LETTERS

Despite the effort of Carl Diem in Berlin to get *The Olympic Review* and *The Bulletin* into the hands of the membership, many countries refused to handle mail from any of the warring nations, which created a problem for IOC President Count Baillet-Latour in Belgium. Seeing this, Sigfrid Edström, the IOC 1st Vice President, sought a way to keep the IOC Membership together. As he was a citizen of Sweden, a neutral country during World War II, international mail could be both sent by him and received from all countries, including the warring nations. Taking advantage of his situation, Edström created the

Circular Letters, which was the only direct contract between the membership form July 18, 1940, until July 2, 1946. Members were invited to send news, which Edström typed on single sheets of paper and sent them on to the membership. A complete list of the Circular letters are:

1. July 18, 1940 (1 Page)
2. August 13, 1940 (1 Page)
3. October 3, 1940 (1 Page)
4. December 10, 1940 (2 Pages)
5. February 5, 1941 (3 Pages)
6. April 21, 1941 (3 Pages)
7. July 9, 1941 (3 Pages)
8. October 25, 1941 (4 Pages)
9. January 8, 1942 (2 Pages)
10. January 24, 1942 (7 Pages, 2 of which are a personal letter, his last, from IOC President Baillet-Latour)
11. February 14, 1942 (4 Pages)
12. February 17, 1942 (5 Pages)
13. June 15, 1942 (4 Pages)
14. October 15, 1942 (5 Pages)
15. January 13, 1943 (1 Page)
16. May 15, 1943 (5 Pages)
17. November 1, 1943 (6 Pages)
18. May 15, 1944 (6 Pages)
19. August 15, 1944 (7 Pages)
20. December 29, 1944 (1 Page)
21. June 1, 1945 (7 Pages)
22. September 1, 1945 (3 Pages)
23. January 15, 1946 (4 Pages)
24. January 17, 1946 (4 Pages)
25. February 14, 1946 (1 Page)
26. April 30, 1946 (6 Pages)
27. July 2, 1946 (4 Pages)

International Olympic Committee Bulletin (Bulletin du Comité International Olympique) - The IOC voted to continue to produce an Olympic-related publication at its 1946 Session at Lausanne, Switzerland. The first edition of the *International Olympic Committee Bulletin* came out in October 1946 and represented the ninth version of the *Olympic Review*. Published at IOC headquarters in Lausanne, the *International Olympic Committee Bulletin* was written in French and English with the occasional submission in German, Spanish, or other languages. The new publication had yet another sequential numbering system.

#1	October 1946
#2	December 1946
#3	February 1947
#4	April 1947
#5	July 1947
#6	September 1947
#7	November 1947
#8	January 1948
#9	March 1948

ACKNOWLEDGMENTS

The publisher would like to thank the following for their invaluable assistance to 1st Century Project and World Sport Research & Publications: Gov. Francisco G. Almeda (Philippine Olympic Committee, Manila); Sheik Fahad Al-Ahmad Al-Sabah (Olympic Committee of Kuwait); Don Anthony; Maj. Gen. Charouck Arirachakaran (Olympic Committee of Thailand, Bangkok); Bibliothèque National de France (Paris); Marie-Charlotte Bolot (University of the Sorbonne Cultural Library and Archives, Paris); Boston Public Library; British Museum and Library (London); Gail Britton; Richard L. Coe; Anita DeFrantz (IOC Member in the United States); Margi Denton; Carl and Lieselott Diem - Archives/Olympic Research Institute of the German Sport University Cologne; Edward L. Doheny, Jr. Library (University of Southern California, Los Angeles); Robert G. Engel; Miguel Fuentes (Olympic Committee of Chile, Santiago); National Library of Greece (Athens); Hollee Hazwell (Columbiana Collection, Columbia University, New York); Rebecca S. Jabbour and Bill Roberts (Bancroft Library, University of California at Berkeley); Diane Kaplan (Manuscripts and Archives, Sterling Library, Yale University, New Haven); David Kelly (Sport Specialist, Library of Congress, Washington, D.C.); Fékrou Kidane (International Olympic Committee, Lausanne); Peter Knight; Dr. John A. Lucas; Los Angeles Public Library; Blaine Marshall; Joachaim Mester, President of the German Sport University

Cologne; Ed Mosk; Geoffroy de Navacelle; New York Public Library; Olympic Committee of India (New Delhi); Richard Palmer (British Olympic Association, London); C. Robert Paul; University of Rome Library and Archives; Margaret M. Sherry (Rare Books and Special Collections, Firestone Library, Princeton University); Dr. Ruth Sparhawk; Gisela Terrell (Special Collections, Irwin Library, Butler University, Indianapolis); Walter Teutenberg; The Officers, Directors and Staff (United States Olympic Committee, Colorado Springs); University Research Library, (University of California at Los Angeles); John Vernon (National Archives, Washington, DC); Emily C. Walhout (Houghton Library; Harvard University); Herb Weinberg; Dr. Wayne Wilson, Michael Salmon, Shirley Ito (Paul Ziffren Sports Resource Center Library, Amateur Athletic Foundation of Los Angeles); Patricia Henry Yeomans; Nanci A. Young (Seeley G. Mudd Manuscript Library, Princeton University Archives); Dr. Karel Wendl, Michéle Veillard, Patricia Eckert, Simon Mandl, Ruth Perrenoud, Nikolay Guerguiev, Fani Kakridi-Enz , Laura Leslie Pearman, and Christine Sklentzas (International Olympic Committee Olympic Studies and Research Center, Lausanne); and Pat White (Special Collections, Stanford University Library, Palo Alto).

The publishers recognize with gratitude the special contributions made for Volume 11 by Marjet

Derks (Netherlands Sports Museum); Stefan Flatow; Kate Griffin; Robert Hoffmann (Presseillustrationen Heinrich R. Hoffmann); Juha Kanerva (Sports Library of Finland); Dan Kulpinski; Lappe Laubscher (South African Sports Historian); Alexandra Lecief Mandl (The International Olympic Committee); Blaine Marshall; Angelika Obermeier, Richard Horn (Bayerische Staatsbibliothek); Patricia Olkiewicz (United States Olympic Committee); and Sherwin Podolsky.

The Publishers would also like to thank the following individuals, institutions and foundations for providing initial funding for the project: The Amelior Foundation (Morristown, New Jersey); Roy and Mary Cullen (Houston); The English, Bonter, Mitchell Foundation (Ft. Wayne, Indiana); Adrian French (Los Angeles); The Knight Foundation (Miami); The Levy Foundation (Philadelphia); and, Jonah Shacknai (New York). And for completion funding: Michael McKie, Optimax Securities, Inc. (Toronto); Graham Turner, Fraser & Beatty (Toronto); and Century of Sport Partnership (Toronto).

And a special thanks to Baaron Pittenger (Assistant Executive Director, United States Olympic Committee, September 1981 to August 1987 and Executive Director, August 1987 to Dectmber 1989).

BIBLIOGRAPHY

Albertson, Lisa H. (ed.). *Athens to Atlanta: 100 Years of Glory.* Salt Lake City, Utah: Mikko Laitinen Commemorative Publications, 1993.

Albertson, Lisa H. (ed.). *Chamonix to Lillehammer: The Glory of the Olympic Winter Games.* Salt Lake City, Utah: Mikko Laitinen Commemorative Publications, 1993.

Anonymous. "Ice Queen." *Time,* February 2, 1948.

Anonymous. "Olympic Puck Play is Marked by Tranquility." *Hockey News,* February 4, 1948.

Anonymous. "Sabotage, Fist Fights and Continued Disputes Peril Winter Olympics." *The New York Times,* January 31, 1948.

Anonymous. "Squalls and Brawls." *Newsweek,* February 9, 1948.

Anonymous. "Underrated Flyers Cop Olympic Crown." *Hockey News,* February 11, 1948.

Associated Press. *Pursuit of Excellence: The Olympic Story.* Danbury, CT: Grolier Enterprises, Inc., 1979.

Baker, William J. *Jesse Owens: An American Life.* New York: The Free Press, 1986.

Ballard, Sarah. "Reflections of a Queen." *Sports Illustrated,* January 27, 1988.

Borgers, Walter. *Torch Relays at the Olympic Games 1936-1988.* Cologne, Germany: Carl Diem Institute, 1988.

Bunch, Lonnie III & Louie Robinson. *The Black Olympians: 1904-1984.* Los Angeles: California Afro-American Museum. 1984.

Bunting, James. *Switzerland.* London: B.T. Batsford, Ltd., 1973.

Carlson, Lewis H. & John J. Fogarty. *Tales of Gold: An Oral History of the Summer Olympic Games Told By America's Gold Medal Winners.* Chicago: Contemporary Books, Inc., 1987.

Chapman, Mike. "The Forgotten Olympian." *Olympian,* December 1988.

Diem, Carl. *The Olympic Idea:Discourses and Essays.* Cologne: Carl-Diem-Institute, 1966.

Diem, Carl. "The Skiing Festival." *Olympic Review,* October 1939.

Eisen, George. "The Voices of Sanity: American Diplomatic Reports from the 1936 Berlin Olympiad." *Journal of Sport History,* Winter 1984.

Espy, Richard. *The Politics of the Olympic Games.* Berkeley, CA: University of California Press, 1979.

Fimrite, Ron. "A Hero in His Native Land." *Sports Illustrated,* September 14, 1988.

Gafner, Raymond (ed.). *The International Olympic Committee–One Hundred Years–The Idea–The Presidents–The Achievements, Volume I.* Lausanne: International Olympic Committee, 1995.

Gafner, Raymond (ed.). *The International Olympic Committee–One Hundred Years–The Idea–The Presidents–The Achievements, Volume II.* Lausanne: International Olympic Committee, 1995.

Gordon, Harry. *Australia and the Olympic Games.* St. Lucia, Australia: University of Queensland Press, 1994.

Guttman, Allen. *The Games Must Go On: Avery Brundage and the Olympic Movement.* New York: Columbia University Press, 1984.

Guttman, Allen. *The Olympics: A History of the Modern Games.* Chicago: University of Illinois Press, 1992.

Harris Norman. *The Legend of Lovelock.* Wellington, New Zealand: A.H. & A.W. Reed, 1964.

Hart-Davis, Duff. *Hitler's Games: The 1936 Olympics.* New York: Harper & Row Publishers, 1986.

Hedin, Sven. "Olympia-Tokyo." *Olympic Review,* April 1940.

Henry, William. *An Approved History of the Olympic Games*. Los Angeles: The Southern California Committee for the Olympic Games, 1981.

Hoberman, John. *The Olympic Crisis: Sport, Politics and the Moral Order*. New Rochelle, New York: Aristide D. Caratzas, 1986

Kamper, Erich. *Encyclopedia of the Olympic Winter Games*. Stuttgart: Union Verlag, 1964.

Laughlin, James. "International Racing Spews Discord." *Ski Magazine*, November 14, 1948.

Lucas, John. "Ernest Lee Jahncke: The Expelling of an IOC Member." *Stadion*, XVII, 1991.

Lucas, John. *The Modern Olympic Games*. New York: A.S. Barnes and Company, 1980.

MacAloon, John J. *This Great Symbol*. Chicago: The University of Chicago Pres, 1981.

Mandell, Richard D. *The Nazi Olympics*. New York: The Macmillan Company, 1971.

Marvin, Carolyn. "Avery Brundage and the American Participation in the 1936 Olympic Games." *Journal of American Studies*, April 1982.

Murray, Bill. "Berlin in 1936: Old and New Work on the Nazi Olympics." *The International Journal of the History of Sport*, April 1992.

Nelson, Cordner & Roberto Quercetani. *Runners and Races: 1,500M/Mile*. Los Altos, CA: TAFNEWS Press, 1973.

Polley, Martin. "Olympic Diplomacy: The British Government and the projected 1940 Olympic Games." *The International Journal of the History of Sport*, April 1992.

Poole, Stephen. *The World Atlas of Skiing*. New York: Mallard Press, 1990.

Powers, John. "How They spent Their Winter Vacation." *Sports Illustrated*, December 16, 1991.

Pringsheim, Peter. "Olympic Preview." *Ski Illustrated*, December 1947.

Riefenstahl, Leni. *Leni Riefenstahl: A Memoir*. New York: St. Martin's Press, 1993.

Segrave, Jeffrey O. & Donald Chu (eds.). *The Olympic Games in Transition*. Champaign, IL: Human Kinetic Books, 1988.

Seth-Smith, Michael. *The Cresta Run: History of the St. Moritz Tobogganing Club*. London: Foulsham, 1976.

Tahara, Junko. "Count Michimasa Soyeshima and the Cancellation of the XII Olympiad in Tokyo: A footnote to Olympic History." *The International Journal of the History of Sport*, April 1992.

Tissot, Victor. *Unknown Switzerland: Reminiscences of Travel*. New York: James Pott & Co., 1914.

Travaglini, M.E. "Olympic Baseball 1936: Was es Das?" *The National Pastime*, Winter 1985.

Wallechinsky, David. *The Complete Book of the Olympics*. New York: Penguin Books, 1988.

Wenn, Stephen R. "A Tale of Two Diplomats: George S. Messersmith and Charles H. Sherrill on Proposed American Participation in the 1936 Olympics." *Journal of Sport History*, Spring 1989.

Weyand, Alexander. *The Olympic Pageant*. New York: The MacMillan Co., 1952.

Young, David C. "Modern Greece and the Origins of the Modern Olympic Games." *Proceedings of an International Symposium on the Olympic Games*, 1992.

Zellers, Margaret (ed.). *Fodor's Switzerland 1979*. London: Hodder and Stoughton, 1979.

PHOTO CREDITS

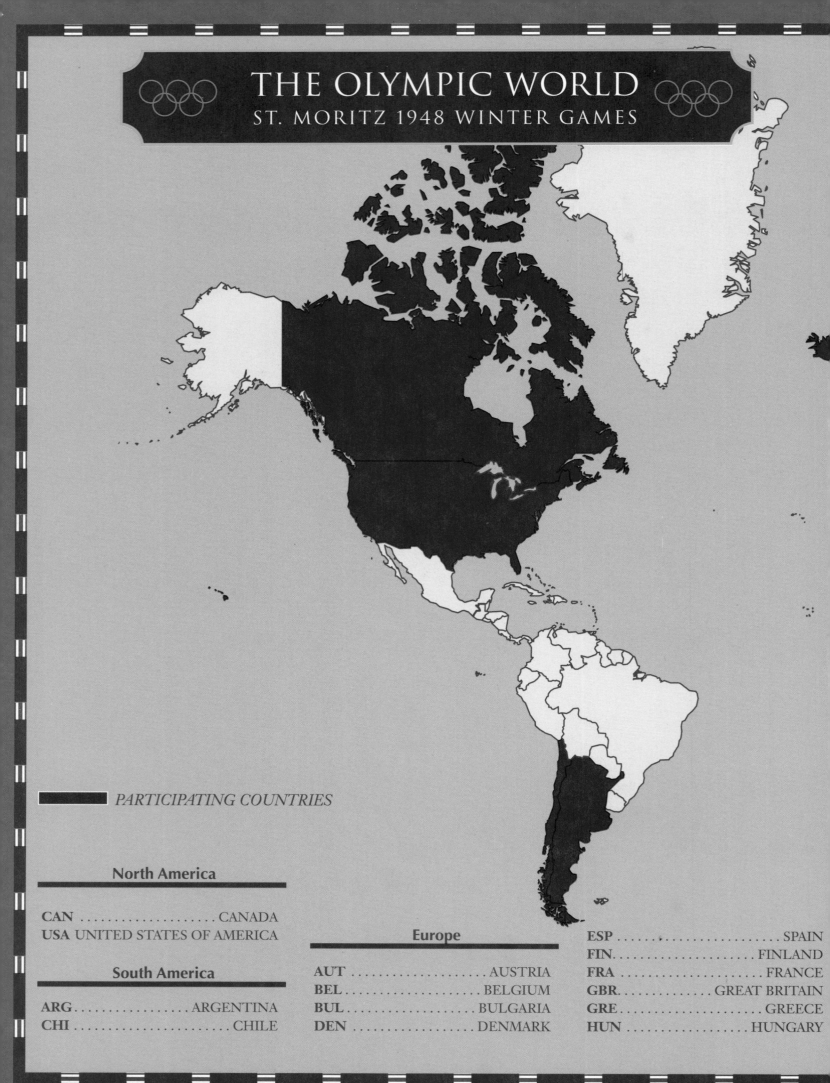

THE OLYMPIC WORLD
ST. MORITZ 1948 WINTER GAMES

PARTICIPATING COUNTRIES

North America

CAN . . . . CANADA
USA UNITED STATES OF AMERICA

South America

ARG . . . . ARGENTINA
CHI . . . . CHILE

Europe

AUT . . . . AUSTRIA
BEL . . . . BELGIUM
BUL . . . . BULGARIA
DEN . . . . DENMARK

ESP . . . . SPAIN
FIN . . . . FINLAND
FRA . . . . FRANCE
GBR . . . . GREAT BRITAIN
GRE . . . . GREECE
HUN . . . . HUNGARY